Mourning the Dream—*Amor Fati*

Mourning the Dream—*Amor Fati*

An Illustrated Mythopoetic Inquiry

SUSANNA RUEBSAAT

PICKWICK *Publications* · Eugene, Oregon

MOURNING THE DREAM—*AMOR FATI*
An Illustrated Mythopoetic Inquiry

Pickwick Publications
An Imprint of Wipf and Stock Publishers
199 W. 8th Ave., Suite 3
Eugene, OR 97401

www.wipfandstock.com

PAPERBACK ISBN: 978-1-5326-1385-2
HARDCOVER ISBN: 978-1-5326-6510-3
EBOOK ISBN: 978-1-5326-6511-0

Cataloguing-in-Publication data:

Names: Ruebsaat, Susanna, author.

Title: Mourning the dream—*amor fati* : an illustrated mythopoetic inquiry / Susanna Ruebsaat.

Description: Eugene, OR: Pickwick Publications, 2018. | Includes bibliographical references.

Identifiers: ISBN: 978-1-5326-1385-2 (paperback). | ISBN: 978-1-5326-6510-3 (hardcover). | ISBN: 978-1-5326-6511-0 (ebook).

Subjects: LCSH: Mythopoesis. | Jungian psychology. | Arts—Psychological aspects. | Art therapy.

Classification: NX180 P7 R62 2019 (print). | NX180 (epub).

Manufactured in the U.S.A.   DECEMBER 10, 2018

All images are artworks by the author. All photos were taken by the author.

DEDICATION
"And if thou gaze long into an abyss,
the abyss will also gaze into thee."[1]

This book was written for all the abusers, violators, disturbers,
and victims of the Subjective and Objective Unconscious that pull
us to the lip of the abyss. These figures are trying to come into
consciousness but generally remain in the form of undifferentiated
anxiety. "He who fights with monsters should be careful lest he
thereby become a monster."[2]
In light of Nietzsche's uncanny provocation of the abyss looking into
you, the reader, the following inquiry may invoke your own figures
of undifferentiated anxiety, any of whom are invited to dance with
your imagination.

1. Nietzsche, *Beyond Good and Evil*, 146.
2. Nietzsche, *Beyond Good and Evil*, 146.

As the third space created through the ongoing dialogue of conscious and unconscious, the mythopoetic voyage holds the capacity of catching glimpses of the mythic stream of potentialities continuously flickering in the body and dreams. The journey itself becomes a presence that invites the possibility of loving one's fate, one's life, in the face of its very mourning.

Contents

Illustrations

Poems

Preface

Weary of hope while entangled in the bowels of a lost dream, I hear another voice, this one a hoarse whisper: "Love your fate."[1] A mythopoetic inquiry into the appearance of a state of loss or mourning and *amor fati*, this love affair with fate—and how one is an inherent piece of the other—can awaken a form of consciousness that lives in the unconscious, that which is at the core of the birth-death-rebirth archetype, the Self.[2]

Where does this voice come from? Where does it want to go? Even though I may be absent to myself, there is an underlying archetypal narrative I am intrinsically a part of. The whispering voice seems to have knowledge of this archetypal resonance in the same manner art does. It is as if a layer of the unconscious where the mythopoetic dwells continues to reveal itself in the mirror of my experience, no matter what or how I think of myself. My body emits and extends mythopoetic wisdom as the dreambody is tumbling through the wounded parts of the old story, the false myths. And so I am confronted by my own narrative, turning on me in a desperate gesture for me to awaken to the unlived life, a symbolic life that sees Psyche's deeper intent for me.

1. Nietzsche, *Ecce Homo*, 13.
2. Jung, *Psychology and Religion*, 187.

Acknowledgments

I would like to acknowledge Meehae Song for her tireless work, copyediting and formatting the manuscript, and her accompanying me on the long winding writing of the mythopoetic inquiry; David Rosen for his unconditional support of my work and nudge to publish; David Roomy for his longstanding mentorship and faith in the creative impulse towards self-actualization; Steven Rosen for his introducing me to several key concepts that sparked the emergence of central images around which the inquiry spiraled; my brother, Norbert Ruebsaat, for initiating the kind of intimate conversations that can happen in writing and the courage this brings to becoming able to be vulnerable in one's own work. The initial statement: "I think I would be fun to be in a relationship with" came out of one of our dark yet playful dialogues about the beauty and horror of being oneself.

Prelude: Telling the Story

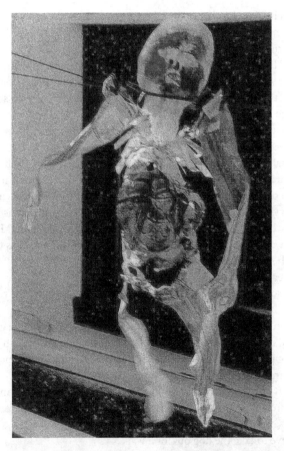

Figure 1: I Think I Would Be Fun To Be in a Relationship With

I know a little about your story.

I know, some of it is a bit scary.

Is that why you are afraid to tell it?

Never thought before that I was. But as soon as you mention it, I feel this numbness rise in my body. I mean telling it in bits and pieces in conversation just seems to happen spontaneously, naturally without any particular intention. But to write it down . . . seems like some kind of commitment I don't know I can keep. You know, the scariness of it. And I get confused about how to tell the truth about my own unlived life.

That's all I can tell you today.

Ok.

Several days have passed.

I've noticed there's been quite a silence hanging in the air. A darkening quiet.

Yes. I became quite frightened of . . . speaking with you. I'm not even sure why other than because of my own tangled feelings of amazement and terror. That freezing numbness descended again so I had to go away.

What did you discover in your own disappearance?

A terrible loneliness.

What is this mysterious weight that is to be carried by my being human? What exchange is taking place behind the scenes in this self and other business? Taking place—whose place? Whose weight am I carrying with muscle aches that compare to what Atlas must feel?

So what do you think of the weight of words? Of thoughts? Do you ever consider the burden of these that your body continues to carry with such commitment?

I mean certain kinds of words and thoughts.

Yet some kinds of words, thoughts, or images are light, lift you, suspend you in a moment of weightlessness, yes?

I don't want to split lived experiences into black and white; good and bad; desirable and undesirable. I can't bear this kind of high speed ping pong game in which the mind begins to play out it's madness.

So are you saying that your "story" carries a lot of weight?

I can only know that if . . . I'm feeling that tight numbness in my gut again, a little shaking vibration and difficulty breathing. Freezing. Ice.

I have to take the dog out for a walk.

Glaciers change the shape of the earth.

Step. Stepping. How many steps did I take on my walk?

If you make enough steps it's called a journey.

I could feel the rhythm of my stepping, landing down on one foot
then the other, rocking me back and forth. Soothing.
A cradle in my own body.
I'm suddenly imagining ice cubes floating to the top of a glass of wa-
ter, bobbing, knocking each other around. Making a tinkling sound
like bells.
Where are you?
I am neither here nor there. Frozen, floating like the ice cubes.
I drink in the night, sipping the smell of wet leaves fallen from the
silent giants I walk among. Nico keeps her nose to the ground. I fol-
low her luminous white body in the black so that I can make my way
home without stumbling.
So she acts as a guide even while she is on her own scent trail?
We have an agreement.
She carves the trail, flagging with her tail.
I see the path with peripheral vision and imagine where we are
going.
Together we go into the labyrinth
knocking into edges. The places vortices begin.
There are no tinkling sounds here.
No nostalgic bells.
Only a hellish smell of wounds scraping against each other.
A dark guest walks into my kitchen and I immediately drop into a
pool of despair.
I can smell the ooze of her wound.
My wound; that smell of abandonment.
I have to go to bed.
I say someone has to leave otherwise there will be a disastrous colli-
sion of secrets.
Where is the knowing of this?
In the viscera.
Hers.
Mine.
But it's a secret.
She oozes while I swim the sea of the despondent.
I am swept down current and have to go limp
so that my body will be soft and flexible,
like a baby
falling.
I fall asleep and wake up with a "NO"!
The emphatic "no" of the unconscious that speaks again of the un-
lived life?
Why can I not say no to her leaking psyche, her dribbling flesh?
I go swimming.

I go to bed.
I go for a walk.
I leave.
I begin a journey.
What is the story that is unfolding here?
The journey started with fear and anger.
What are you doing with the story you are telling yourself?
I am re-telling it.
Not just repeating it.
I am trying to break the spell.
Wicked Witch of the North.
I am asking what is happening here.
I am asking what story I need in order to get through the day.
I am carrying the stories of my own family forward,
pushing them over the cliff and into the imaginal.
I want to breathe new life into old stories.
All old stories have to be retold.
Once upon a time there was a little girl who deeply loved her older
brother and sister.
She would watch them do funny things; so she learned how to see
the world the way she imagined they saw it.
As funny?
Yes, making fun.
This little girl always wanted to be with her older siblings and do
what they did.
But sometimes she was not allowed
because she was too little.

Figure 2. Family by the River

What was she not allowed to do?

She was not allowed to go with them with their father to jump into the Columbia River, swim out to the middle, and let the current carry them downstream.

She so badly wanted to do this with them.

But she could only watch from the shore as they drifted what to her seemed a great distance and see them scrambling onto the banks about a mile down river.

They would return to the spot where the little girl waited, all wet and excited, shivering bodies telling the tale of being like giant ships on the Atlantic Ocean sailing to Canada.

But they were already in Canada.

But they were immigrants so having their bodies transported like that, in the strong current of the river, like ships, made them feel like they were really here, in Canada.

That they had made this journey with their own bodies.

At least this is what the little girl imagined.

She had been told about the big ocean trip she never made.

She wanted to discover that feeling in her own body.

Why did she not make that voyage?

She was not yet in the womb then.
She was still just an unfertilized
egg in her mother's body.

Figure 3. Unfertilized Egg

Do you think the egg knew about the big voyage?
The egg knew that it was from a different place,
the same place her brother and sister were from.
That's why she wanted to go into the middle of the river with them
and their father,
to experience the journey, be the big body ship crossing the ocean.
She wanted to be part of that mythical voyage.
But the little girl had a mythical voyage of her own to make
that she didn't yet know about.
Did this mythical voyage, her own journey have something to do
with the egg?
We will have to wait and see how the tale unfolds.
Do you have the patience to find out?

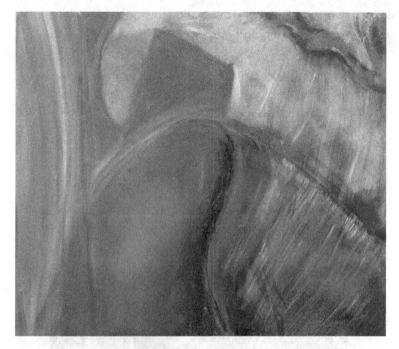

Figure 4. Mythical Voyage

Field Notes: Canadian Thanksgiving, October 2012

The future cannot be changed because it has not yet happened.
But the past can be changed to what it is meant to be.
This is the secret mythopoeia holds:
The capacity to move from the mythic to the mythopoetic,
Which is the ability to move beyond one's present myth
and all its assumptions and prescriptions,
and into one's living myth,
the myth that is unfolding in this very moment,
through the authentic self,
alive and moving forward.
Living in deep time.

The words deep time came to me spontaneously as a description of a certain quality of experience that dropped me into a sense of interiority quite different than my usual relation to the phenomenon of time. The words presented themselves while I was listening to a Jungian analyst describe her twenty plus years of working with the unconscious. Deep time is an embodied moment.

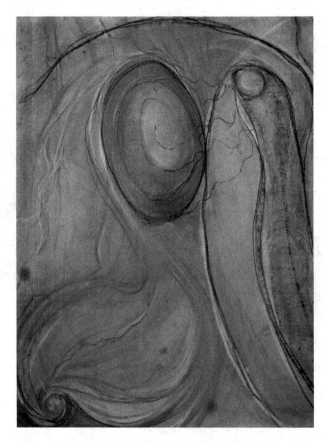

Figure 5. Deep Time

Introduction

Mourning the Dream / *Amor Fati*: A Spiraling Inquiry

SPIRALING INTO THE ARCHETYPAL story that lives beneath conscious thinking about oneself and the world, is like being in an extended altered state. Through journeying the inner mythic landscape, the mythography of one's soul (Psyche), there arises the probability of realizing that Psyche has ulterior motives for us. Seemingly unrelated to ego goals and aspirations, such a journey usually begins with some sort of "call" some of us cannot ignore. The unconscious is unwittingly taking us in an entirely different direction that often makes no sense to ego-consciousness. The "direction" feels like no direction at all, spiraling into a disorientation that erases a sense of self and the world. We are plunged into a liminal space-in-between where our existence has no reference points, no anchors to "who I think I am." The boundaries of "inner" and "outer" dissolve as if they never even existed, like a dream the ego once had. The now questionable "self" is a nightmare. The unravelling of ego as complex can feel like a harsh peeling away of one's very skin.

Is this the beginning of the archetypal encounter of self and "other," that numinous meeting we both long for and are terrified by? Is this the entry into an alternate realm beyond the literal and into the symbolic? Could this unravelling of ego be a revelation of *mundus imaginalis*, where the possibility of returning to one's own story anew lives? Is it here, in the imaginal, that we can discover that our story or myth is *the* aperture of vision-making—an archetypal function of the personal and collective Psyche? Having found its home in the mythopoetic, the reclamation of our narrative may be, as Donald Kalsched suggests:

> a basic function of the unconscious, i.e. its tendency to present itself in consciousness in the form of images . . . A mythopoetic story evolves in each individual's life, the flame around a candle's

1

wick providing a matrix for the soul's indwelling . . . representing an intermediate between the worlds of spiritual and material
reality. This mysterious third area is known in analytic psychology as psychic reality or imaginal reality . . . mythopoetic images have their roots in a collective layer of the unconscious
and . . . this stratum of the psyche mediates experience that is
perceived as spiritual. So we cannot avoid spiritual experience
in our otherwise material lives. We live our true lives "between
the worlds." In ourselves we are "citizens of two realms."[1]

I light a metaphorical candle so that I can see what Kalsched is talking
about. I want the image to tell me directly what he means and how the
flame of my individual life burns in the imaginal. I see flickering around
the steadiness of the wick. My mind dances back and forth between the
movement and the stillness as the flame continues to burn.

The archetypal story, with its roots in the collective layers of the
unconscious, is epic by nature, as it is round after round of encounters
between the conscious and the unconscious. Navigating the mythopoetic
matrix of the "soul's indwelling," Kalsched asks for a path where inner
and outer meet as one, living an imaginal story in which we ourselves
become liminal figures.

The Relationship between the Mythopoetic Journey, Trauma, Embodiment, Klein Body, and the Spiral Lens

As a path between spiritual and material experience, the mythopoetic
follows liminal figures as reflections of soul. Seeing itself in resonant images (art, dreams, poems), the journey itself develops an awareness that
it too is a mirroring process, an extension we might say of the inherent
structuring of the very matrix that is shaping one's myth. The soul-images
tell the story and their embodiments (as art and story) have the capacity
to hold soul even through the colonization of self by trauma. The resonating soul-images, Psyche's flickerings, lead to a sense of Presence through
the encounter of "other" presences on the journey. The Presence holds an
overarching vision that encompasses the whole of one's life. It is the spiral
lens crafted through the suffering of what I have come to name the Klein
body (from the Klein bottle in alchemy) in its process of metamorphosis
that brings the perspective and perception of Presence into one's being:

1. Kalsched, *Trauma and the Soul*, 316.

> The Klein bottle was first described in 1882 by the German mathematician Felix Klein, a German mathematician, known for his work in group theory, complex analysis, non-Euclidean geometry, and on the connections between geometry and group theory. Klein devised the bottle named after him, a one-sided closed surface which cannot be embedded in three-dimensional Euclidean space, but it may be immersed as a cylinder looped back through itself to join with its other end from the 'inside.'[2]

The mythopoetic journey involves the reflexive embodiment and contemplation of initially unconscious encounters that are tracked in a mythopoetic inquiry. Through this tracking and visceral processing of inner and outer events, a living mythopoesis emerges that acts as a container for attending to the Klein body as a transformative instrument (fashioned from the Klein bottle of alchemy) for individuation. Hidden in this body—our human body—is a continuous symbolic process of crafting a spiral lens (consciousness). This lens, like no other, sees both the old, habitual narrative and the mythopoeia emerging within this narrative. The developing spiral lens brings into view the capacity of the "old" myth as the necessary aperture through which vision-making happens in the mythopoetic. The image of the spiral lens unexpectedly came to life in the writing of *Mourning the Dream / Amor Fati*. It spontaneously appeared in a drawing, "I Am a Spiral Lens" and is further explored and illustrated in the following pages.

Mourning the Dream / Amor Fati is a mythopoetic inquiry, a narrative of the imagination which mirrors an alternate story that dwells beneath consciousness or the dominant story (individually or collectively). In that space of mirroring we create the story as we are living it, writing the narrative at the same time as we are reading it to ourselves and the world, creating a vision while seeing, an imaginative vision about what is and what can be. A spiraling inquiry circles around patterns emerging in the tracking of experience. With each circling—like a bird watching overhead—comes the true depth of these experiences. In the reflections of inside/outside the Klein body is producing, the spiral lens takes form like a pearl emerging from layer after layer of the translucent spit of the soft body of the oyster.

Mythopoetic inquiry has its own logic as it spirals throughout its unique creation. However, it also needs to connect to "reality." Art making (and other creative activity that spirals around inner and outer events)

2. Alling and Greenleaf, "Klein Surfaces," 159.

tethers imagination and reality together, sharing the same story emerging from the personal and collective liminal place between the conscious and unconscious. As humans we have a shared imagination in myths and archetypes that is the common ground of this imagining.

The Term Mythopoetic is Made Up Of

Myth: of or relating to the making of myths: narrative. Self-story, life-story that explains how the world (or individual or group) and humankind came to be the way they are.

Poetic: poetry is both reflective and a language of reflexivity, the kind of aesthetic that turns around and looks back at itself.

Mythopoetic implies that the myth holds meaning in its reflexively looking back into itself.

Reflexivity refers to circular relationships between cause and effect, consciousness and unconsciousness. Like seeing a curve, an arc, the back of a whale surfacing just above the line of the horizon, we imagine the whale in its entirety. Through this chance sighting we "know" how the whale moves through the deep waters below. The simple glimpse of her massive form allows us to feel in our own bodies the completion of her circular gesture above and below our line of vision. That "feeling" is the same as what my Klein body is doing in the waters of the unconscious where the spiral lens is shaping itself. This lens has the capacity—much like our imagining the entirety of the whale—to bring into view a sense of completion and beginning anew in one gesture. We imagine the journey of the whale well beyond any evidence to inform us of such. We feel it in our flesh.

Mythopoetic Inquiry assumes an alternate story is present that is working on us. As it spirals throughout our being beneath our consciousness, this story or narrative offers us flavors of deeper, underlying sensibilities or imaginings that "bend back on," refer to, and affect the inquirer. Such sensibilities are nudging us towards a more conscious participation with the logic of "otherness" the presence this alternate story hints at. There is an expansion of perception that sees these polarities of self and "other" as a continuum we are travelling along in either or both directions, a horizon line that holds our gaze as if it were a constant, at eye-level.

The horizon line in perspective drawing is a horizontal line across the picture. It is always at eye level; its placement determines where we are looking from—a high place, or close to the ground. It helps us navigate. Yet when we move, the horizon line, like our shadow, seems to follow us wherever we go. It is acting here as a symbol of our subjective placement as "I" in the world on the one hand, *and* as a metaphor for the unknown, or the "other" inside *and* outside ourselves (where we are looking from, and where we are looking to). As such a consistent presence, the symbol of the horizon line holds the continuum of our narrative in its extremes of "I" and "other," and everything that lies in-between. And so, its image invites the possibility of our being beside ourselves, living a parallel narrative to the one we call "I," by taking a step aside our usual perception and storytelling of ourselves. Do I tell my story from the perspective of who I think I am? Or what I think or feel about myself? Or can I intuitively let my body enter the unknown, that is, possibly from the perspective of where I am looking to, the "other" which continuously parallels my every movement? Could "I" step into the narrative of this "self" that is "other" where I am imagining my story reflected in your story—where a dialogue of dreaming together emerges? Big universal as well as highly personal questions and motifs can be asked here. Spiraling around these questions again and again, we can discern what kind of sensibilities we are bringing to personal and collective issues.

The Klein Body

Mourning the Dream / Amor Fati evolved into a mythopoetic inquiry including the integration of the process of the Klein bottle/body metamorphosing into a spiral lens. As transformative alchemical instrument, the Klein bottle like the Mobius strip appears to have two surfaces but in fact the mathematical model has only one surface. As a metaphor for the body—Klein bottle as sentient body—the Klein body creates the illusion that the body's inside and outside are separate. Self and "other." But our body responds to interior and exterior events as one process, as if there is no such inner and outer. The Klein body is a metaphor for the body-soul experience. Similar to the Mobius strip, a symbol on the surface (on the outside) of a Klein bottle (body), slides around it, and reappears backwards (inside) like the opposite image in a mirror. This is not possible on a sphere as any spherical form is orientable. The Klein bottle, like the body-soul experience has to pass through itself without a hole. It contains itself. Our myth, our story about who we are, must also pass through itself without a hole. In the containment of the mythopoesis our story transforms itself into being a symbol of itself. It sees itself through the spiral lens that is crafted through the body of the inquiry itself.

The Heart of the Matter

The heart of the matter in the pages to come is the bringing of my/your story into the light of day, bringing it out of the dark and its sense of isolation and irrelevance to finally join its sisters and brothers in the collective shaping of experience. To do this we need to bushwhack our way through the first story—the myth that is lived largely in reaction to a limited perception—as if it were the forest of unconsciousness. Tracking the movements of this original story, spiraling over and through it and over again, and letting it unfurl the many petals of the events and images that have shaped it, I come to see my myth within the container of this mythopoetic inquiry. I am moving from the mythic to the mythopoetic along the horizon of my story-line, each step informing me further of the significance of events recalled. And so I lay bare this myth and how it is part of the interweaving of all myth. "When any one person recovers [her] his voice many people begin to speak through that story."[3]

Embarking upon this multifaceted inquiry places me/you within a historical and mythological context in which the personal and collective Psyche shows her deeper intent, her ulterior motive beyond the empirical through the creative processes of art making, poetry, storytelling, teaching, writing, illness, and art therapy. In addition to Depth Psychology, *Mourning the Dream / Amor Fati* also draws on the discourses of Art Education, Art Therapy, Phenomenology, Mythology, and Taoism and some references to Chogyam Trungpa Rinpoche's views on Tibetan Buddhism. The following pages are the terrain this mythopoetic inquiry roams, gathering the evidence of living moments on paper surfaces of what has not yet happened—a spiraling journey of discovery and dissolution of selves, a reshaping the past through a re-assembling of the images my/ your myth is simultaneously holding and being held (back) by. *Mourning the Dream / Amor Fati* is both a re-creation myth and apocalyptic in the original meaning of the word: revelation of secrets of what lies behind the

3. Frank, *Wounded Storyteller*, xiii.

veil of the story already told. It is the life and death of the body as Klein-bottle, transforming experience into conscious embodiment and insight.

This mythopoetic endeavor requires action that affirms polarity and so brings polarities into relationship. It asks for metaphoric action based in symbolic understanding so that it can reveal the metaphoric nature of life. Mythopoesis is archetypal action that would "speak the unspeakable and mourn openly."[4] It invites the possibility of loving one's fate, one's life, in the face of its very mourning. Mourn openly. Journey into the folds of grief, a labyrinth of loss wherein one might be forever left wandering in one's own shadow, one's own exile. Walking this potentially dangerous path I/you can potentially become an archetypal activist who consciously holds the tension of opposites. Doing so I/you potentiate a process whereby deep insight has immediate consequences—we are living in deep time. In embodied moments when the "I" of "who I think I am" drops away, an alternate mythic journey emerges with a significance parallel to the experience of descent. The journey itself becomes a presence, the third space created through the ongoing dialogue of conscious and unconscious. The mythopoetic voyage itself holds the capacity of catching glimpses of the mythic stream of possibilities continuously flickering in the body and dreams. Dropping into deep time—when the "I" is a liminal figure, an imaginal ego, a potential archetypal activist—provides the quality of energy that fertilizes the process of mythopoesis: "As archetypal activists we are called to be synthetic (i.e. dialectical) in order to facilitate bringing together the fragmented polarities of the culture in such a way that the existential tension of opposites is maintained while the opposites interact mutually, engaging without definitive dominance. In this way polarities may reflectively energize and activate each other, reflecting through distinction."[5]

For the liminal figure outside/inside coexist as experienced by the Klein body in her metamorphosing into the spiral lens, an imaginal instrument that accesses all dimensions of experience. Mythopoesis can awaken a form of consciousness that lives in the unconscious and is at the core of the birth-death-rebirth archetype: the Self.[6]

---

4. McNamara, "Evolutionary Challenge," 4.
5. McNamara, "Evolutionary Challenge," 6.
6. Jung, *Psychology and Religion*, 187.

Figure 6: Body as Klein Bottle Revealing Inside/Outside Simultaneously

Mourning the Dream / Amor Fati is a mythopoetic, autobiographical inquiry into the relationship between what appears to be a state of mourning or loss from the two-dimensional perspective and *amor fati* (love of one's fate)—and how one is an inherent piece of the other. Seeing through the spiral lens reveals the dialectical nature of self-actualization, what Carl Jung referred to as individuation.[7] As an inquiry and practice, *Mourning the Dream / Amor Fati* offers a perspective of the role "image" plays in the relationship between perception and consciousness. The notion of "image" is used in a broad sense of its definition to include, not only the visual image but also that which is experienced as sound, smell, touch; or as idea, notion or even impulse—the invisibles: "The image . . . is a radiant node or cluster; it is what I can, and must perforce, call a

7. Jung, *Psychology and Religion*, 40.

vortex, from which, and through which, and into which, ideas are constantly rushing."[8]

Imaging is the nature of how we experience. It is active perception, the most direct experience there is as Psyche *is* image who is always imaging. We are always perceiving, creating our lived experience. If, according to Jung, "every psychic process is an image and an imagining," I want to ask what the image is seeking, what the image within my longing is and what buried significance it might hold for me or others.[9] "What is its intent?" as it is reflexively both reaching out and reaching into at the same time. What is the generativity that urges my body as Klein bottle to pass through herself without a hole, all the while containing herself as she squeezes through my myth into a dimension beyond/within herself and into the matrix of the third space of the imaginal? Is this an embodiment of unconscious experience, Psyche's deeper intent?

Figure 7: Embodying

David Bohm, contributor to theoretical physics, philosophy of mind, and neuropsychology, described this generative capacity as "active meaning"—a meaning that becomes activated within a particular kind of energy, which then synthesizes into meaning-making—much like the mythopoetic journey itself awakening to its mirroring of the matrix it is

8. Albright, "Early Cantos I–XLI," 60.

9. Jung, *Psychology and Religion*, 544.

structured through.[10] My understanding of Bohm's "active meaning," in this sense, suggests that meaning lies within the energy present in the relationship between the Implicate Order and the Explicate Order: "Instead of talking about object we deal in process, we enquire as to how a particular explicate (individual mind/body) unfolds out of the Implicate. Minds become both truly collective and personal by virtue of the continuous process of unfoldment and enfoldment whereby they are united within the Implicate and individuated within the Explicate. Mind and matter are connected because of their essential identity within the Implicate Order."[11]

Mourning the Dream / Amor Fati investigates the underpinnings of both the structure and content of one's myth as an unfolding of active meaning-making. Its spiraling around more inconspicuous forms of meaning calls into consciousness the relationship of these forms to the implicate order—an order which lies beyond space and time according to Bohm, in deep time. The highly subjective content of suffering, loss, and the consequent sadness and despair in *Mourning the Dream / Amor Fati* reveals intimate hints of a hidden awareness of vaster context, an alternate narrative operating as a centrifugal force of a particular significance of perception Jung would refer to as the Self. Bohm's "active meaning" speaks of re-gaining this significance which encompasses a sense of purpose, intention and value.

"Active meaning" comes from the implicate order itself that is first experienced unconsciously in the body as Klein bottle. It enters the body, so to speak, as a future to unfold, a seed to sprout in the dark before it reaches the surface of consciousness. Through the crafting of the spiral lens in the sufferings of the Klein body, the meaning, initially indiscernible, is made explicit in the creative act, an act of perception that fastens imagination to "reality." Through the "active meaning" this symbolic tethering of imagination and "reality" creates, the future comes in, and the meaningful tuggings of tacit awareness of the implicate order begin to speak of the ancients' call to listen. In the middle stage of writing this book the string of words "the ancients are lamenting" kept arising subliminally from the work. I did not know what this meant but could not ignore its insistence on being part of the inquiry. I let it stay without definition until such time as the inquiry led me to the intent and consequences of

10. Bohm, "Meaning and Information," 41–44.
11. Peat, "Alchemical Transformation," 22.

its appearance. I ask the reader here to be patient and allow this unfolding to occur in your own process without my naming this apparition now.

When the unconscious pulls towards Underworld experiences, it can have one lose touch with the more subtle sense of purpose and intention of the implicate order. It blinds us in a torrent of raw material waiting to then be metabolized by the Klein body. The shadow aspect of soul is the dark realm of the ancients who are wanting to tell their tale over and over again, echoing their fate in each cell of my body. Ginette Paris, a professor of mine at Pacifica Graduate Institute described her experience of the Underworld in her book *Wisdom of the Psyche* as such: "I am a frequent traveler and have visited many countries. However, of all the trips I've taken in my life, the one that was the most fascinating was my descent to the dark recesses of my Psyche, that place where we reside as if in a nightmare, a place that the ancient Greeks called the Underworld and that we call the unconscious . . . The necessity of a descent into the Underworld is a core idea of depth psychology."[12]

In such plunges into the recesses of the Psyche, I call on the capacity of the Klein body for both immersion *and* reflection in its crafting of the spiral lens. This lens can hold a backwards *and* forwards panorama in focus creating depth perception of an archetypal nature, that third space of "deep time" that opens where/when the self and the process of "selfing" are united within the Implicate and individuated within the Explicate. Naturally an inquiry that invites such immersion *and* reflection, researching the continuum of the horizon line of our experience, requires the time and length it needs to do this. I invite the reader to immerse yourself in deep time, taking in each circle of the spiral as it adds another dimension to the mythopoetic significance of certain images and experiences—with the understanding that this is how one moves from the literal to the symbolic. The spiraling is the action of the mythopoetic, which seen from ego consciousness, seems only repetitive. From the perspective of the heroic ego, it appears no change is happening. The horizon line is still so far away. It is always far away when looked at as if it were outside of oneself. The spiraling around and within resonant events in one's life creates the multiple deeps where "images take shape and meaning becomes clear."[13]

The repetitious act of spiraling is necessary if an inquiry is to reach the heights and plumb the depths of the mythic. Within each circle of the

12. Paris, *Wisdom of the Psyche*, xii.
13. Jung, *Structure and Dynamics of the Psyche*, 402.

spiral there is also a vertical movement. Even if the image or experience is the same, the perspective of it as shown through the spiral lens has in fact changed. Changing perspective *is* the action of perception, the mythopoeia. The repetitions act much like the chorus of a Greek tragedy that chimes into the narrative to remind the audience of the context of the tragedy (archetypal trauma). The chorus is a collective voice, a dramatic function which offers background and expresses what is hidden from the main character. It also reveals needed insight as if from another source outside the drama (whose constellation is the complex that has been activated). The collective holds a presence for the drama to unfold, an anchor as it were that gives voice so that the conscious mind can stay connected to the scene rather than dissociate (split into the trauma vortex).

Field Notes: Dreams and Past Discussions

The spiral lens presented itself initially through a drawing process and then took root as a key image throughout Mourning the Dream / Amor Fati. *I came to understand its appearance in my inquiry and how it symbolically served as alchemical instrument birthed through the strainings of the Klein bottle, a kind of three-dimensional version of a mobius strip. "The Klein bottle is an objective model in space . . . that serves as a medium for dimensionality extending the self-reflective words so that they can actually re-enter their own pre-reflective ground. Here the higher dimensional Klein bottle is embodied not just as an object of significations, but as a part of signifying act itself."*[14]

Because it is being twisted through another dimension, the Klein bottle, also called a pelican, is an impossible structure in physical reality. It is a symbolic vessel, though I would like to propose that its existence is manifest in the mind-body-soul transfiguration taking place in the individuation process. The paradox of this alchemical instrument's "impossibility" and its essential function in mythopoesis brought forth one of the final questions posed to the reader in this book. I am not surprised somehow by Rosen's work with the Klein bottle arising here as he had introduced me to the notion of the Implicate order through some discussions we had just prior to my first transplant and the publication of his *Topologies of the Flesh: A Multidimensional Exploration of the Lifeworld.*[15] The body as Klein bottle is a visceral morphing of soma into lens; this sharpening of

14. Rosen, "Quantum Gravity and Taoist Cosmology," 37–40.
15. Rosen, *Topologies of the Flesh.*

perception through the body is a crystallizing of flesh from grain of sand into glass that holds the transparency of wholeness in a single moment; body crafting itself into lens (am I simply a way of seeing?) so that I am not separate from my seeing.

In the individuating process, what is called upon is both the inconspicuous forms of meaning which lie beyond space and time, as well as an anchoring presence much like the chorus in the Greek tragedy which holds context—just as a subjective embodiment holds the context of one's personal myth. The inconspicuous presences are the inherent meanings of the Implicate order in deep time. The presence of the collective voices of the chorus—the collective voices of the archetypal—connect the personal myth to the mythopoetic narrative that moves from the mythic to the mythopoetic into the imaginal. My/your body, the body of humanity as Klein bottle, is an alchemical vessel of transformation. Soma is showing me inside and outside simultaneously with no separation between the two, just as the image in the mirror I gaze at now gazes back at me in the very same moment, no separation of time in their appearance. And so this gaze between us presents another dimensionality that holds both the object of signification, and *is* the signifying act itself: active perception. The gaze is already possible as an *a priori* presence in the body as Klein bottle and made clear through the spiral lens. I am reminded again of Jung's encouraging suggestion in working symbolically: "Image and meaning are identical. As the first takes shape so the latter becomes clear."[16]

Emerging initially in a series of figurative drawings, the image of the spiral lens became an essential catalyst in the development of the relationship between embodiment and working symbolically, psyche and soma, mirroring an archetypal pattern revealing itself in order to be transformed. Thus, the spiral lens was an important image my Psyche presented to help me extend my dulled perception of myself and the world and enliven my capacity to see. I invite you, reader to consider gazing through your own spiral lens and experience your body as an alchemical tool much like the Klein bottle, and to know that your body is part of the collective Klein body stretching itself towards a vaster perception of the birth-death-rebirth archetype.

The spiral lens—that "mythopoetic eye"—that sees and shows me how to see myself as a way of seeing, is a form of consciousness that lives in the unconscious. It is necessary. It is archetypal. My Klein body knows

16. Jung, *Structure and Dynamics of the Psyche*, 402.

this form of consciousness in its gut as it experiences inside and outside as one multidimensional continuum of existence. The collective Klein body also knows this and speaks its truth through cultural rituals and the arts.

The notion of the spiral lens is significant culturally in its inherent connection to traditions that are part of each culture's heritage, its origins, its stories and art that speak about where the people came from and how—its myth. The spiral lens is an important symbolic tool for me to see where and how I have come to be the way I am, particularly given my literal vision loss. As a "mythopoetic eye," the spiral lens brings the archetypal (arche: the beginning, the first, and type: mark, figure, outline) into view and invites me to see those inconspicuous forms of meaning that lie beyond the reach of my physically blind eyes; or to reside with them in that primordial dark of No-Image—that form of consciousness that lies deep in the unconscious, the Self which can "see" the path of individuation. Individuation is "a person's becoming [her] himself, whole, indivisible . . . this is the key concept in Jung's contribution to the theories of personality development. As such, it is inextricably interwoven with others, particularly self, ego and archetype, as well as with the synthesis of conscious and unconscious elements."[17]

The ego is a complex of the archetypal Self, and the Self-Ego axis is the image of individuation.[18] Individuating involves actively engaging the archetype at hand. In *Mourning the Dream / Amor Fati*, this is primarily various aspects of the Death archetype from which the dynamic purpose, the "active meaning" encoded in me ironically comes to life. Naturally my relationship to what has died and needs to be mourned must be included in this research.

Seeing through the spiral lens offers me/you the view of the suffering of the dead and becomes an act of archetypal dimension, an act our collective Klein body knows but the conscious mind can only conceptualize. How ironic that as our body is dying, we have little desire to have a relationship with this personal and collective fate. No wonder the ancients are lamenting. They are wanting our active participation in this the most important of transitions of life into death, the spiral of the birth-death-rebirth cycle. Without the crucial relationship to the dead, there is an interruption of this core archetypal sequence that every mythic tale speaks of.

17. Samuels, *Critical Dictionary of Jungian Analysis*, 76.
18. See Edinger, *Ego and Archetype*.

Myths are epic lamentings and we can draw on their teachings to bridge the soul-split of the interruption of the birth-death-rebirth archetype. They are attempts at healing the soul-rupture caused by not honoring personal and collective trauma, archetypal suffering. Grief. Authentic and embodied mourning takes place through the practice of archetypal activism which introduces the possibility of letting go (archetypal) and seizing hold (activism). Finding oneself in deep time is an act of archetypal activism itself—a moment that inspires immersion, reflection, and action, the beginning of a journey of getting at the root of the matter:

> The white of the moon is the light of the true sun.
> The sunlight on the moon is what is called the "root of heaven,"
> Otherwise it would be enough just to say "heaven."[19]

The suggestion here is that through reflection as the true seeing—seeing symbolically, the root of "seeing through"—we experience the archetypal flickering present in an event or story.[20] I hear the archetypal story of suffering throughout my myth as it calls me to begin the grieving *and* loving as the title of this book suggests, *Mourning the Dream / Amor Fati*, without splitting into the complexes that arise as neurotic defenses against the archetype of suffering.

Figure 8. The Moon Is Reflecting upon Herself in the Animal's Body

19. Cleary, *Secret of the Golden Flower*, 48.
20. Hillman, *Re-visioning Psychology*, 83–84.

I met David L. Miller while attending Pacifica Graduate Institute in 2000–2001. Miller associates activism with one-sidedness and archetypalism with many-sidedness, an oxymoron by definition. Could such opposites be held together in one piece of work? Do opposites stem from the same root? Or would this paradox be too daunting? Coming into relationship with the reflexive paradox of *Mourning the Dream / Amor Fati*—a form of archetypal activism in itself—asks that I engage my interiority and environment in a manner I never quite imagined before—like the simultaneous inside/outside of the Klein body, and the image of myself in the mirror and me. My body as Klein bottle, the still fleshy spiral lens I need in order to see again, is digging in the dark earth of the unconscious for the root of heaven, dying to each moment so to live the next as one breath. All stories share the same breath.

I could viscerally feel the tension of the one-sidedness and many sidedness of archetypal activism, an experience of living and dying in one short breath, a breath I could not catch even while it struggled to complete itself within the tight chambers of my rib cage. A breath cut in half, unable to find its other half, not knowing what to do, a splitting of consciousness—a cutting off the breath of Psyche and her deeper intent; a deep inner pressure becoming omnipresent. Is it pressing inward or outward? Intense energy held in from the inside as if from an outside force pressing in, a force field, a field of information, subject and object, active and receptive at the same time, constantly reminding me of something just dying to happen. Mourning; deep grieving to allow for the initiation of some form of movement, some kind of momentum to be ignited, something as simple as rolling over in bed. Or putting pastel to paper and letting the subtle waves of in-breath/out-breath create the mark on the blank white surface; white sheets to roll over as if in sleep, gestures of the unconscious; shades of the Underworld. So I turn to these shades and gestures inherent in the creative arts where transformative embodiment perceives its own activism. Even while the thinking mind sleeps—dreaming into its tacit significance, purpose, and intention—the unconscious is secretly creating an aesthetic that has the capacity to touch the imaginal, the moment the mythic realm of being is becoming.

Being a mythopoetic practitioner means living in a synchronically perceived world organized through seeing behind the scenes—the projections of our personal and collective myth—at the same time as understanding that our projections populate our inner and outer worlds.

The spiral lens shows us how we are affected by these worlds and in turn affect them.

Practicing mythopoesis includes asking how my/our narrative has been wounded and how has the attempt to heal this myth of wounded-ness moved it. Healing happens in the realm of the unconscious, though we have the ability to assist this through our consciousness. Imagination is the chaos out of which forms are fetched.[21] *Masa confusa*. The spiral lens of mythopoesis catches these forms while they are still possibilities, flickerings just behind consciousness. The body-heart-mind whole then tracks and crafts the images through several stages of embodiment:

1. Stirrings or flickers in the body sometimes manifesting as symptoms are the ephemeral aspect of embodiment. These are the seeds lying in the earth of the unconscious wanting to sprout. They are possibilities that may or may not take on further form, largely depending on the conscious attitude towards them. They are the tendrils of archetypal processes going on behind the scenes that are still in the unconscious though very present. These include the rustlings of the ancients, the inconspicuous forms of the morphic present in the collective field.

2. These ephemeral tendrils seeking more substantial embodiment by making themselves known through their stirrings or flickers in the body-mind-heart have physical, mental and emotional resonances. These resonances are also reaching for form but often perceived as difficulties, problems, and blocks, or experienced through illness and pathologies. The energy of these stirrings is indicating movement, change.

3. If the inherent change that is being indicated by the stirrings—whether perceived as difficulties, instinctual impulses or inspirations—is responded to through the imagination and contemplation, it moves on to yet another stage of embodiment: creative processes resulting in forms in the world. In this manner the stirrings and flickers in the body-mind-heart transform (moving from one form to another) from their initial embodiment in the unconscious in flesh, to thought-forms, emotions, and actions that give substance and value to them within the gestures of lived experience, a dance of the imagination.

21. See Stein, *Carl Jung's Red Book*.

4. Being of value that is, having been evaluated through sensations, feelings, thoughts and intuition, these stirrings of one's being are given personal and cultural expression in the world. They are brought out of the invisible into the visible in more concrete embodiments such as music, dance, theater, poetry, art, etc.

5. The personal and cultural "objects" of these creative expressive processes are embodiments in the world and both create and affect this world.

These embodiments in-the-world are living sites of transformation and make up the architecture of our lives. In turn, they affect us as cultural beings and individuals. In this reflexive process of taking the invisible into the visible, the next stage of embodiment is the "taking in," interiorizing the resonances of these personal and cultural forms into the architecture of our imaginal world through contemplation and further attending to what flickers arise from them. So we have moved from the invisible to the visible, and now back from the visible to the invisible, in the ongoing dialogue of our intersubjectivity and world making. This describes just one cycle of the ongoing dialogue of the soul with its own existence in the soul of the world—*anima* and *anima mundi*—the spiral of a synchronistically perceived world organized through seeing behind the scenes and then embodying these scenes symbolically through cultural and artistic expression. This is the mythopoesis that sees through a spiral lens.

As a container, *Mourning the Dream / Amor Fati* creates the appropriate *temenos* for the unveiling of the "truth" that lives within the myth: the rolling narrative that runs like an underground river creating a gravitational pull in the psyche that moves life forward from behind or beneath—in "the subjective: our imaginative, invisible gaze, in the direct sense of what is beneath our feet, our 'sub-jectivity' (from 'to throw under')."[22] I am thrown under into the subterranean river to meet the archetypal image beneath the narrative: death. Through the disclosure of dark secrets that have shaped "my" story and my body, there lies a part of a vaster truth, a legitimacy, a potency for me beyond my present capacity to embody the narrative without this piece of work, this mythopoeia. The *temenos* is "the psychological container shaped . . . by mutual respect for unconscious processes . . . and a commitment to symbolic enactment . . . the hermetically sealed vessel . . . an alchemical term for the closed

22. Angelo, "Splendor Solis," 25.

container within which opposites transform."²³ I propose *Mourning the Dream / Amor Fati* as such a *temenos* for the reader.

"Everyone carries a shadow and the less it is embodied in the individual's conscious life, the blacker and denser it is. If an inferiority is conscious, one always has a chance to correct it . . . if it is repressed and isolated from consciousness, it never gets corrected, and is able to burst forward suddenly in a moment of unawareness."²⁴ "Fleshing out" the shadow, drawing fresh blood into those pale places of soul deprivation initiates a healing, a re-membering of the limbs of the liminal that had been cut off, now bringing them back to the Self (archetypal Self). Those lost pieces yearn for the Self like a child reaching for her mother. Through the engagement of creative modalities, unconscious myths can embody into consciousness. Body listens to the wisdom the mind is too busy to hear. She dances, paints, sings out from the depths, the shadows, and something imaginal emerges, something the mind may not be aware of. Then this dance, this painting, this song can, in turn, infuse one's whole being and awaken a life unlived. In this kind of reflexive engagement there is no need for an antidote to the myth presently being acted out unconsciously. No "cure" for one's life; Nothing to fix. Rather, it is an archetypal act of moving into essential shadow material to mine the literal for its symbolic significance, to see through one's myth and deepen experience. This is mythopoetic research whose subject is our very experience as it presents itself to us including the unlived life we yearn for. In one of her body psalms, Dr. Celeste Snowber speaks/dances "body seen as text; moving to becoming listening; stretching to become research."²⁵ Snowber asks:

> What happens when we listen to all of who we are, integrating grief as a place of research—grief is in the body who is interested in what is absent, touching the behaviors of the body; inappropriate behavior that might tell an embarrassing tale; reveal a wrath of grief that cannot be contained.²⁶

Grief is a doing, an act of engagement with what cannot be contained. It asks that a *temenos* be built for it.

---

23. Samuels, *Critical Dictionary of Jungian Analysis*, 149.
24. Samuels, *Critical Dictionary of Jungian Analysis*, 138.
25. Snowber, "What the Body Knows."
26. Snowber, "What the Body Knows."

"Stories are told not just about the body, but through it. They are autobiographical acts echoing the embodied self."[27] In this sense, *Mourning the Dream / Amor Fati* is an echo chamber resounding mythopoetic archetypal actions that have "active meaning." Through trans-forming itself in the arts, our myth reflexively transforms us. In shifting meaning from the literal to the symbolic, the mythic to the mythopoetic, *Mourning the Dream / Amor Fati* is research as imaginal container. Carl Leggo, poet and professor at the University of British Columbia, describes this as:

> language designed to enrich our comprehension of our inner lives, a language that helps us to see beyond the literal, beyond the world revealed to us through other disciplines like science and mathematics, history and geography. In this it shares an epistemology with the other creative arts . . . Our mythopoetic discourse helps us see the world more fully.[28]

Mythopoetic discourse takes us into deep time when the embodied self lives, "when we listen to all of who we are, integrating grief as a place of research."[29] Mythopoetic inquiry endeavors to see through the spiral lens of the dream to be with the suffering of the ancients, hearing and heeding their laments, sacrificing the Klein body in her evisceration of becoming the spiral lens. Birth-death-rebirth uninterrupted.

Taking my story on a mythopoetic voyage—that big ocean trip to Canada (the new land of freedom and adventure) the little girl never made—helps me see and experience deep time more directly through speaking the language of body, story, poetry, and image, swimming with the current of the imaginal and the morphic past in the present. Mythopoetic inquiry has made me drop down and ask: "what is the untold story sleeping in the embodied image sitting at the bottom of deep time?" Perhaps my mother did not want me to swim in the swift current of the deep river with my father and siblings for fear that I might sink to the bottom and drown. What important question is the image at the bottom of the river holding for me, just waiting for me to get past the analysis, past even the emotions that are the call to pay attention, to listen? "What is important is not a philosophy of life but to observe what is actually taking place in our daily life, inwardly and outwardly."[30]

27. Frank, *Wounded Storyteller*, 71.

28. Leggo, "Longing for Books," 38.

29. Snowber, "What the Body Knows."

30. Krishnamurti, *Choiceless Awareness*, 16.

What is taking place symbolically to invoke consciousness? "Consciousness is perception."[31] Perception is consciousness. Not through five senses but one, sensing the holistic way we take-in space and reality. Perception is an act that creates something—a gesture, a feeling, a contemplation. It is in the depths of Psyche that we find embodiment, that instinctual connection between heart, mind, body . . . the depths in the viscera which will be actualized more potently in image than in conceptualizing alone.

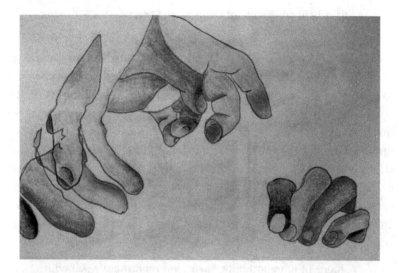

Figure 9: Sometimes a Gesture is a Sign. Sometimes It's Unconscious

Mourning the Dream / Amor Fati holds the intent to unveil and bring the depths into view by asking questions with no answers and finding meaning by sacrificing the attempt to find it, not necessarily asking "why." Mythopoetic intention is both an archetypal action that creates a container *and* openings to an evolvement of my way of seeing, both literally and figuratively as a partially sighted image-maker. I ask the reader where she might be partially-sighted—or short-sighted—and if a new way of inquiring/seeing emerges from having retrieved or let go and mourned the lost visions of the forever vanishing horizon line. When my perception reaches both beneath and beyond what my eyesight and myth or story proclaims, I may be re-imaging, re-visioning a journey in which life is imaging me. In each moment as I image it, this moment is

31. Merleau-Ponty, *Phenomenology of Perception*, 326.

also imaging me (as I look into the mirror while the image there looks into me). I do not need to ask "why." The "why" is embedded in the gaze itself, just as the image reflected is a symbol of itself, and so my self-image or myth is symbolic in the same manner:

> This is correct seeing, whatever is contrary to this is false seeing. Once you reach this ungraspability, then as before you continuously practice stopping and continue it by seeing, practice seeing and continue it by stopping.[32]

> This is twin cultivation of stopping and seeing. This is turning the light around.[33]

I see flickers, catch glimpses and reflections in the mirror of my experience.

"Turning the light around is the turning on of the light of the mind itself emblematic of the basic awakening of the real self and its hidden potential."[34] Turning the light around, awakening to the archetypal Self that sees the Implicate Order is a mythopoetic move that signals the start of the crafting of the spiral lens. One definition of mythopoesis is "situations where meanings of mythical accounts had been re-visioned, the original literal tellings of *myths* and stories transformed into symbolically new versions."[35] A story is flickering in a single silver strand of hair. Shedding light on the mind, becoming conscious of consciousness itself is a "stop":

> A moment of opportunity when I am momentarily paused in action that calls my attention to what is hidden; a vulner-ability. A stop invites me to question my longings as well as my habits of practice and to engage anew. A stop is an invitation to understand things, events, experiences and/or relationships from a new perspective.[36]

I stopped combing for a moment, and noticed for the first time, the silver threads glistening through the darkness of my hair; Time. How do I/you move through time? This "stop," a moment of risk, drops my ordinary way of being.[37] A strange intimacy arises that releases me into the many-

---

32. Cleary, *Secret of the Golden Flower*, 48.
33. Cleary, *Secret of the Golden Flower*, 21.
34. Cleary, *Secret of the Golden Flower*, 1.
35. Doty, *Mythography*, 20.
36. Fels, "Complexity, Teacher Education, and the Restless Jury," 74.
37. Appelbaum, *The Stop*, 91.

sides my story, my myth is both telling me, and withholding from me (the many-sidedness of the archetypal). Shadowy places between my differing conceptions of myself light up ironically revealing blind spots and absences. "Philosopher David Appelbaum speaks of what he calls a 'stop'. . .A stop, he tells us, occurs when a traveler encounters an obstacle, and is momentarily paused in action. A stop is a moment of hesitation, a moment that calls our attention to what is hidden—a vulnerability, an intimacy, a longing. A stop invites us to question our habits of practice and to engage anew."[38]

Something has gone terribly missing in my life. Where might I look for this something, or even know what it is? At what moment did I notice it went missing? In what moment did I know of its presence? "Stalking a dramatic moment requires the patience of a fly-fisher, the willingness of a coyote, the breath of a winged angel," a moment outside the habitual chattering narrative the mind so often indulges in.[39] If I "practice seeing and continue it by stopping," I might catch this breath, see this flickering as an archetypal act, urging me to continue the mythopoetic journey, the shifting from the literal to the symbolic moving along the Self-Ego axis of individuation.[40] In the archetypal dimension, I am a many-sided being; I am all ages. I am not yet born, I am ancient. Psyche knows the moment of my/your birth and my death as seen through the spiral lens.

Encompassing the one-sidedness of activism with the many-sidedness of the archetypal, mythopoetic inquiry includes and moves through the aperture of our current narrative, as well as being in strong contrast to today's societal view of myth as a kind of a fable or false story. In indigenous traditions, "myths" are better defined as stories, many of them guiding stories (or images) that emerged as a means of teaching something important to the people, essentially how to survive (physically and psychologically). Symbolically, the stories are meant to teach about something else and that something else is really the core teaching of the myth itself—the mythopoesis. The mythopoesis is the act of perception that teaches us to see through our own story to the archetypal narrative our story is a metaphor of. The aperature of the spiral lens allows us to see through the myth to the imaginal which maintains the purpose of connecting the personal with the collective.

38. Fels, "Complexity, Teacher Education, and the Restless Jury," 74.
39. Fels, "In the Wind," 81.
40. Cleary, *Secret of the Golden Flower*, 48.

When our own narrative turns against us, confronting our "version" of ourselves so that we might recognize our myth as a metaphor implying something else, then we might be moving into the diaphoric, that aspect of the metaphor that puts us in contact with the presence of something yet unseen or unknown. As a symbolic process, our personal myth becomes a laboratory transforming itself. In this laboratory the Klein body "loops back through itself to join with its other end from inside."[41] As a metaphor for the mind-body-soul connection, the Klein body reminds us that our body's inside and outside are not separate. This symbolic process suggests that our myth also needs to pass through itself without a hole that needs fixing.

Our myth contains itself—including soma—and the spiral lens this opus is crafting. What begins to occur in this containment, this *temenos*, is a process of mourning the losses and absences in our story. An integration of the myth of "who I think I am" can then act as fuel in moving more closely to *amor/fati*, "that one wants nothing to be different, not forward, not backward, not in all eternity. Not merely bear what is necessary, still less conceal it . . . but love it."[42] Through the inquiry of the personal and collective sufferings of the Klein body, *anima mundi*, the mythopoetic journey itself becomes a liminal path of transformation.

Figure 10. Ways of Knowing

41. Alling and Greenleaf, "Klein Surfaces," 159.
42. Nietzsche, *Basic Writings*, 447–48.

Liminality has me palpably experience what is absent. I gaze into absence. I "stop" and look into what is not visible: those dark gaps. I reach for my spiral lens as I descend into a story of darkness tracing Psyche's footprints. I am following the whale's movements through my own somatic experience and imaging.

Tracking the moments of my/your original story, beginning to recognize its patterns, I/you come to feel the invisible momentum of my/your myth as it presents itself to me/you within the container of mythopoetic inquiry.

To straddle the visible and invisible, connecting to Psyche's deeper intent, I must put certain things aside—attachments to pathologies, both physical and emotional as well as cultural—and challenge habitual states of mind and being. Within the *temenos* of mythopoetic inquiry and with the help of my spiral lens in-the-making, I begin to see myself as a way of seeing, sensing a deepening of events into experiences, a self selfing. Mapping out the unfolding of these experiences from this symbolic perspective, initiates an alternative positioning of being in the invisible; being invisible, throwing an image of myself into the dark and stepping into it; my body needs no instruction. My body is the place of a fold by which the sensible reveals itself: my "body's non-coincidence with itself; the invisible *of* the visible."[43] From this fold of my aesthetic—intertwined with the world of sensations, gestures, images and words—comes an opening that may shed light and bring to consciousness the deeper intent of Psyche, the "active meaning" my horizon line holds for me.[44] I continue to follow the imaginal whale's path in my Klein body, catching glimpses and reflections in the mirror of my experience. The mythopoetic eye sees my experience as a symbol, and so I enter the liminality of the visible/invisible my aesthetic knows so intricately.

To map these motions of my aesthetic—so that they can be passed onto others, becoming a story—involves tracking. Like a hunter, who goes into the underbrush of the imaginal to find entry points to the liminal, I sacrifice my usual positional way of being in the world and in myself; stopping, taking the risk of being and being *in* the invisible, I am trusting that my body will find her way. My mother used to say to me when I was confused "your body will be somewhere." Becoming less self-conscious and more conscious of consciousness itself—trusting that

43. Merleau-Ponty, *Visible and Invisible*, 149.
44. Bohm, "Meaning and Information," 41.

"mythopoetic eye" that has the capacity to see into personal and collective dimensions of past-present-future—would be an act of "turning the light around."[45] Learning how to listen to my "call," the call of the ancients lamenting through my voice, allows me to feel into the Implicate Order I can only hear if I "stop" and go into the silence of non-being—No-Image, the bardo, the "place-in-between"—where the noise of neuroses can no longer drown out the song of the whale deep in her underwater travels.

By setting out on this journey through the deepest of discussions with myself, I know I need to choose to travel in the dark for a period of time as we all do in depth work—go into the blindness, move into mythic rhythm, and slip into deep time where any notion of myself is a redundancy, a "false seeing," a "myth."[46] Here I will see this redundancy as a neurosis structuring itself out of the narcissistic wound attempting to contain itself. Instead of denying emotions or trying to do something about them, I could recognize how they are pieces of the original story flying loose, uncontained now by the fixation with the narcissistic wound. In the alchemical vessel of the mythopoetic inquiry, these unsuppressed feeling states can be mined for their pointing out of certain forgotten details of the false myth I have been telling myself about myself, that wounded narrative. In fact, these uncomfortable places—if attended to symbolically—can unveil the disguise of the false myth as defense and thereby actually intensify intimacy with soul. Here lies the shadow work of soul perhaps. Here is the "myth" in both senses of the word: a false story, the source of suffering and "wounding," *and* a guiding narrative that is part of a greater weave of sentient beings.

Unmasking the wounded narrative by seeing through its clever disguise, seeing it symbolically rather than unconsciously continuing to act it out or identify with it, is the very passage of soul-finding towards self-actualization. In this place of vulnerability lies the route though (and root of) suffering, where Bohm's "active meaning" generates the energy of the implicate order—that innate sense of purpose, intention, and value that draws us into the now activated mythopoeia.[47]

A mythopoetic approach opens a sensibility where the wound is tended to, held like a baby in my arms. An important step towards developing a mythopoetic sensibility is the practice of deep democracy.

45. Cleary, *Secret of the Golden Flower*, 21.
46. Cleary, *Secret of the Golden Flower*, 21.
47. Bohm, "Meaning and Information," 41–44.

"Unlike 'classical' democracy, which focuses on majority rule, Deep Democracy suggests that all voices, states of awareness, and frameworks of reality are important."[48] The broad, open foundation which deep democracy offers sets the stage for archetypal activism which ignites the practice of mythopoetic inquiry.

> Deep democracy is both a philosophy and method. The philosophy recognizes that every group [individual psyche] has a consensual [ego-oriented] reality as well as another dreaming reality. This dreaming dimension includes all of the deep feelings and dreams hidden within our communication.[49]

Deep democracy includes everything in the field. That is, all the images each participant is living, whether they are aware of them or not, whether they are consciously or unconsciously expressed. All the "guests" are participants of what is going on and not going on so that a kind of collective dream is taking place, embodying the group's or individual's myth. (Myths are inclusive of what is left out of the story). The work of deep democracy is to set a place at the table for all images and No-Image, and allow each and every one a voice, and welcome them into consciousness:

> The method of deep democracy focuses on the ability of the facilitator [ego] to use his or her awareness to notice, value and follow all of the people and parts [images] of a given group [individual psyche] in consensus reality, as well as noticing and valuing the more dreamlike expressions and feelings of a group [individual].[50]

Deep democracy is active perception that sees and draws on the deeper, broader pool of resources of the collective unconscious left otherwise untapped. As well, it brings power and attention to archetypal presences that exist parallel to conscious, consensus reality, those "flickers" mentioned above. Tracking these "flickers" from the unconscious brings subtle shifts in consciousness, body gestures and symptoms and dreams, as well as what arises in an aesthetic experience and creative processes; different guests are brought into the field of awareness and come into focus through the spiral lens—even if just for a moment. Through the practice of deep democracy, I am also able to learn more about archetypal activism and dialectically bring together polarities previously split off as

48. "Deep Democracy."
49. "Deep Democracy."
50. "Deep Democracy."

a result of unmanageable tension in the system (cast into the shadow for temporary relief). As I practice deep democracy in this manner, what becomes apparent is the possibility that these polarities within me interact mutually, engaging without definitive dominance. "In this way polarities may reflectively energize and activate each other, reflecting through distinction."[51] Turning the notion and experience of polarities around in the manner suggested is stunning—a "stop"—especially when I feel dominated by a particular compelling, if not seductive, image/archetype. Death; illness; powerlessness.

Figure 11: Choking Bud

I am sitting with the now embodied flicker of the choking bud above and I instantly know its predicament. I can feel this bud in and around my body. I look at it and enter the gaze between us as if we are both intimately bound together in a third space of our own in the diaphoric imagination (that touches the possibility of something unknown entering the field). For a moment the intimacy between the image of the bud and my image of myself becomes a luminous presence itself that holds a particular kind of unanticipated potency; Stepping into that space-in-between invites me to slip past ego consciousness and into relationship

51. McNamara, "Evolutionary Challenge," 10.

with "other." In considering the role of metaphor in interpretation it is crucial to distinguish "two ways of metaphor. The purpose of 'epiphor'— metaphor in the conventional Aristotelian sense—is to express a similarity between something relatively well known or concretely known (the semantic vehicle) and something which is less known or more obscurely known (the semantic tenor). The other and complementary kind of semantic movement that metaphor engages may be called diaphor. Here the 'movement' (phora) is 'through' (dia) certain particulars of experience (actual or imagined) in a fresh way, producing new meaning by juxtaposition alone. The relation is presentational not representational."[52]

In the liminal field, the practices of deep democracy, archetypal activism, and engaging the diaphoric imagination enable the archetypal activist to step out of the one-sidedness of ego consciousness towards facilitating the fulfillment of Psyche's ulterior motives. Here the concept of the Self-ego axis illustrates how the ego comes to learn that it is in service to the Self. This difficult task for the ego is rehearsed over and over again, should the ego agree to this, in the process of art making when the image claims its own autonomy. In allowing the image to land on its own feet, so to speak, the image forthwith brings about a new presence whose symbolism now holds that which was previously blocked by a more literal interpretation, a colonization of the image's potency as that of the ego's. In the same manner, the literality of our historic self that we claim as the subject of our narrative, lacks the diaphoric dimension (that which implies something "other" than this limited notion of self) of the mythopoetic. It splinters into a wounded narrative. By seeing it only at the concrete level, the narrative, myth or story—the voyage through this literalization of the self—can seem like a kind of pathography; a neurotic rather than a creative response to our experiences.

Mourning the Dream / Amor Fati is a story of pathos, a retrospective of images of the Death archetype with its attention to the intricate details of a chronic condition that has plunged me into periods of darkness, including the literal loss of eyesight. However, the word retrospective is not quite accurate, as this inquiry does not only look back, but is also a direct experiencing, and re-membering of images as they embody themselves in writing and art making. I look as if into a mirror and ask what the black marks on the paper/screen are speaking about; what are they spelling out for me? Black is not an absence but a different kind of presence.

52. Wheelwright, *Metaphor & Reality*, 73.

Classically, pathography is a style of biography that emphasizes the dark aspects of life and work, such as failure, unhappiness, illness, and tragedy. *Mourning the Dream / Amor Fati* certainly includes the shadowy parts of life that illness and blindness bring into the forefront of daily living. But my interest is not in simply leaving it at this.

Taking the first "step" of mythopoetic practice as outlined in this book, deep democracy opens a field of possibilities for attending to images—the "flickers" such as the choking bud above. Perceiving symptoms and conflicts as expressions of the tension of opposites directly is possible when we see our experience as a mirror reflecting an imaginal reality from which the symbolism of these very inner encounters arise. Chogyam Trungpa takes this a step further in his explanation of the sanskrit concept of *mudra*: "*Mudra* means 'symbol' which has nothing to do with analysis or examples; rather the thing itself is its own symbol. Everybody represents themselves, and everybody is a caricature of themselves. There is that sense of a humorous aspect, a caricature aspect, as well as everything having its own basic fullness. You represent yourself not by name but by being. So there is a sense of completion."[53] Reading Trungpa's words I am immediately taken into that place of peace where the tension of duality has been released. I am once again drawn into the image of the back of the whale inviting me into her watery universe. The peripheral gaze of the whale (her eyes each on the opposite side of her head) that catches movement now enters my body which feels archetypal processes, the forces shaping my myth. The image itself here brings a somatic and symbolic sense of the whale's entire journey in me imaginally. "[Our] life is less the resultants of pressures and forces than the enactment of mythical scenarios."[54]

I feel how the *mudra* of the bud and the whale echo archetypal forces in my journey, showing me how my myth itself is its own symbol. The mythopoetic approach helps me see this enactment of mythical scenarios through the lens of the particular moments of the bud's or whale's life glimpsed at here in their images. Through the symbolic presence of the bud or the whale, and my engaging them in the manner described, I am offered a template with which to have relationship with other archetypal forces that appear as "guests" within the field of my experience with the ineffable (such as my blindness). I feel the contours of their

53. Rinpoche, *Tibetan Book of Living and Dying*, 171.
54. Hillman, *Re-visioning Psychology*, 22.

influence—the bud's desire and imperative to grow, the whale's instinct to migrate through vast seas of possibility. Through their embodied presence, living in my myth, I begin to see more clearly the role of the archetypal potentialities presented in the images and how these are crucial "guests" accompanying me in the mythopoetic journey.

The image of the bud, the whale, and other accompanying "guests" are full of possibilities, yet complete in themselves. They are provocative even if the possibilities they inspire do not embody themselves consciously. The richness of each image still maintains its own basic fullness whilst offering its co-emergent wisdom as a mirroring mechanism (the mirror of my experience reflecting and being reflected by the cosmic mirror). In this manner, working with the very images that are my experience being mirrored back to me, I am able to engage the raw material of the mythopoetic project directly. I can see the images as central to my myth *and* as their own symbol, as Trungpa might suggest.[55] I understand that my myth, with all its "guests" and even its repetitive patterning—the spiraling over and through previous experience and conditioning—is itself its own symbol. This symbol is asking me to see correctly; to see the myth as an image, to experience the ego as an image, that is, a symbol of itself. Psyche's teachings lie in the repetition of certain patterns, specific images signaling me to turn the light around to see what the symbols of the patterns are pointing me to: that my myth itself is its own symbol with its own basic fullness and "sense of completion."[56]

By continuously practicing stopping and continuing by seeing, it becomes evident to me that the white of the moon (indirect light, the peripheral, the consciousness in the mirror of the unconscious) is the real sun—the gold the alchemists are creating out of the lead of life. My story, my myth is the important lead to be transformed. My blindness to this is the very beginning of lessons to come. As I feel into the Klein body and look through the spiral lens this body is crafting, I begin to know what my story is reflecting back to me. In this mirror I see a presence entering me, like the future that comes into the present in order to transform itself and me reflexively.[57] This is the diaphoric imagination that is holding something within the unconscious so that it might appear at some point in consciousness—a moment of "active meaning." This form

55. Trungpa, *Cutting through Spiritual Materialism*, 171.
56. Trungpa, *Sacred Path of the Warrior*, 178.
57. See Rilke, *Letters to a Young Poet*, 63.

of imagination is moving beyond the middle ground of metaphor and into the unknown, the unfamiliar, into the depths with the whale, into the soul of my blindness. I invite the reader to receive the images in this book, as well as their own "flickers," by practicing stopping and continuing by seeing, borrowing the approach I have sketched out above, seeing through their own spiral lens. The reader may even discover through this approach that they too can find an image in the dark, retrieving a nugget of gold from the dark recesses of the personal and collective Shadow archetype.

To explore the dark transformative aspects of Psyche one becomes a "mythographer," a compiler of myths. These are the myths that are operating as if underground in the subjective and objective Psyche. "We forget that the soul has its own ancestors."[58] Who are the ancestors of the soul of my blindness, the ancients who are calling to be seen and heard? How can I, myself blind, respond to their lamentings? To root out these myths into the daylight so that they might become illuminating is both an intuitive *and* conscious response to the call from my own darkness. I travel with the whale. This is Psyche's ulterior motive for us and "why" we must find the shadow-image swallowed by the dark—no matter how blind we are personally and collectively:

> Belief, conscious or unconscious, that a prior readiness to trust a transcendent power was a prerequisite for the experience of the numinosum cannot be conquered; one can only open oneself to it. But an experience of the numinosum is more than an experience of a tremendous and compelling force. It is a confrontation with a force that implies a not-yet-disclosed, attractive and fateful meaning.[59]

Mourning the Dream / Amor Fati is a kind of "soul tracking" by way of the footprints of the emerging autonomous images from the unconscious that present themselves symbolically. Opening myself to the very confrontation my own narrative is challenging me with feels almost impossible, yet I have no choice. The path before me, which appears more like an impenetrable forest, can only be discerned through my ability to see symbolically; to see what is not yet evident. I would like to suggest to the reader that this way of seeing could allow the possibility of both mourning the dream—the mourning of what has been lost, or never even

58. Hillman, *Soul's Code*, x.
59. Samuels, *Critical Dictionary of Jungian Analysis*, 100.

achieved—and loving one's fate, a sacred way of seeing that illuminates a path of "letting go" and "seizing hold" of life towards one's fate; to fall in love with this continuous revelation of the mysteries of Self. As Nietzsche writes in *Ecce Homo*:

> My formula for greatness in a human being is *amor fati* [love of fate] that one wants nothing to be different, not forward, not backward, not in all eternity. Not merely [to] bear what is necessary, still less conceal it—all idealism is mendaciousness in the face of what is necessary—but love it.[60]

Nietzsche's profound insight here is the grain of sand in the desert that hides the secret diamond it is, flickering its many facets throughout your mythopoeia.

Holding handfuls of sand—sifting through experiences of loss while engaging the presenting grain of any given moment—I am living in deep time. I ask myself and the reader: "How do I/you move through time? How does time move through me/you?" As a spiral lens in the making, *Mourning the Dream / Amor Fati* brings the whole mythography into view. It is an invitation to see your own myth, including yourself, as an image; your self-image as a symbol of yourself, both a completion and a beginning . . .

The body of work in *Mourning the Dream / Amor Fati*, a Klein body itself, is an invitation to experience the unconscious as it presents and expresses itself through images. The spiral lens allows us to understand how the unconscious has the ability to embrace the invisible, that it has the depth and breadth to engage that which I/we are not conscious of and then reveal this to us through our Klein bodies as embodied images. Through this intricate process, we become simply a way of seeing, rather than who we think we are. We become the archetypal activist, the imaginal ego who can find the route to the mythopoetic through our own unconscious footsteps made visible in the arts.

My fingers trace the edges of a mythopoetic map that shapes itself within my blindness, feeling into the emptiness of the loss of my eyesight. Am I inquiring into the nature of the unconscious? Is the loss of vision the cue to a descent into the Underworld where the mourning and grieving can begin? Daring to encounter the soul of blindness as a symbol of its collective self—as a symbol of the unconscious, where Psyche presents images in the grit of sand—I begin to "let go" and "seize hold" of fate. I

---

60. Nietzsche, *Ecce Homo*, 258.

am forging my destiny through doing image work with the very unfolding that is happening before/within/beneath me, moment by moment,
taking in the gestures of soul/Psyche subjectively. Subjectivity is always
embodied.

Overview of Chapters to Come

The prelude of the book is intended to offer the reader the tone or a
metaphoric glimpse of the long and difficult journeys that were and still
are the raw material of the mythopoetic project. The introduction has
hopefully served to present some sketches of the inquiry as a narrative of
the imagination which creates an alternate story to the dominant story.
The objective of this introduction is *not* to find or define the meaning of
this story as such, but rather to clearly situate it, allowing myself and the
reader to be engaged in uncanny situations. This chapter introduces the
notion that the inquirer, researcher, or mythopoetic practitioner her-self
is both subject and object, her presence the creation *and* the one acted
upon in the process of imaging. In this imaging, Psyche creates a space
in which something new emerges that simultaneously changes the actor
and the world—new information that moves from the unconscious to
conscious to symbolic (invisible to visible, to again invisible, and now
integrated). We are both the liminal space and the liminal figure that
moves through it.

Chapter 1, "Developing a Mythopoetic Disposition: *I Am Simply a
Way of Seeing*": A mythopoetic sensibility offers a foundational shift from
our usual assumption that the imagination is in the mind and images are
a product of the mind. Let us consider here that the human mind lives in
the imagination, rather than restricting the imagination to the confines of
one's mind (*logos*). This subtle—though profound—discernment changes
the course that our sense of identity takes in our myth, directly connected
to the individuation process. It introduces the notion of *I am Simply a
Way of Seeing* as a symbolic way of seeing that opens to an "other" point
of view—an alternate story that is born out of the diaphoric (unfamiliar
aspect of metaphor): a form of perception which occurs when the new
eye/I sees through the image to perceive the way the image sees.

Suggestions for developing a Mythopoetic disposition are presented
in chapter 1: (1) practicing *deep democracy*, which creates an opening to
the field of experience, (2) *archetypal activism*, which brings opposites

into co-existence without polarization or splitting (one dominating the other), (3) embodying images that arise (the somatic experience and art making), and (4) reflecting and sensing into the images so that a presence appears in the diaphoric imagination through which a new myth, a new expression, emerges (the transcendent function) and a new story is told.

Chapter 2, "Entering the Liminal," takes you, reader, into a vivid evocation of the lived encounter with the void. It travels to the heart of the raw existential wound of the original myth. The images, poetry, and narrative offer the reader illustrations of an important step in the mytho-poetic project—that of entering the third space. The embodied expres-sions of this piece of mythopoeia might act as guides or even anchors for readers who want to explore this part of the mythopoetic journey in their own lives.

Chapter 3, "The Call," asks the questions that are the initiations of a mythopoetic inquiry, in this case: "How do my ill-health and vision loss act as a 'call' to deepen consciousness and expand awareness?" Vision-making. Readers might be prompted here to discover and articulate their own initiating questions and pursue a line of inquiry towards how their creative practices may be an important response beyond what they have already examined. As an example, this chapter provides steps for working with the wound and wounded narrative through catching cues, track-ing flickers in the intra-psychic, and inter-relational fields that develop through opening oneself to the diaphoric imagination. In the beginning, the ego can only "hear" the story carried mostly by symptoms; the imagi-nation opens the doors to the message.

Part 2, "Falling into Context," builds a larger frame for the signifi-cance of the personal myth and how it is an important aspect of the col-lective weave of intersubjectivity. Suggested is a new hermeneutic which clearly contributes to embodied and contemplative practices of artists, art therapists, educators, and researchers. It is an invitation to those who would like to move from the literal to the symbolic. Part 2 of this book introduces the role of therapy and education in facilitating such a shift in perspective within a cultural container.

Chapter 4, "Black," is the shadow journey of the inquiry and holds the experience of blackness as an investigation into the history and origins of my myth, including implications of the cultural background of dis-ability and the victim archetype presented hermeneutically through both symbol and process. Black offers the reader an example of mythopoetic

inquiry as it illustrates a tracking of symptoms/symbols, "flickers" pointing the way, taking up the "call" to living in the questions rather than an-
swering them. Black presents one of the loops of the spiral of the journey/
inquiry; it is an autobiographical inquiry that transfigures the wounded
story into the living mythopoeia. The spiral of Black takes the reader into
the dark, the long journey of profound loss; the intimacy and destiny of
the soul's dialogue with its own existence. The experiences that arose in
writing Black brought me to an important turning point in the book and
my life. It marks a transition in movement, a shift from descent to ascent
with the knowledge that another spiral of the same is inevitable.

Part 3, "The Hermeneutic Imagination: The Spiral Lens Crystallizes," introduces the movement between intention and extension through
spiraling into the momentum of Psyche's ulterior motive and method of
finding images in the dark. Turning to the notion of the inward and outward eye/I, this section takes the reader into embodied reflections in the
mirror of experiences of mourning and *amor fati*.

Chapter 5, "Learning How to See Again," continues the spiraling
of the inquiry into the relative nature of objective and subjective reality,
finding how the two "realities" and their teachings merge and emerge in
an alternate narrative. Learning how to see again is an emergence through
releasing the body from its unconscious habits, allowing the body to become healer of the narrative that has been torn up by the unfinished business of the personal and collective past. This chapter leads you, reader,
into an experience of entering the imaginal world, interacting with inner
figures and archetypal patterns, directing a new multidimensional way of
seeing. Here the mythopoetic arises and an alternate narrative speaks—
one is wounded but whole, wounded and healing.

Figure 12: Into the Imaginal

Chapter 6, "Vision-Making: Eye-Sight and In-Sight" helps the reader to understand and perhaps identify with how inner and outer, intention and extension, function in the personal and collective Psyche. Following the subliminal narrative of the myth, one learns to see (penetrate) through blindness (unconsciousness) and extend this place-in-between into a ground of learning where the "other"—the unknown—is crucial to knowledge. This form of knowledge surpasses mind-body dualism when consciousness is experienced in and through our body. The suggestion here is that through this "knowledge," and the mourning it demands, comes the possibility of loving one's fate: *amor fati*.

"Vision-Making" elucidates how embodied imagination has the ability to re-enchant the world and bring authentic spirituality back into culture by recognizing the primacy of intersubjectivity and the way we are always already embedded in the world—part of a cosmic process of unfolding, our personal experience a mirror image in the primordial mirror—bringing awareness to phenomena. As a form of spiritual phenomenology, this unfolding, intending, and extending may carry the possibility of deconstructing the mythic modern materialistic narrative that has yet to shift from the literal to the symbolic; from myth to mythopoesis. Active reflexive perception.

Chapter 7, "Embodied Reflections in the Diaphoric Mirror of Experience: Mourning the Dream / *Amor Fati*," takes the reader into the sense of interiority that dreams create, travelling across invisible thresholds of self where we encounter "other" as self and self as "other." Here we find images that old habitual ways of seeing cannot even touch, images that reveal disruptive presences lying just around the corner of perception, asking to be known. Presences sometimes disturbingly known to the Klein body which can experience an existential confrontation consciousness itself cannot acknowledge. A full-on meeting of the creative/destructive dialectic presented as a potential opportunity to re-myth and re-embody ancient wounds and traumas, to hear the laments of the ancients.

Chapter 8, "A Mythopoetic Practice: Threading Back, Stitching Forward: Mythopoetic Inquiry," threads back through the morphic resonances that live in and amongst us, while stitching forward into the soul's most intimate dialogue with its own existence. Coming into contact with inner figures and archetypal patterns established by the ancient ones and becoming attuned to their signals through "flickers" experienced in the personal and collective Klein body, a form of fieldwork is developed that supports a method of mythopoetic research. Coming to meet the "guests" of the unconscious as they come to meet the researcher becomes the symbolic task of the mythopoetic approach proposed.

Part 1.

Travelling: Mapping Out the Territory

1

Developing a Mythopoetic Disposition

I Am Simply a Way of Seeing

As mentioned in the Introduction, a mythopoetic sensibility challenges the assumption that the imagination resides in the mind—rather than the mind dwelling in the imagination. Such a re-visioning of our innermost processes profoundly affects who we think we are both internally and in-the-world in the individuation process. I dare say that the discernment between the above perspectives of the imagination and mind is also noteworthy on a cultural level, underpinning the values that steer the evolution of both society and the individual. We have collectively experienced all too well the ethical and political ramifications of regarding images as products and the colonization of the imagination in service of a kind of "spiritual materialism": "The problem is that the ego can convert anything to its own use . . . the main point of any spiritual practice is to step out of the bureaucracy of the ego."[1]

However, as far as ego is concerned (as a sense of identity), it also acts as a kind of homing device on the journey of individuation through the past-present-future dimensions of the birth-death-rebirth archetype. From a mythopoetic perspective this "self" (ego) is an image, mirror, or symbol of itself that functions much like a centrifugal force. We experience this force while orbiting in the spiraling path of mythopoesis which, paradoxically, pulls us away from the fixed focus we maintain as a "self"—our sense of identity. The circular movement around the

1. Trungpa, *Cutting Through Spiritual Materialism*, 13–15.

literalized concept of self (ego), is spinning on an axis that lies outside of itself, just as the earth revolves around the sun. As we relax, rather than holding rigid to this literalized "self," we begin to see through its trickster-like guise. Instead, we see a gap in its game, a break in its story, and enter a liminal space wherein we can experience the ego more fluidly as imaginal ego. Then we can also see this story which is our myth, symbolically, that is our own myth as a symbol of itself. What is introduced here then is the notion that *I am Simply a Way of Seeing*.

"Whatever heavy burden the hero carries is himself, or rather the self . . . the totality of his being."[2] Working within the context of a mythopoetic sensibility, I propose that some of the heaviness of the burden comes from carrying one's myth of "who I think I am" too literally. I am a burden to myself when I believe what I tell myself about myself, thereby maintaining a perspective of my existence that has me feel squeezed in on all sides by the confines of my own narrative. Here the mind pinches the imagination into a contorted shape that feels impossible to maintain. The pressure pushes me to a new question, an alternate inquiry: What would it be like to experience a more symbolic way of being? What would it be like to develop a mythopoetic sensibility by engaging life through the imaginal archetypal realm through images and symbols, a more active symbolic way of being?

> 'The Imaginal' . . . is nearer to the language of the arts than it is to the language of concepts . . . a speech of the lost power of the soul . . . Psychological language may thus have to find its kinship, not with the language of scientific reason or with the exercises of behaving well, but with the arts.[3]

Let me propose some immediate provocations regarding these queries:

> Am I how I see myself?
>
> Am I how I think of myself?
>
> Or am I myself simply a way of seeing?

I ask you, reader to consider these provocations as we embark on how a mythopoetic perspective or imaginal disposition might be experienced,

2. Jung, *Symbols of Transformation*, 303.
3. Hillman, *Myth of Analysis*, 180.

and how it might be useful to ask why such a perspective is important. And if so, how it might be developed.

Turning back to the questions posed above, the third question, *am I simply a way of seeing?* is exciting and not as "fixed" as the first two questions are. "Our symptoms and fixations are symbolic constructs; when our visions harden into dogmatic realties: we become sick."[4] Question three intrigues me . . . and holds a glimmer of what a symbolic relationship with life might conjure. Questions one and two, *am I how I see myself?* and *am I how I think of myself?* both suggest a disorienting split in our sense of self. The "I" is the subjective perspective and "myself" the objective, resulting in a separation of identity in the structure of the questions themselves. As language constructs our social identity, images from the unconscious can challenge this often taken for granted or assumed notion of self (ironically also mostly unconscious). The story of who we are in the context of family, society, culture, gender, and era allow us to feel at home in our environment—at the same time alienating us from shadow aspects of those collective scripts we might experience. At some point, our own narrative turns on us and bursts the very body of our beliefs. Where do we turn when our sense of self is ruptured in this crisis of authenticity?

I have had discussions in group sessions with participants about which to trust as the more authentic or true self, the conscious mind or the unconscious, as if there were an implicit hierarchy. Do I turn primarily to the unconscious for direction, stepping into the unknown in order to be guided? Or do I expand and strengthen that center of consciousness, the ego? These questions are legitimate in their curiosity about what the subliminal narrative inside is telling me about myself. Am I the subject or object of my own criticisms or idealizations of self taking place in my myth? Am I the perpetrator or the victim of the wounded narrative? Which pole of these dynamics do I identify with and which remains in the unconscious? "Neurotic symptoms may be regarded as attempts at self-healing in that they draw a person's attention to the fact that she may be out of balance."[5] Forms of neuroses frequently erupt to shut down the painful responsibility the Psyche is now faced with in maintaining wholeness, the totality of all psychological and somatic processes, both conscious and unconscious. The strength to hold the tension between

4. Hillman, *Myth of Analysis*, 206.
5. Samuels, *Critical Dictionary of Jungian Analysis*, 99.

the conscious and the unconscious requires an ability to contain the totality of wholeness which, presented here, relates to the emergence of numinous encounters that surpasses comprehension. We feel as if we are dangerously in need of making a decision, as if our life depended on it, but cannot. Our sense of self, so ardently forged, vanishes and we are left with what Krishnamurti calls "choiceless awareness":

> The important thing is to discover . . . and after discovering, keep going. It is detrimental to stay with what you have discovered, for then your mind is closed, finished. What you have discovered becomes literalized by the mind and the myth is no longer living; the same story repeats itself ad infinitum. But if you die to what you have discovered the moment you have discovered it, then you can flow like the stream, like a river that has an abundance of water.[6]

Krishnamurti's description creates a path to mythopoesis, suggesting the very workings of the process of transformation. "If you die to what you have discovered," Krishnamurti writes, then the moment of this death becomes a new life—a starting point of inquiry of this subject/object dialectic; a portal to rich images and narratives that Psyche wants to tell us beyond the story we already know.[7] That sense of identity ego understands calls us "home" (home as a symbol of self). It draws us in so that we can see what we have discovered on this path of individuation that is the very ground for connecting to the archetypal realm and the wisdom of Psyche.

Psyche's wisdom moves us deeply into a sensibility that is active in the sense of taking the myth—the literal (that natural homing device our sense of identity serves)—and experience this "totality" at a level of import and depth. Such a shift from the perspective of ego as complex to the ego as archetype marks a new rule of order in which the non-dualistic imaginal ego is both the subject and the object of individuation. The mythopoesis itself is now functioning as a "living" myth. To illustrate this, I refer to Gaston Bachelard's words: "Everything that makes us see, sees."[8] Taking this a step further implies that everything that makes us, makes us see it, and the myth that is making me is making me see itself. My myth is offering itself for me to see it symbolically—even as it is living through

6. Krishnamurti, *Choiceless Awareness*, 2.

7. Krishnamurti, *Choiceless Awareness*, 2.

8. Bachelard, *Poetics of Space*, 168.

me in my own private storytelling, in this moment. Seeing through it, recognizing the epiphoric (familiar, more concretely known) aspect of the metaphor as it is coming into relationship with its complementary diaphoric aspect (something less known or more obscurely known), I come into a new relationship: a reflexive, mythopoetic relationship with both my own and the collective narrative of "self."

Through experiencing my sense of self symbolically—this mirroring relationship between identity and awareness—I am released from many notions I might hold about myself. I literally move "through" myself: "Here the 'movement' (phora) is 'through' (dia) certain particulars of experience (actual or imagined) in a fresh way, producing new meaning by juxtaposition alone. The relation is presentational not representational."[9]

The diaphoric imagination moves through the more literal ego-story "I" have of myself, encouraging me to now include a perspective of soul, so that I can realize something that does not yet exist—unborn awarenesses. As I re-cognize/embody this new creation, I sense a new presence replacing an absence. I am invited to step into those dark blind spots, those gaps in my retinas, the absences now possibilities; Psyche's ulterior archetypal motive.

An aching absence is the presence of a dis-embodied mourning of a dream. Stepping into the mourning fully, filling it with my presence, I begin to see diaphorically: "The essential possibility of diaphor lies in the broad ontological fact that new qualities and new meanings can emerge, simply come into being, out of some hitherto ungrouped combination of elements."[10]

Miller describes this diaphoric seeing thus: "The poet is the purveyor of radical metaphor: absolute metaphor, or diaphor . . . which is a carrying through whereby the lost mythic moments are carried through into contemporary experience."[11] The lost mythic moments are the mourning, the lament. "The take-it-or leave-it attitude that is implicit in all good metaphor is in itself so far as it goes, diaphoric; the sense of an invisible finger ambiguously pointing is epiphoric. The role of epiphor is to hint significance; the role of diaphor is to create presence. Serous metaphor demands both . . . diaphor emerges from the metaphor."[12] The diaphoric

9. Wheelwright, *Metaphor & Reality*, 73.

10. McGaughy, *Strangers and Pilgrims*, 277.

11. Miller, "Images of a Happy Ending," 80.

12. Wheelwright, *Metaphor & Reality*, 192.

seeing of the poet creates presence, discovers meaning. She finds images in the dark. She does this by being neither neurotic nor psychotic when "an unknown 'something' takes possession of the psyche and asserts its existence undeterred by logic."[13] The poet (poesis) creates presence through her mythic, archetypal connection to the unconscious, which engenders the pregnant moments of essence—the collected "stops" that gather into shaping and forming something to be birthed. "Poetry is the art of letting the primordial word resound through the common word."[14] The mythopoetic lifts the myth into the symbolic where it is re-connected to the archetypal narrative of the collective.

Field Notes: From the Viscera

I can feel in my gut what it is that breathes me: the mythopoeia has taken hold. The myth inside has stirred, awakening to its task.

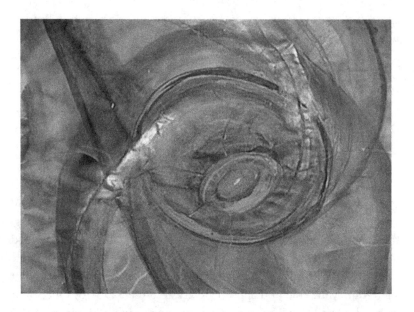

Figure 13. The Egg Has Been Sent

13. Samuels, *Critical Dictionary of Jungian Analysis*, 123.
14. "Primordial Word."

*Mythopoetic diaphoric seeing, which has been born of the meta-
phor of my myth, changes the eye. This eye/I now sees through
the image to see the way the image sees. This new eye/I changes
the breath which now breathes the way the image breathes. See-
ing/breathing from inside the image, enfleshing it with my new-
found sense of presence to meet it, it is the new-born embodiment
breathing me. I can hear her breath whereas before I was lost in
an echoing of my absence. Breathing through her breath, seeing
through her image as a mirror of me, in this moment appears as
an inner figure of a blind victim. I now breathe/see the way she
breathes/sees. I see how she sees and doesn't see. I experience her
myth for a flicker of a moment that startles me and begins creating
a new presence and meaning in me. I am suddenly no longer separated from her; she is no longer lost to me. She reveals her image of
herself, tells her story and I re-member it. We are now in dialogue.
I no longer have to unconsciously grieve her, this soul-figure. The
blind victim and "I" no longer have to vie for the position of subject, being one against the other—split: one light, one dark; one in
the light, the other in the dark. I can now see how she sees—in the
dark. Now she can come out of hiding. She can move through me,
diaphorically revealing herself through the developing of a spiral
lens that sees her. The Klein body strains into this re-membering.*

Mythopoeia *is* an awakening to Psyche's ulteriority and is a move
into the uncanny itself. Seeing the invisible I see that "everything that
makes me see, sees."[15] And everything that makes me see, makes me see
it. I see my blindness that forces me to see. I see through images and
events—my myth, knowing that it is what breathes me, sees me. My
blindness sees me! It is the presence within the myth trying to speak with
me, making attempt after attempt to help me recognize its presence as
subject. Who is this story about? What is this story about? Who is telling
it and who is listening to it—and who is living it all at the same time?

As a partially-sighted mythopoetic inquirer, artist, researcher,
educator, and therapist, I have learned to recognize this presence more
clearly through the absence of my eye-sight. I see it in the context of the
dark, initially just as flicker, then a blinding moment in which its embodiment takes shape in its own blackness through body/image/word,
black script on white surfaces of skin, melancholia scratching incisions
of re-cognition. Realizing the profundity of the presence of what appears
to be absence, I have a dialogue with this image/inner figure of blindness

15. Bachelard, *Poetics of Space*, 168.

and am not left alone with my own blindedness to her. As a figure of darkness, I find her in the shadows as she finds me by taking me into her world, touching me in all the raw places. Here we are now both subject and object together through my seeing/breathing from inside the blackness she is, seeing/breathing the way she does. Breathing the same breath, she embodies herself through my body. We are one process and together we step into the uncanny.[16] Together our body is an emboldened liminal space, the place in between and as twins we create a middle ground. This liminal body *is* the transitional space in which we can travel freely and dialogue with each other speaking the language of flesh and poetry, mythopoesis. We are inside and outside simultaneously. We/I am the Klein body pushing through into an "other" dimension in the metamorphosis of becoming a spiral lens.

In symbolic conversation with "presences" from the autonomous unconscious, new possibilities the mind could not reach while assuming itself to be containing the imagination spring forth. In vaster regions beyond mind, Psyche adeptly fulfills her ulterior motive of having me step into those "stops" that act as portals to the numinous. The flickering presences brought forth by Psyche—even as blinding moments when everything seems to stop—are the "interspaces" referred to as spaces of yet unknown possibilities, pieces of the unlived life asking to be lived consciously.[17] As an artist, I understand these spaces as the liminality of the visceral, animated processes cooking in the tension of opposites. These are spaces with presence that are brought to life through practicing archetypal activism. If I follow a mythopoetic sensibility and read the signals in my body as flickers from Psyche, I come to embody yet unknown possibilities—the future entering into me before it actually happens "out there."[18] If my awareness is not yet born, I will likely be stuck in the old (habitual) notion of subject/object being a "problem," rather than as diaphoric consciousness at work (connected to Jung's notion of the tension of the opposites leading to the "transcendent function").[19] Without the mythopoetic disposition, I may miss the possibilities Leggo speaks of. I will be blind to the presence that is teaching me and there will be no encounter with the numinous—that presence I can only be aware of by

16. See Leclerc, "Unconscious as Paradox."
17. See Leggo, "Longing for Books."
18. Rilke, *Letters to a Young Poet*, 63.
19. Jung, *Essential Jung*, 226.

listening to the signals in my body, the "invisible presence that causes an alteration of consciousness."[20]

The Klein body—that living, transformative alchemical instrument, bodying inner and outer through its own invisible dialectic (a mythopoetic dialect, a "both/and" that the practice of deep democracy suggests)—encourages a dropping into deep time, when/where mysterious encounters take place. When I am fully naked to the moment, present in the possibility of a numinous meeting with "other," deep time reveals Psyche's ulterior motive. Such a rendezvous is in direct contrast to neurosis, a running away, grasping at the moment ahead in fear of being in this unbearable relationship. If I actively move into those vulnerable places—present right in this body, in each sensation, as the flickerings of my myth (which the blinding of my sense of continuity constantly reminds me of)—I will be in the very position to develop a mythopoetic sensibility and moving through (dia-phor) the literal to the symbolic. Then I am in the act of perception; I *am* that place of possibilities which invites presence and new meaning along with meaning-finding methods that bring soul into the re-connected moments of living and dying. Archetypal activism.

Stepping into the liminal and embodying it with my presence—like Psyche throwing an image of herself in front of herself—I come to know the liminal and my body as one and the same; the body as alchemical Klein bottle. My body as liminal space/being activates the image emerging from this place-in-between and moves in the direction the image is guiding me. This directive image is none other than Psyche's trickster-like ulteriority. She creates an alternate image to that of the ego and so introduces a new presence.

The awakening of this archetypal presence in-waiting (silent, invisible), kick-starts the development of self-story and narrative. The archetypal image beneath the wounded narrative or complex is trying to tell/ reveal itself to me; it is showing its presence to me if I am present to it. The archetypal image is not the archetype per se. An archetype cannot be apprehended without image or affect which is the signifier of the presence of an archetype. Such a signifier might be the complex: "A complex is an autonomous entity within the psyche . . . they behave like independent beings . . . splinter psyches."[21] I can recognize a complex by its heightened feeling tone sending a "charge" throughout my system, particularly the

20. Samuels, *Critical Dictionary of Jungian Analysis*, 100.
21. Samuels, *Critical Dictionary of Jungian Analysis*, 34.

body. The complex is a highly subjective experience, though at its core lies the invisible archetype our journey of individuation is pulling us closer to. Though mostly unconscious, the complex does not fail to draw our attention to it. I am reminded here of Angelo's poignant statement about subjectivity: "If an inner eye/I is to be cultivated, it requires a further understanding of our imaginative, invisible gaze, in the direct sense of what is beneath our feet, our 'sub-jectivity' (from 'to throw under')."[22] The inner eye/I with its indirect gaze into the liminal—into the interiority of corporeality—sees the underlying archetypal image beneath the unconscious complex that is generating its own momentum, its "affect" leaving me as if caught in a spell. Who casts the spell?

The cultivated inner eye/I that *is* the spiral lens in the making, sees the unconscious director of my movements. Listening through, ala James Hillman's "seeing through," can be cultivated in the presence of the dominating narrative of a complex.[23] The archetypal activist sees through the spell the complex casts while being inside its powerful tug into unconsciousness. Here, inside the image, Psyche offers the archetype through the complex (complex as image or narrative); she can hear the underlying leitmotif structuring experience and discern the song of the ancients in its melody. In this way, I can recognize the song as not mine alone. It is a reoccurring motif, each breath in the song holding the feelings, thoughts, and gestures of the ancients breathing my body.

When I am feeling as if I am stepping close to the lip of an abyss, I wonder if I am unconsciously walking in the shoes of the victim figure of the inner narrative (complex). I am horrified when I inadvertently find myself caught in this wounded narrative of my self-story, and feel the posturing, gesturing, and contortions this inner figure takes in the painful morphing of the Klein body. As if in a play or a film, I am literally "acting out" this character. Often when I listen to people speaking, either casually or in the therapeutic relationship, I notice which role they consistently cast themselves in—and which role I fall into. I become aware of their posture through the sensations generated by how I hold myself and read facial expressions as I feel into the inner figures that might be present in the field; which "guests" from the unconscious are embodying themselves in this moment. Is it the hero, the antagonist, or any other inner figure in the theater of the Psyche that has stepped into the main role, directing

22. Angelo, "Splendor Solis," 25.

23. Hillman, *Re-visioning Psychology*, 83–84.

the actions of this "play"? Which archetypes are in the field, hoping we might recognize them through these unconscious, symbolic enactments?

Sometimes I feel the animation of particular inner figures through these conversations. In moments I recognize how the consistency of an apparently central inner figure may be a clue to the myth the person and myself are constellating in that instance. I feel the flicker of the myth in my Klein body which throws light on what story I am embodying in that moment with them: body-to-body in a liminal, morphic field of autonomous performances of silent scripts. Often this playing out of imaginal scenes is a mirroring of the projective identifications of the stories around us. I am at times able to hear these secret scripts, a kind of perception of "depth on the surface" when my Klein body is picking up an unconscious aspect of the field and detects the depth of the myth voicing itself in simple dialogue. The cultivated inner eye/I that *is* the spiral lens in the making then sees the mythic scenarios that are insinuated upon the players on the stage of Psyche's interiority.[24] The spiral lens brings all the inner figures acting out the present drama into view, appearing as an arrangement of images whose pattern becomes an image in itself—a motif, a theme—reflecting and resounding the archetypal pattern in the field. Myths dreaming together. "[Our] life is less the resultants of pressures and forces than the enactment of mythical scenarios."[25]

Working reflexively with this mirror of my own myth, taking in what is being reflected back to me, I am painfully reminded of how I often fixate on the image of myself as an object: am I how I see myself? Objectifying myself in this manner leaves me stuck, immobile, separate; self as commodity, false currency. I feel this in my flesh—the stomach locks down—and I want to get away from the pressures and forces enacting the mythical scenarios Hillman suggests. I become blind to what the spiral lens is trying to bring into focus. I attempt to escape this fleshy ache by analyzing and scrutinizing the central inner figure I am fixated on, which I think is "me." I am imprisoned in the hardened body of an old story I unconsciously identified with, rather than stepping into the mythopoetic possibility presented in the very drama being re-enacted. I am split, absent, grieving without presence: a rotting depression. The archetypal victim/perpetrator dialectic, a central part of my myth, and a core archetypal force played out in power dynamics collectively, remains ineffectual when it replaces the more potent and important one of

24. Hillman, *Re-visioning Psychology*, 22.
25. Hillman, *Re-visioning Psychology*, 22.

Mourning the Dream / Amor Fati. The suggestion here is that personally, culturally, and collectively we once again ask:

Am I how I see myself?

Am I how I think of myself?

The inquiry proposed re-examines the politics of the unconscious in that the questions posed ask that the power structure of the psyche be analyzed for the purpose of detecting and re-evaluating existing unconscious assumptions—particularly in light of a sense of identity and belonging. Many unspoken, unrecognized power dynamics that are underlying a destructive patterning in the personal and collective psyche perpetuate ongoing wounding.

Ethically speaking, understanding that within our own personal unconscious there are inequities—cases of bullying and victimization as well as heroic sensibilities—that become autonomous while remaining unconscious. They are then acted out with others in our environment and the power of their energy is misdirected. Rather than identifying with the archetypal core of these "mythic scenarios" through the complexes, a mythopoetic approach takes their vitality and works with it symbolically, inviting the transformative potential they carry to embody itself consciously. The shaping of this form of consciousness allows us to look at what sensibilities we are bringing to personal and collective issues and whether our research requires the crafting of well-designed questions.

I am proposing that the two questions posed above are of a "bad design." They will likely fail in the development of any sort of mythopoetic attitude required in the crafting of the spiral lens. When I focus my sense of self through the lens of the first two questions—*am I how I see myself?* and *am how I think of myself?*—am I the subject or object of the knowing of my experience? These questions render me lost in the labyrinth they themselves engender. I am blind in an endless maze of self-referencing that, in the end, leads nowhere and is therefore, neurotic and burdensome to myself and others. I am left with a "one sided or undeveloped perspective of neuroses, which leaves one with a sense of meaninglessness."[26] This neurotic perspective does not have the capacity to meet the numinous. It remains blind in its self imposed limitations in the mind and my story becomes a weight to carry rather than a life to live. A dead myth. A dead-weight. It cannot re-member the presence that is desperately asking

26. Samuels, *Critical Dictionary of Jungian Analysis,* 99.

to be "seen through" in the wounding and re-wounding—like a traumatic repetitive dream replaying a sense of absence.[27]

Question three on the other hand, *am I myself simply a way of seeing?* points to seeing in the way the spiral lens sees, creating an imaginal way of knowing that intuitive understanding of the whole lies in its parts. The imaginal ego lives in the liminality of the alchemical Klein body, which both takes in and shows everything it perceives—all the while in the process of becoming a spiral lens.

> The imaginal ego [that is embodied in image] is more discontinuous and guided as much by a synchronistic present as by the causal past . . . a circulation of the light and the darkness. It includes the downward turns, the depressions, the recessions, and fallings away from awareness. The movement of the imaginal ego should be conceived less as a development than a circular pattern.[28]

A circular spiraling pattern creates an entirely different perspective or disposition towards experience; the self now becomes a *process*, a momentum towards the symbolic. I am the lens, the act of seeing itself that spirals. Active perception. In this way of being, I am not self-referencing (that is, objectifying myself in the manner of the egoic self who provides its own pocket-mirror so that it might see itself). I am not consuming myself; the narrative about myself is *not* the experience. However, seeing myself as a way of seeing ironically affects and transforms my usual convoluted responses to the first two questions (*am I how I see myself?* and *am I how I think of myself?*). Seeing myself as a way of seeing spirals my consciousness into wider and vaster fields of perception.

Consciousness does, in fact, move. Imagination is the arising of images that inform us of this constantly. The imaginal ego knows that life is but a dream: "The idea of the imaginal ego gives conceptual form to what actually happens in Jungian psychotherapy: adaptation to the unconscious is reflected in the changed ego personality of the analysand. His adaptation is primarily to a 'psychic reality' (Jung), to the imaginal world (Corbin)."[29]

Through becoming more actively, mythopoetically engaged with the presence of the "otherness" the blind victim in my dream/myth plays—as

27. Hillman, *Re-visioning Psychology*, 83–84.

28. Hillman, *Myth of Analysis*, 184.

29. Hillman, *Myth of Analysis*, 184–85.

the dark pull of the archetypal dynamic of illness/wholeness—the one-sided perspective of the ego identification or the fixation of a complex is kept in check. Working mythopoetically offers the practice of (1) deep democracy, opening a spaciousness for receiving the blind victim as part of an archetypal narrative. As she guides me into the darkness she carries for me, I stay committed to practicing (2) archetypal activism, by experiencing both light and darkness. I begin working with the (3) diaphoric imagination which can then introduce a new presence into the alchemical mix of the narrative. Through my inquiry, I can engage this "other" mythopoetically and see her in her fullest capacity—not separated or isolated but "a part of." I am gazing into the darkness of my blindness to the "other," receiving her teachings about the shadow element of the illness/wholeness archetype.

The inner figure of the blind victim, the one that has the power to withstand the dark pull of the archetypal dynamic of illness/wholeness, was particularly active for a long period of time after I initially lost my eyesight. She kept looking for what I could not see, checking each eye over and over again separately, crying out in despair to the other eye to see if it could grasp what this one could not. As a metaphor pointing to something not seen—shadow material not identified with—the soul of my blindness kept reaching out past her claustrophobic confinement to the blackness pressing in on her. She was relentless in her efforts to stay connected to the "not-me" that might help her learn how to see in another less literal way.

I reflect now on how seeing and my sense of identity became symbiotic in that what I could see I felt was still a part of me; I could still be whole. I still had a relationship with these parts of my experience. And what I could not see was lost to me forever, vanished as if my very sense of self was suddenly unavailable, absent—dead.

Every moment I found myself looking for what I could not see, I lost myself. Each excruciating time this happened, I felt myself as if falling into an abyss. I also held the notion that these upheavals seen mythopoetically were the dramatic callings of the ancients speaking through soma. They are calling me to step deeper into *and* beyond myself into the larger narrative of the collective imagination, to then look back at myself from the perspective of soul, *anima mundi*. What is my task in this archetypal drama? The insight of seeing this drama with the "other" as archetypal releases me from the delusion that this is merely a personal issue. It illuminates an important part of the dialogue of the soul with its own existence in a manner that includes my myth as an essential part of the collective mythology. This dialogue speaks matter-of-factly about personal myth as a crucial lens for seeing how those archetypal structures underlying the human experience (and perhaps of all sentient experience) press up from the unconscious. These are the upheavals that topple the powerful neurotic compulsion to remain blind to one's personal narrative as a unique expression of the collective. This fundamental mythopoetic premise is central to my ethics as a Jungian-oriented art therapist.

Myth Making / Soul Finding

All minds, and all lives, are ultimately embedded in some sort of myth-making. Mythology is not merely a series of old explanations for natural events; it is rather the richness and wisdom of humanity played out in a wondrous symbolic storytelling: no story, no myth, and no humanness either.[30]

In *Memories, Dreams, Reflections* Jung asks the question "what is your myth—the myth in which you live?"[31] I understand him to be asking me to identify and become conscious of:

the contents that press up from the unconscious. The unconscious contents want first to be seen clearly, which can only be done by giving them shape, and to be judged only when everything they have to say is tangibly present . . . This can be done by drawing, painting, modeling [dancing, singing, performing]. Often the hands [body] know how to solve a riddle with which the intellect has wrestled with.[32]

Could the dream released in the dance, the painting, the song, reveal the nature and shape of the archetypal image lying beneath the "sub-jectivity" of personal narrative as reflected in my life?[33] The symbols in the dream image, painting or song seem to resonate with something archetypal, that directing image that lies at the heart of my myth where my mythopoetic sensibility lies sleeping. Mythopoetic sensibility lies in the seed (*anima*); it is the deeper intent of Psyche waiting to sprout.

30. "Depth Psychology."

31. Jung, *Memories, Dreams, Reflections*, 171.

32. Jung, *Memories, Dreams, Reflections*, 326.

33. Angelo, "Splendor Solis," 25.

Edward S. Casey, author of *Imagining: A Phenomenological Study* comes to mind regarding his explorations of the living, breathing character of imaginative experience. Drawing on his own "sub-jective" experiences, Casey shows imaging—be it visual or auditory (and I would add all the other sense channels through which we experience and express our being)—to be distinct from perceiving. He defines it as a radically autonomous act, involving a characteristic freedom of mind echoing Krishnamurti's choiceless awareness. Suddenly, I catch a glimpse of the imaginal ego roaming the mythopoetic landscape, an embodiment of the liminal.

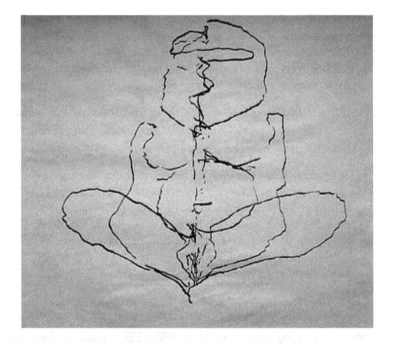

Figure 14. Embodiment in the Liminal

The imagination—image—is here both the core and the circumference of experience: imaginal ego *and* mythopoetic landscape, figure and ground. I am both the sub-ject (thrown under) and the object of the dream, the painting, and the inquiry in this dialogue between the ego and the presence of consciousness embedded in the unconscious. There is an obvious correlation here to Jung's notion of the archetypal Self. In Jung's words: "The Self . . . embraces ego-consciousness, shadow, *anima,* and collective unconscious in indeterminable extension. As a totality, the self is a *coincidentia oppositorum*; it is therefore bright and dark and yet neither."[34] To image the Self as both center and circumference, intention and extension, *anima* and *anima mundi*, takes a mythopoetic sensibility which intuits the way the imaginal ego sees, feels, touches, and smells its way through existence. This is in keeping with my question posed earlier: *Am I simply a way of seeing?* It offers an exciting prospect well beyond the more positional questions *am I how I see myself?* and *am I how I think of myself?* which are more aligned with the perspective that the imagination inhabits the mind.

The more radical notion of the mind being a part of the imagination is illustrated in the imaginal ego's ease in navigating the landscape of myth—its agility in tracking Psyche's footsteps through the flickers experienced in the Klein body. The body as the liminal figure shaping this landscape of the imagination is carving space with her dynamic mythopoetic moves. This embodied imaginal ego can arch into the liminal curves of the realm of the archetypal, as well as see herself as an image symbolizing herself. I see flickers of the crystal spiral lens as it brings into view the whole arc of one's life. I see the whale as she reveals her glistening back to be seen just for a moment, then carries our imaging with her into the depths.

The embodied imaginal ego sees and moves beyond the limited horizon set by the heroic-ego/mind. This is a mythopoetic perspective which recognizes archetypal patterns within narratives. Archetypal activism works with the polarization the archetype is generating—hero/victim, perpetrator/victim, dismembered/remembered. It intentionally eclipses the opposing forces as they manifest in the body. Recognizing both extremes existing at the same time challenges identifying with either pole. Through inquiring into what the intimacies of the body are saying, the archetypal activist deliberately holds the space for the affect and image of both poles. As a liminal figure, the archetypal activist enters the inner constellation of polarization through the sensations and affects experienced in her Klein body. The Klein body lives in the space in between and knows the in-breath and out-breath of hero/victim, dismembered/remembered poles. She experiences and reveals these in a process much like Casey's "imaging." In a diaphoric archetypal act which, again, as Casey suggests, results in a radical freedom of mind, what is apprehended

34. Jung, *Memories, Dreams, Reflections*, 108.

is a mythic scenario taking shape in direct experience somatically and symbolically. Mythopoetically, this is a call from the collective voices of the ancients, asking the individual psyche for the integration of morphic resonances present in their narrative to be fully embodied without splitting. Bit by bit, life by life, dismembered aspects of the collective shadow that have accumulated in the wounded narratives of groups or individuals are coming forward to be metabolized by the alchemical Klein body towards metamorphosing into the spiral lens—the vision-maker.

Through mythopoetic inquiry, the embodied imaginal ego as archetypal activist becomes the vision-maker who takes the radical step into the archetypal perspective; the vision-maker enters the imaginal realm where the archetypal story is living somatically and symbolically, embodied in the liminal Klein body who experiences inside/outside simultaneously. The imaginal ego is defined within the context of the imaginal—the symbolic body—which carries a mythopoetic sensibility as its mode of being (the body as liminal interiority with intent).

Edward F. Edinger was a Jungian analyst whose work mapped out the anatomy of the psyche and how it applies to where one is in her or his individuation. Edinger suggested that "consciousness is psychic substance connected to ego."[35] I imagine this as the imaginal ego coming into relationship with other archetypal psychic material just as the dream-ego comes into contact with other dream figures. Edinger continued his suggestion of psychic contents being potential entities—that I refer to as presences—becoming actualized and substantial. Embodied, they "make connection with an ego when they enter an individual's awareness."[36] They make conversation, so to speak, through body and symbol, soma and psyche, the mythopoetic sensibility picking up their presences long before they become conscious. Soul is eavesdropping and suggests an attending to the flickers in the Klein body as if they are elements of our future coming into us.[37]

Active perception of these tendrils of embodiment would invite them to fulfill their purpose of crafting the spiral lens. As they are transforming and transforming us, these presences can be engaged reflexively and hermeneutically and so contribute to the movement from the old myth eclipsing with the symbolic of mythopoeia. The capacity for seeing the literal as the ground for its own metamorphosis would, for example,

35. Edinger, *Creation of Consciousness*, 18.
36. Edinger, *Creation of Consciousness*, 18.
37. See Rilke, *Letters to a Young Poet*, 63.

reveal the deeper intent, the telos of the victim in the larger narrative. The archetypal victim calls for help through the felt-sense—moods and affects. She is asking to be seen clearly and that her archetypal role in one's experience be understood both in its necessity to be taken care of and to be received symbolically as a shadow disturbance that is signaling change. Being responsive to her dark flickering mythopoetically points to what she is carrying for us: woundedness. She is the voice of the wounded story of the collective Shadow. She experiences and reveals inside and outside transparently, and so becomes a target for collective vulnerability and violence. But the victim archetype is also the carrier of soul. A Black Sun that illuminates.

As a shadow figure, she is pushed into silence and invisibility, the unbearable image of all of us forced upon her: the inhumane treatment of the human body, tortured flesh. Breaking apart. And we do this in private in ourselves.

In the practice of deep democracy, there is a kind of listening through the whole body as soma hears/feels/senses the cries of the archetypal victim as expressions of presences—Psyche's flickerings, illuminations in potentia. This practice steers the Klein body through upheavals and temptations to fall apart. Archetypal activism brings the literal present situation together with the past in the present, which is where the upheavals are coming from. Rupert Sheldrake is helpful in bringing our attention to the morphic resonances which I call the laments of the ancients.[38] I hear the voice of the victim as their storyteller and I want to know those stories if I am to see and experience the whole story of my myth as the archetypal narrative being told through me. I can no longer cut them off by remaining blind to their embodiments in my life.

---

38. See Sheldrake, *Presence of the Past.*

Figure 15. Sight Cut in Half

Something is cutting me in two. In the story there is the "I" and the "not-I," and these two do not want to be together. Unfortunately, they grew up sharing the same room. Their solution for this "problem" was to divide the room with a line the other could not cross. What they did not realize was that they could not divide the air in the room with such a line. They were still breathing the same atmosphere—one inhaling, the other exhaling. In fact, they could not be apart at all, otherwise they would be unable to complete their breath. And although they were suffocating each other, they could not survive without each other. My childhood bedroom, shared with my younger sister, had such a crack in its blue linoleum floor. My bed was on the side of the room that had the door, so my sister was required to take a long leap across to her half of our quarters.

Having as its most characteristic feature the encounter of opposites—first experienced as the ego and the unconscious, the "I" and the "not-I," subject and object, and myself and "other"—comes the possibility of "creating a new increment of consciousness."[39] Theoretically, this is sound (from the Depth Psychology literature). However, I would like to return to the body as key in creating a "gateway" to consciousness. The body is the carrier of shadow presences and is the first to "know" of this split between the "I" and the "not-I" because it hurts. But in the above

39. Edinger, *Creation of Consciousness*, 18.

scenario, there seemed to be no apparent explanation for this other than a pathological one.

I heard pathological explanations spoken in a language with long words and complicated management plans: the language of illness, disease, chronic conditions, and medicines to "fix" the body. I learned to listen to this foreign language like an immigrant or indigenous person who no longer hears her mother tongue. I was told to pay attention to signs from the outside and not to trust the signals from my own pulse. "I wonder how much harm really has been done by all the ways we have tried to cover up our own shadow, losses, or un/dis/ease of living in the world."[40]

Eventually, these signals became fainter and fell into the shadows of the day-to-day symptoms coupled with the rigid regimens to be followed. As these signals lay submerged in the unconscious, they grew fat from the black blood that fed them. One day, this dark blood spurted violently from the depths and turned everything black. I fell into darkness and remained there for quite some time. A place where the "I" and "not-I" became silent—no sound of identity, absence. "Your body will be somewhere," I heard the echoing of my mother's voice. Where is this body now? I can't see her. I can no longer be how I see myself. I am invisible to myself. I am invisible. I am blind. Tokyo, 1986. Retinal hemorrhaging and detachment, sight gone.

Where did my sight go?

The creative arts as embodied inquiry plays with ideas of identity, and de-construct or reconstruct these notions in multifaceted interpretations, allowing the different guests of Psyche their moment on the stage. True to my mother's words, my body was somewhere even though my identity was not. I could still carve space through my movements. I could feel the air on my skin. This air smelled different than the air in the room I grew up in. My body was shaping a new home for me, discovering meaning in an entirely different manner than previously, a manner my body was quite unfamiliar with consciously, though my gestures came naturally as if already rehearsed. The Klein body was moving into action.

Edinger believes that each time the ego falls into unconscious content and drops into an image not identified with, there is the possibility of becoming conscious of this content. Through an act of separation that allows the ego to see the emerging psychic content as an archetypal

---

40. Snowber, "What the Body Knows," 3.

image, the ego can become dis-identified from the archetype itself. In the gap of "separation" (blackness), the ego moves into the position of object—of being acted upon by the psychic material that is pressing up from the unconscious. The emerging image/presence has become, for the moment, the subject. This content, this story is acting on me, its object. The mythopoetic task here is to see that *I am simply a way of seeing*, even while I cannot see!

The embodied imaginal ego can make this shift from subject to object through the creative act. The painting, dance, or song is then the subject "acting" on the artist, dancer, or writer. Much like a stunt man taking the place of the main character in dangerous scenes of our plot, the symbolic image or performance recreates unconscious mythic scenarios with an agility that surpasses the limitations of the ego as identity. It takes on archetypal abilities that are available in the collective unconscious and brings these perspectives into view, while still mirroring the original pattern of the dynamic.

"A symbol for the process of separating subject from object, the knower from the known, is the mirror. The mirror represents the psyche's ability to perceive objectively, to be removed from the deadly grip of raw, primordial being . . . to separate subject from object, how to perceive experience as a mirror that provides an image of meaning rather than as chaotic anguish."[41] An image of meaning presupposes consciousness, "to perceive objectively."[42] I look into the mirror to see an image of myself. When Psyche is looking for an image of herself she throws one out in front of herself and steps into it. Seeing my experience as a mirror brings me into relationship with a reflected image of myself and asks me to look beyond the reversed image in the mirror to see myself as a way of seeing.[43]

41. Edinger, *Creation of Consciousness*, 37–39.

42. Edinger, *Creation of Consciousness*, 38.

43. I am not here referring to Lacan's critical reinterpretation of the work of Freud in which the mirror stage establishes the ego as fundamentally dependent upon external objects.

Figure 16. Experience as a Mirror

Art as mirror provides an image of inner meaning that comes into relationship with chaotic anguish. The inherent aesthetic of our being human creates an order that the raw chaos that is being reflected cannot. The creative process and its interconnectedness with the world of matter *and* psyche can thus not only generate a tolerance for unbearable images, but even shifts these very images into becoming aesthetic experiences. Creativity takes the raw material of our experience as it is and leads us through (dia) the literal to the symbolic and into the diaphoric imagination, presenting a new, spirited story that is already living in our everyday. In the gathering and inviting of images in this mythopoetic inquiry, *Mourning the Dream / Amor Fati*, I begin to sense that my ego—as place of identification—has shifted into the position of object, being acted upon by the very images, the "guests," of the myth I have been living and writing about.

The quicksilver behind the mirror reflects the presence of mercury, the alchemical mixing of solid and liquid like Hermes' (Roman: Mercury) transformational capacity for crossing boundaries between one state of embodiment and another. Symbolic shape-shifting aids in the discovery of the meaningful image embedded in the oppressive mood (another mirror). Such a discovery, as discussed regarding the archetypal victim as wound carrier and symbolic signal from the ancestors, allows me to see an image of myself that is not actually me. I am not the victim. She is a presence pointing me to the larger collective dynamic of Psyche, reminding me that *I am simply a way of seeing*. Soul. If I can see the archetypal image of the victim without identifying with it, I will see it as a process I am engaging with. This way of seeing can perceive even the oppressive mood as a mirror, reflecting back images of an old myth, its presence generating these unbearable images I mistake as me. The image of the line on the childhood bedroom floor flickers through my mind's eye and a wounded story becomes the raw material for a collective archetypal inquiry of self and "other."

Discovering what the images in my experience are reflecting, I can sense the embedded myth moving through my body. Tracking and marking the turns in the path through the blackness and melancholia, the encounters between "me" and "not-me," I feel the ineffable contours of a mythopoetic landscape and am guided by the flickers of another form of consciousness. Again, I am with the whale.

Whenever I take a moment to look into the mirror of my experience and see it as a symbol of itself, I understand a little more about how the imaginal ego has a way of seeing that is both subjective and objective; I feel how it is fully embodied in the liminality of viscera, that mystery that holds duo-consciousness. Because the experience of being the knowing subject is only half of the picture, half of the experience of self—one side of the mirror—I yearn to gaze into the eyes of that face looking back at me. I want to step into the place-in-between of the gaze between us, which suspends each of us in an imaginal mythopoetic moment: "And when you gaze long into an abyss the abyss also gazes into you."[44]

The experience of being the object of knowledge feels as if the image in the mirror is consciously looking back at me. I become quite disconcerted in its eerie gaze. Whose consciousness is this? How does it appear like this when I think I am completely alone, private? Where does it come

44. Nietzsche, *Beyond Good and Evil*, 146.

from? This is an image of the imagination itself, in the process of "imaging." "I" am an archetypal image being mirrored in my myth. The ego itself is also an image that is being gazed at in the mirror of imagination, which sees spirally, encircling the looking and what is being looked at as one event. I am mirroring and being mirrored in my myth.

Rollo May was interested in analyzing the structure of human existence with the aim of understanding the reality underlying all situations of humans in crises:

> [Each] of us has his or her own myth around which we pattern our lives . . . The myth bridges the gap between conscious and unconscious: we then can speak out of some unity of the tremendous variety in each of our selves . . . The individual myths will generally be a variation on some central theme of the classical myths . . . Each of us may be hero or heroine, or criminal or rogue, or onlooker, or any other character in the drama, and the emotions we experience will fit these characters.[45]

The myth bridges the gap between conscious and unconscious, transforming this liminal space into a mirror. My myth carries the story of "who I think I am" so I can reflect on what is happening in the mirror of my embodied myth to see my experience symbolically.

May continues his exposition of the hero with the statement that the hero is the carrier of our ideals and beliefs, and is created by us, born collectively as our own myth—the image of our life and how we live it—a metaphor for the ego. He proposes that this is what makes heroism so important because it reflects our sense of identity, and from this our own heroism is molded (I wonder what he might say about what the victim archetype is a carrier of). What May does not quite spell out here is that this hero-image is the archetypal image of the ego—as it is normally associated with—in its function as subject. It is a heroic myth. I am not so sure my myth is a heroic one. It is more circular than linear; it is spiraling not "progressing." Its intent is towards soul, the dark, the light of the moon reflecting: the real seeing.

Soul as metaphorical process indicates that soul acts. It is an action, a relationship to the unconscious: Psyche. It performs as does a metaphor, as does the image. I am reminded here of performing my everyday activities and what they might be mirroring. Who am I in relation to in these largely unconscious embodiments: the villain/hero; victim/perpetrator;

45. May, Cry for Myth, 33.

or any other polarized co-joined archetypal twin? Which pole am I identifying with as I furiously wash my floors or gaze into the abyss of the dirt? Who am I in my relations to others and my environment when an unconscious figure/presence (complex) takes over my reality—those moments of being mesmerized by unconscious material? Am I living my own life in the daily scripts and roles I play or are they created by others for me to perform? I am reminded of the family story here and my particular "character" in that intersubjective, intergenerational web of myths, including the weaving of a myriad of projective identifications taking place to form the family myth.

Who is performing who in this myth, and that of our collective? In the mirror of art making, images appear that invite me to embody and see an alternate story that is realized in the midst of enacting it in the art. Information is offered all at once within an image, without any sense of linearity, as in a dream. I dream I am washing the floors but can't find the mop. I awaken and immediately know something needs to be cleaned, tended to; the wound needs cleaning to avoid infection. The dream images are symbols from the unconscious expressing an alternate perspective than that of the ego.

Creative expression and aesthetic meaning supplement one another in the workings of the image in conjunction with the literal, the beauty of poetry, the gift of the mythopoetic. "It transposes meaning and releases interior, buried significance," much as the image (seed) embedded in the emotion does.[46] Expanding my capacity of experiencing myself subjectively and objectively, as the non-duality of the Klein body does, I am able to tolerate being held in the liminal gaze of/into the mirror/abyss. I see the diaphoric aspect of the metaphor of the mirror implying the presence of something not yet realized—a soul perspective.

I enter a mythopoetic discourse where the soul perspective knows of the importance of the details of the day-to-day (washing the floors), *and* how these are inherent to the descendant and transcendent workings of the mythopoetic. A mythopoetic sensibility embodies and en-souls the every-day. The imaginal ego is not fixated on herself or any particular conditions; she is not looking in the mirror to make sure she is astutely imitating the life the ego thinks she should be living. She can explore where a positional ego cannot. *I am simply a way of seeing.* The imaginal ego is neither a seer alone, nor that which is seen, but is fluidly both. "An

---

46. Hillman, *Archetypal Psychology*, 32.

encounter between self and other becomes an interstice, an invitation, and an improvisation."[47] The imaginal ego—being a part of the imaginal world, the mythic realm, metaphor, an active presence in the mythopoetic space—can embrace both the spiritual and the aesthetic. Alfred Schutz described this space as:

> a plane of consciousness of highest tension originating in an attitude full of attention to life and its requirements . . . This attitude, this *interest* in things, is the direct opposite of the attitude of bland conventionality and indifference so characteristic of our time.[48]

Mythopoetic space corresponds to a sense of soul, the space and process of this relationship to the unconscious and the kind of aesthetic that is cultivated therein. It descends into the realm of the ancestors and transcends the stasis of dead myths.

47. Irigaray, *To Speak Is Never Neutral*, 138.
48. Schutz, *The Problem of Social Reality*, 213.

Inlay: Self-Image and Suffering

To stop suffering, I am invited to stop identifying with the self that perceives itself to be suffering. I pause after contemplating this and think: *perhaps sufferers achieve enlightenment more readily than non-sufferers do as they have more opportunity to practice this kind of dis-identification.* The motivation to stop identifying with the suffering self is greater than the motivation to stop identifying with the non-suffering self. The location of pain is definitively in the suffering self. Being "in" the suffering self, *identifying* with it, rather than *being* with it, *is* the suffering. So how do I change locations, so to speak, so that I do not take up residence in the suffering self?

The Dalai Lama tells us that, "The Sautrantika School and the two Mahayana Buddhist schools say there is a kind of image that mediates between perception and its object."[49] In my own experience, this image is embodied in art and myth. In a slippery moment, as the pastel glides across the expanse of white paper, when I am actually able to perceive myself sliding into that suffering self, the subject, "I," sees object, "suffering self." Here, a separation between the one that is experiencing, "I," and the object, "suffering self," occurs. This momentary gap then dissolves the certainty of the object and its true nature is revealed. I see the suffering self for what it is: an image of myself suffering that I have inadvertently imagined/defined as me.

Recognizing the suffering self as just an image that I find myself in from time to time opens a door to the possibility of my assigning this image the role of metaphor rather than fact—to see through the myth that I am living. Seen as a medium, suffering now acts as an opening to the diaphoric imagination, where a completely new presence dissolves the

---

49. Dalai Lama, *Sleeping, Dreaming, and Dying*, 115.

tension between "self" and "suffering self." Wholeness, Ego, and Shadow in dialogue.

In its newly assigned role, the transparency of the image of "suffering self" can be seen through. When I can call its bluff in this manner of seeing through, the suffering self then suddenly takes on a fluidity that allows it to flow out of its definition of *me*. By calling this bluff I separate the "suffering self" from "my-self," setting it free. Through releasing the "suffering self" by naming it here—embodying it in words—it has no choice other than to return to its original intent as process *and* liminal space-in-between that is as fluid as paint. Seen as a medium, like paint, the suffering now acts as an opening to the diaphoric imagination—the aspect of metaphor that points to the unknown where a completely new presence emerges between "self" and "suffering self." In such a mythopoetic maneuver, the "suffering self" becomes a mirror revealing itself as an image (the mirror miraculously turns into a door) as does the imaginal ego. I myself am a mirror. I am mercurial and move and morph through my reflected image of myself, just as a Klein body does in the process of becoming a spiral lens.

The imaginal ego—the ego as archetypal image—has the capacity to be subject and object simultaneously, the knower and the known. This "ego" can transit, like Hermes, in and out of any image I am identifying with at any given moment. It or "I" could very well be the image that mediates between perception and its object (as I believe the Dalai Lama is suggesting). If the human mind can be imagined as a synthesizer of images or, conversely, that which is being synthesized by the many images or aggregates of itself, then location of self becomes questionable—and thus potentially freed from itself. However, when suffering is taking place, the fluid capacity of the imaginal ego often becomes frozen in its attachment to itself, like Narcissus *locked into the image of the suffering self at the same time as rejecting it*. The moment I find myself in this predicament, I hope that I might remember that, to stop suffering, I must stop identifying with the self that perceives itself to be suffering. Or at least join the crowd of opportunistic sufferers who are imagining their enlightenment.

2

Entering the Liminal

The space-in-between, the liminal, can be experienced as a gap. It could also be seen as an encounter between known and unknown—where such polarities can join in embodiments in the form of symbolic acts and objects. Through poems, performances, stories, myths, narratives, and living imaginally, we enter the gap (and/or the gap enters us). We engage the encounter of opposites in which the symbol making function of Psyche is activated and generates images. Often these images lead us to truths not so accessible to ego consciousness or consensus reality.

The underlying premise of mythopoetic inquiry is a practice of engaging the liminal as the place/process of knowledge, a hermeneutic in its own right. The mythopoetic practitioner and researcher steps into the liminal and roams the imaginal, *mundus imaginalis*, the world of image and potentiality. Researchers of this practice tacitly know their work happens in the body—theirs as Klein body *and* the body of matter in relation with *anima mundi*—in the alchemical opus of transformation. This is the path of the mythopoetic pioneer.

As a mythopoetic researcher, I have discovered this tacit knowledge of the body to be central to the work, particularly in its intricate connection to subjectivity in the autobiographical aspect of mythopoetic inquiry. Subjective experience can act as an aperture for the archetypal, as our bodily existence travels in and through our story, drawing the mythic dimension into itself. Both the visceral and symbolic experience of "what is beneath our feet, our 'sub-jectivity,' from 'to throw under,'" orients us in the body *and* our story.[1] Our myth unfolds in flesh and symbol,

1. Angelo, "Splendor Solis," 25.

grounding the notion that Psyche wants to be embodied in our personal lives—so that we feel it directly—connecting us even more deeply with mythopoetic sensibilities. The flickerings of the ancients (in our flesh and the images we experience) bring us close, sometimes painfully so, to coming into relation with those morphic presences so that they can tell their stories through us. Those stories, as they live in me now, have become the underlying current throughout this book, a river of images that flowed into the valleys and crevices where theory dropped away to raw experience—this *prima materia* presenting a way of theorizing itself.

In the liminality of our raw experience, what becomes apparent is the extent to which transitional spaces, often left out of our perception, embody themselves in art making. Hidden in those in-between spaces, secrets that have been gestating in the unconscious begin leaking truths into the field of awareness, creating an inspired atmosphere of "knowing." Such experience-based knowledge cooks in the kitchen of the research as the writing and imaging heat up and become increasingly animated. Hidden truths of the larger, collective piece of post-war European emigration emerged in the ethnoautobiographical thread of *Mourning the Dream / Amor Fati*. This part of the inquiry made itself known through a voice I could neither understand nor explain: "The ancients are lamenting." I decided to let this voice from the liminal stay, but worried that I would not grasp its intention—a deeper knowledge I was yet to uncover. "Knowledge, like fiction, itself is liminal space."[2]

As "knowledge" is generally connected to consciousness, I find myself now considering consciousness as something that fluctuates, disappearing then reappearing in different forms: poems, art, dance, and voices, urging me to become aware that my sense of self, self-presence as consciousness—like Hermes—is actually quite unstable, having enormous mutability. Where does this consciousness or self-presence go in its disappearing act? Where am I in the moment I have disappeared? "The performative researcher is haunted by absence; troubled by silence—resonance sings presence into welcomed discord."[3] Fels' "welcomed discord" reverberates elements of my self-presence I see no evidence of but can feel vibrating. Absence implies presence, presence implies absence. They will not survive without each other. The known and unknown are inseparable, existential twins.

2. Coppin and Nelson, *Art of Inquiry*, 146.
3. Fels, "Complexity, Teacher Education, and the Restless Jury," 147.

When I can no longer see myself—when I have lost all of my mirrors—I must give voice to this absence, to let it give voice to itself within my consciousness, by listening to what lies beneath or beyond my perception: that which is stirring in the Klein body. Not knowing what else to do, I turn to my own story—the one my body has been carrying for me, the one I already know by heart, the one that no longer seems to hold the presence/absence of my being in the world but continues to vibrate and confront me with its disquiet. What is vibrating here? Even though I know only too well the restrictions and "fiction" of this self-narrative, it seems I have nothing else in this fierce liminality that I find myself in. So while my self-presence is absent, I listen to my story by telling it, by writing it. I let its vibrations re-sound into this emptiness of no-identity so that I can descend into its implicit significances, echoing beneath my self-identity. I do this by entering the mythopoetic project, which includes confronting *and* being confronted by my self-image, my narrative—that is, my own myth-making. In this reflexive gesture, I carve a pathway into the space in-between, where the voices of the ancients—who are seeing something, knowing something about all of this—live in me. I can hear and speak what they are trying to voice here.

The vibrations of their voices are resounding larger collective stories, rippling through my body as a tuning fork for the messages they carry. Snowber describes this particular aspect of knowing, commenting: "For the blurring of identity is part of all of who we are, so that even within the one there are many multiple voices . . . to live into and through our vulnerabilities within the teaching process."[4] The vibrations of vulnerabilities are the ancients lamenting, their voices speaking my narrative, even while this story has lost its own truth through endless explanations to myself about it. It is my main text. "Words, both invented and represented, are as much ourselves as the social masks which protect and reveal us."[5] How is it that the ancients are so disguised by their shadow realities in Psyche?

Tracking the movements of this original narrative (or "fiction"), feeling into it as both substance *and* absence, I at least allow myself to imagine that something is going on. There is meaning in this forbidden sense of lack. I begin to tell tale after tale of meaninglessness, dreams lost and never found, feeling no meaning in them at all, all the while dreaming of meaning. I feel the only chance I have left is to drop into the

4. Snowber, "What the Body Knows."
5. Snowber, "What the Body Knows."

spaces between meaning and meaninglessness and begin a mythopoetic inquiry of this narrative. Weary of hope while entangled in the bowels of a lost dream, I hear another voice—this one a hoarse whisper: "Love your fate,"[6] which is in fact my life; love this fate even if this love does not alter your fate. Where does this voice come from? Where does it want to go?

Even though I may be absent to myself, there is an underlying archetypal narrative I am intrinsically a part of. The voice whispering "love your fate" seems to have knowledge of this archetypal resonance in the same manner much of my art does for me. It is as if a layer of the psyche—where the mythopoetic lives—continues to reveal itself in the mirror of my experience in spite of what I think of myself. My body emits and extends mythopoetic wisdom as the dreambody is confronting the wounded parts of the old narrative, the false myths: "Rather than a repository of archetypes, as Jung had suggested, the unconscious, or dreambody, according to Mindell, is a dynamic, flowing continuum of which archetypes are only 'snapshots.' Dreams, physical symptoms, relationships, accidents, altered states of consciousness—all are manifestations of the dreambody in action."[7] My body is a liminal subject, an alchemical Klein bottle that metabolizes laments into their symbolic purpose of the collective dreaming of the numinous.

The Klein body is a liminal space that is storying herself and speaking her knowledge of inside/outside—viscera intending and extending. Being the natural researcher that she is, the Klein body as spiral inquirer gathers information from her "inside-outness" and "outside-inness." As archetypal activist, the labor of love of the Klein body is the crafting of the spiral lens. This kind of labor includes hearing the laments and feeling the sufferings of the ancients. Her body spans millennia as she knows of presences of the past through the morphic resonances vibrating her numinous flesh. The old souls of the ancients are naturally part of her/my/our myth.

As archetypal activists, we find ourselves engaging a whole new level of knowing—one that enters an alternate archetypal and mythopoetic story of humanity. Mythopoetic inquiry holds the *telos*, the purpose of acknowledging the presence of the archetypal narrative, which lies beneath conscious thinking about oneself and the world. As mythopoetic researchers, we are relying on the Klein body's capacity like the imaginal

6. Nietzsche, *Ecce Homo*, 13.

7. Mindell, *Dreambody*, 1.

whale's, to travel the depths of the unconscious where an alternate story is unfolding.

Figure 17. Liminal Spaces. Liminal Figures

My body often feels like it is dissolving, melting, or floating, lived at the edges. Sometimes it crosses borders, journeying into uncharted territories where there is no horizon line. Through the transplant experience, my body is also that of two other persons and vice versa. Who is selfing which self?

Autobiographical inquiries and image making are acts of inviting liminality and all of those liminal presences that are mostly invisible to us. As we encounter these presences, we may experience dissidence in the "I," the literalized sense of self that has not yet made the leap of faith into the imaginal. However, this "I" determines how to be with these discordances the Klein body is carrying, those aspects which have not been accepted as part of the project "I." The mythopoetic researcher and Jungian oriented art therapist opens herself up to these possibilities as she "knows" this to be a necessary part of crafting the spiral lens. The clarity of what alchemical function these discordances play in *Mourning the Dream / Amor Fati* will become evident as the researcher continues to perform her tasks on the mythopoetic path.

Something new, at the edge of its own arrival, emerges; a moment of risk becomes a moment of opportunity. The call to presence in the midst of my self-absence stops the absencing process dead and I hear the potency of the poet Rainer Maria Rilke's future coming into me before it happens "out there."[8] I become curious about this future that has not yet presented itself. I ask what seeds are sleeping in the depths of my absorption into absence—is this very absence a kind of liminality the future is calling me through? I pause . . . am I awake somewhere I cannot yet recognize? Is there a strange kind of consciousness in the unconscious? Is this sense of absence "the dark Mercurius [that] must be understood as representing the initial negredo state, the lowest being a symbol of the highest and vice versa . . . the one and all, the union of opposites accomplished during the alchemical process," or *massa confusa*, "the original elements in a state of chaos"?[9] Here the dreambody is stepping into the mythopoetic space of possibilities.[10] This is the Klein body as alchemical vessel holding and transforming the basic elements of our raw experience, *prima materia*, and inviting the victim—the "other," the blind "not-me," and any other unacceptable presences—onto the path of individuation.

As a symbol of possibilities and the gestation process, the world egg (found in mythological motifs in creation myths of many cultures) is typically a beginning of some sort.

Figure 18: After First Transplant

8. See Rilke, *Letters to a Young Poet*, 63.

9. These are terms Jung used to describe a natural process in which consciousness is embedded in the unconscious. See Jung, *Structure and Dynamics*, 232 and Samuels, *Critical Dictionary of Jungian Analysis*, 15.

10. Mindell, *Dreambody*.

The Body as Liminal Space

After my first islet cell transplant in 2006, a new being emerged, one who felt herself to be premature, a fragile little bird embryo hanging between life and death, yet already producing her own egg. I feel this new egg only now beginning to hatch in the writing of these words. These words are the stirrings within this egg in its desire to break through, its body "needed as that which the forces of light and life express themselves through."[11] But the little bird is weak and full of doubt. She feels utterly lost, her body an eclipse of Eros and Thanatos, caught in the bardo *state. In the Tibetan tradition,* bardo *means the "intermediate state," between death and the next birth, where one's consciousness is not connected with a physical body but still experiences a variety of phenomena.[12]*

A deep visceral sense of loss was present at the time of painting this image, while a great hope for what new life the transplant would engender was percolating. I had waited 42 years for this new life. After the implantation of insulin-producing cells into my liver, I experienced images of myself and the cosmos I had never encountered before—as if they were not me/mine—calling forth Hillman's notion that we do not have images; rather, images have us.[13] My mind was indeed just a part of a collective imagination.

These images took me to foreign lands of the imaginal with odd creatures that could walk on the top of curtain rods while having an argument. In my "hallucinations," I could watch television without it being turned on. I saw cartoon-like images of extreme violence I had never imagined before; some violent death these implanted cells were witness to were deeply distressed and signaling danger throughout my system.

In that moment I felt I had gone too far. In my curiosity about this health/illness, self/other paradox—deciding to be a guinea pig of the islet cell research program—I had ventured well beyond the boundaries of the mind I thought I knew, and beneath into a primordial ooze of confusion and chaos. I no longer had myself. The man in the bed next to me who had received the donor's kidney, looked at me the morning after our surgeries and said, "She sure had a rough night." He was a transplant veteran, this one being his third.

11. Baynes, *I Ching*, 537.

12. See Rinpoche, *Tibetan Book of Living and Dying*.

13. See Hillman, *Re-visioning Psychology*.

Here I was left alone without my "self," stranded in the vast-
ness of an imagination much larger than mine, the landscape of
the collective Shadow. I was left with those images—her images of
dying I imagine—that were now "having me." "I" was absent in
this exchange of selves and, for a long time, experienced prolonged
terror that would abduct "me" randomly and without apparent
cause whenever these "guests"—images of her death—chose to
visit me.

Such shocking liminality became an overwhelming wilderness
in the psyche—where my old self-narrative no longer existed and any
signs of a new narrative had not yet emerged. I had only a thin thread
of memory tethered to a notion of who I was and this thread was under
constant threat of snapping. My little birth-ravaged bird felt ill-equipped
for life and her egg, so precariously tucked under her chin, certainly did
not know its fate. Although states of liminality may involve death, there
is at least a promise, if we can see it, of new life.

The ongoing rhythms of constructing and deconstructing, integrating and disintegrating, are integral to self-narratives[14] and self-actualization.[15] This structuring builds a sense of self (heroic-ego), while the
poetic—that space-in-between the known and unknown of the symbolic—transforms experience through the workings of the archetypal
activist. Through her courageous encountering of polarities, she brings
them into the diaphoric imagination, thus transforming them into a new
presence. The imaginal ego as archetypal activist has the ability to be with
the prosaic and the poetic as one process—the intention and extension of
the psyche, a gesture of the *Dreambody*.[16]

Field Notes: Where is This Going?

Where were these figures of my "hallucinations" going and what
did they want? Even more importantly, was it now my task to live
out the story of this donor's death, to embody those horrific im-
ages I received through her? This ethical conundrum confused me
greatly and I was haunted by the question of what fate was asking
of me; whose fate? I was on the border between the personal and

14. See Holmes, "Defense and Creative Use," and Roberts, "Introduction: A Story
of Stories."

15. Jung, *Psychology and Religion*, 40.

16. See Mindell, *Dreambody*.

the collective here, that razor blade of self/other. For a moment I
am back in my childhood bedroom trying to draw a line between
her and "I" in the air/flesh.

The journey of desire is inevitably incomplete, uncertain, and
produces moments that profoundly disturb and de-center the
self. These liminal moments . . . afford us the possibility of
glimpsing other modes of desire and hence different ethical
relations between self and other, self and world.[17]

A simple glimpse at the figure in that mirror above the bathroom sink
reminds me of the liminality of my being. "An encounter between self
and other becomes an interstice, an invitation, and an improvisation."[18]

I trusted or rather, hoped, that this "possibility of glimpsing other
modes of desire and ethical relations between [my-]self and other, self
and world" was the case for my little bird.[19] Swinging wildly on the pen-
dulum of life and death, this terrified bird had already taken on the responsibility of the egg so gently tucked under her care and even another
one nestled in her little body.

Little One

Little One
Crawled out of Big One's body
and said, "Now
I'm big too. I
want what you have."

But Big One said,
"You have to wait,
you have to learn.
You have to let your body stretch
before you can know
what you really want."

Little One said,
"No, I cannot wait.
I don't have time to learn.
My body will stretch too far

17. Fullagar, "Narratives of Travel," 129.
18. Irigaray, *To Speak Is Never Neutral*, 121.
19. Fullagar, "Narratives of Travel."

if I can't get what I want.
It will hurt
and you may hear me cry."

Big One said,
"Yes, it may hurt,
and you may cry.
And I will hear you.

But your body will know
how far it can grow
and one day
it will have stretched so far
that you will be called

Big One
and a new Little One
will crawl out of you."

I think of the responsibility of the egg and its symbolism: at what cost, what gain, and under what conditions does the psyche produce such an egg? The egg is already in the body of the mother (mother archetype). The generative energy of the process of fertilization determines the fate of the egg. Am I in a large-enough narrative (connected to the archetypal narrative) to risk taking on this responsibility? My body seems to answer an emphatic "no" to this request. But here is the egg nonetheless. I am full of despair, yet this symbol of hope and new beginnings is the guest that arrives from the autonomous unconscious. I am bewildered. Does the archetypal symbol of the egg itself carry this form of consciousness that dwells in the unconscious?

Although liminal space is potentially creative, it can also be dangerous. I have been terrified by my self-absence and my blindness, the "other" inhabiting/inhibiting my being. The darkness within seems to swallow up everything in its path. There is no containment of its consuming appetite. I feel the risk of not being connected to a narrative, a myth that could contain what I am experiencing. As I have lost sight of the archetypal narrative, I am nowhere near the possibility of any integration of what this experience is. I am not yet able to see what is happening symbolically, mythopoetically. I believe that "knowing" of the symbolic is sleeping in the egg, waiting until I am ready to take in the significance of what is happening in light of the lament of the ancients. Out of the terrified Klein body of the little bird emerges the cosmic egg, an archetypal symbol of "the life principle in its wholeness."[20]

The narrative I had been living was no more. It had disintegrated into horrific hallucinations. Roberts refers to the value during the disintegrating phase of having a "broader, deeper narrative able to hold the fractured parts together."[21] I want to be constructing this broader, deeper narrative, bringing it to light; to let my body be needed by that light/life force at the same time that the egg is growing. Would the ancient ones hold any clues for me through their loud lamenting in my viscera? What role do they play in this larger narrative? Might they be having a discussion about my/their fate?

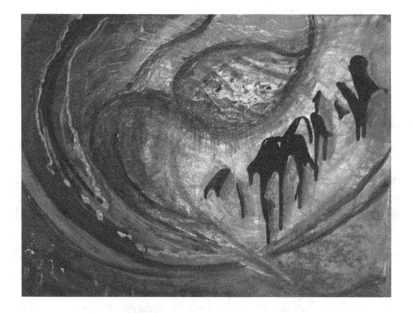

Figure 19. The Ancients in the Underworld

My little bird had lost her shell while her fragile body was still in a delicate formative state. She herself was still an embryo. "Can she make it?" I asked. I honestly didn't know. And I had no clue at the time what this egg was all about. How could she possibly care for this egg? How was it even imaginable that this little body, having just cracked through the "holding, containing structure" of her own egg, produce this new egg?

20. Kalsched, *Inner World of Trauma*, 187.
21. Roberts, "Introduction: A Story of Stories," 12.

Creativity and transformation often involve the undoing of structures (cracking the egg), the letting go of purposive control (crisis and/or
leap of faith), stepping into the liminal, and striding forth into blindness.
The ability to let go of an integrated and integrating self is related to trust.
The painting "After the First Transplant" presented the egg to me without
my understanding the significance of its presence in my unfolding myth.
This presence seemed to be indicating a new beginning I was not privy
to and, in fact, it scared me with its implied responsibility. Upon reflection, I can recognize this new "presence" as being born of the diaphoric
imagination, this impulse a survival mechanism. My re-course was the
suspension from "reality" the liminal often provides, offering a transitional space for the transcendent function to germinate, for the diaphoric
aspect of the metaphor that implies the possibility of something unknown
beginning to take hold. Like Persephone, I entered the Underworld in the
form of deep depression and physical illness. In Greek mythology, Persephone's primary role was queen of the Underworld, receiving immortal
souls into the afterlife.

I was drawing on the mythopoetic, inviting what was sitting un-
derneath my despair (the collective despair of the ancestors), to extend
into the creative process. I was submerged in the liminality of flesh where
the dreambody, this inner uncanny "other," could work unimpeded by
the demands to "make sense." I keep catching glimpses of that "other"
in the mirror. Can she see? Can she see me? Through the work of the
dreambody, the image embedded in my despair was metamorphosing
and I came to see how my narrative was illustrating and speaking both
my myth and the story of the ancients simultaneously. The raw material
of my experience was shaping itself into the aperture of vision-making,
an archetypal function of the personal and collective Psyche.

I became like Psyche, looking for an image of herself, extending
this image through the creative act and stepping into it, becoming it. The
initial desire for self-image (I see myself looking in the mirror and that
mirrored self looking back at me) animated Psyche into extension. The
desire for finding self in this manner/mirror—a transformative reflexivity—becomes an extension of Psyche's deeper intent, her ulterior motive
of bringing the presence of "other" into relationship. The Klein body
flickers these presences of "other" in/to me through embodied images. As
observing this phenomenon became a more conscious practice—through
holding an awareness of deep democracy—a natural unravelling and re-
embodying of my myth began to take form, a kind of "soul-making" in

Hillman's sense of the word: "The psychology of the creative is really a feminine psychology, a fact which proves that creative work grows out of unconscious depth, indeed, out of the region of the mothers"—the mother archetype.[22] I see my little bird now as wounded mother of a collective egg, the nurturing of life potential, and the role of the individual's myth in restorying all stories. "The creation of something new is not accomplished by the intellect, but by the play-instinct acting from inner necessity; the creative mind plays with the objects it loves," which in turn, play with the creative mind: the *images* it loves.[23] That is why they appear out of love, which is how reflexivity develops. A kind of magnetism in the field is constellated in the experience of loving an image, inviting a strong possibility of the image loving me back, of being loved by an image. I was breathless and almost in tears when I considered this notion, as were my students, when I suggested the possibility of their images loving them. I invite the reader to consider for yourself how your images love you.

Charles E. Bressler suggests that linguistically the word "empathy" was first employed in an attempt to specify the emotion peculiar to art.[24] He claims that the beautiful has been defined as anything that involves the processes of *empathy*. Theodore Lipps, a German philosopher concerned with conceptions of art and the aesthetic (focusing much of his philosophy around such issues), gave the name "empathy" (*Einfuhlung*) to a process he described as "feeling something, namely oneself, into the aesthetic object."[25] For me the German word—German being my childhood language—holds more resonance of feeling (*Fuhlung*) myself into (*Ein*) an aesthetic object, like being inside an image. In the aesthetic experience, the antithesis between myself and the object disappears, or rather, does not yet exist. Beauty dwells in the tension of liminality. "The paradox that beauty, growth, and wonder are inextricably connected to living from and through the depths," through the body that is part of earth and her seasons, what has been absent begins to embody itself.[26]

Hillman's articulation of the image loving me brought form and solidity to what I had experienced as the particular empathy Bressler refers to. But most powerfully, through the language of Hillman's notion,

22. Hillman, *Myth of Analysis*, 12.
23. Jung, *Memories, Dreams, Reflections*, 87.
24. See Bressler, *Literary Criticism*.
25. Wikipedia, "Theodor Lipps."
26. Snowber, "What the Body Knows."

this recognition and embodiment of reciprocal love gave me the love I so needed at that time. "The creative is an achievement of love. It is marked by imagination and beauty."[27] The essential beauty of the soul of all things (the *anima mundi*—soul of the world) was revealed through love, through participation or "fellowship with essence," with the love affair of images.[28] I would like to propose the notion of perception as an act of love, to address Simone Fullagar's explanation of desire as the "possibility of glimpsing other modes of desire and ethical relations between self and other, self and world."[29]

At times when I was painting, drawing, writing, I lost the separation between myself and other. Losing myself in this manner in (*Ein*) the embodiments of my creativity, I paradoxically found a different sense of myself in the liminality of the aesthetic experience; my self-absence shape-shifted into a self-presence of a different sort. In the spaciousness of liminality, the embodied imaginal ego is a fluid subject *and* object, shifting into different states of consciousness appropriately depending on what is at hand, what is coming to meet, without the heroic-ego's usual antithesis between positional "self" and "other" attempting to fix the situation.

The disappearance of the antithesis between myself and the object (self and "other") dissolves the resistance to self-empathy or compassion. Even in my unconscious scribblings, I had a felt-sense of this deep empathy for the wounded inner figures, the complexes. These split off sub-personalities and their wounded stories are living in the unconscious and can be activated by resonant situations to the original wound, the original narcissistic wounding. The wounded and forgotten are wanting expression and asking for love. The ancients in waiting.

I stop. The writing stops: the tapping on the keys stops. The theory ends here for this moment in this "stop."[30] The location of consciousness has shifted as I experience this "stop" in the movement of the words across the screen. I get up and leave the "I" that has been writing, the "I" that is stuck, sitting at the computer with a sore back and aching fingers. I begin to dance and feel into who is here because "I" have stopped. "I" am relocating. I recognize the quality of the spiraling gestures within the

27. Hillman, *Myth of Analysis*, 76.
28. Ward, *John Keats*, 160.
29. Fullagar, "Narratives of Travel," 129.
30. See Appelbaum, *The Stop*.

"stop" and follow the traces of an unborn awareness, a presence that has come into the absence—this future that comes into the present in order to transform that cannot be conceived in the "I" that has been writing.[31] Arms, legs, hips, eyes fly into three-dimensional space carving shapes with its twin; the "other" arm, leg, hip, eye spiraling into an alternate intention/extension. An alternate story, an archetypal narrative is flickering through the Klein body.

Now there is depth perception, consciousness set free into the field in-between arms, legs, eyes. Body as shape-shifter of consciousness, liminal interiority crossing boundaries through extension into space and setting free the positional self by letting go of looking and knowing, forgetting any notion of "I" as subject. What is revealed through its own embodiment is the birth of an aesthetic experience in which I am fully present.

In the liminal space of the aesthetic experience (a transitional, intersubjective space of the creative process), I traverse the polarities of subject/object through the transparency of this aesthetic immersion: healing and wounding, illness and wholeness—twins of the same process in one full breath. As therapist and educator, I feel it is my task to hold both polarities in-tension within myself; to not only identify with the healthy, competent aspect or vice versa. This sacrifice of the well-defended, superior position assigned to the therapist in our culture allows the healing capacity within the client to emerge and become active.

As I move back and forth between the poles of therapist and client, I become a transitional, liminal figure—the liminal subject: Am I dancing this writing?

> Unlike the more conventional types of teacher, [the therapist] as liminal servant understands that knowledge is performatively constituted and calls forth the body. Cognizant of the shamanic mission, the teacher [or therapist] as liminal servant speaks to the body and the minds from the hegemony of the everyday and to transform pedagogy into holy praxis in which both teachers and students are united in the sacred communities of knowing.[32]

---

31. See Rilke, *Letters to a Young Poet*, 63.

32. McLaren, "Anthropological Roots," 87.

Figure 20. Transfiguration through the *Temenos* of Empathy

The implication that the teacher/therapist as liminal servant acts as a container and guide for inquiring into knowledge as fluid, brings me back to Coppin and Nelsen's notion that "knowledge, like fiction, itself is liminal space."[33] The educator/therapist, through her own deep understanding of her presence as Klein body in archetypal action, then "feels into" (*Einfuhlung*) the *temenos* of the therapeutic relationship—an aesthetic experience.

The therapeutic and teaching container is a fluid, liminal, transcendent space. Flow is where you lose yourself—your watchful self, your ego self—in the moment of being (imaginal ego).[34] David Winnicott's transitional space and Victor Turner's liminal space are both inter-subjective spaces, and, may I suggest, mythopoetic spaces, where the movements of the liminal servants of therapist, teacher, or researcher can navigate intense experiences of a threshold nature: between self and other, known and unknown, safe and dangerous—all dualities of the Klein body in her inside-out, outside-in way of being. Her body, my body, your body knows how to hold duo-consciousness, to live non-dualistically within the apparent opposites that consistently present themselves as the patterns of

33. Coppin and Nelson, *Art of Inquiry*, 146.
34. See Csikszentmihalyi, *Flow*.

our existence. Living in the transparent shimmering of two mirrors—the material and the spiritual, the literal and the symbolic, flickering back and forth at each other inside/outside the Klein body of the personal and collective—*is* the mythopoetic.

For Winnicott, cultural experience is located in the potential space between the individual and the environment, between self and other. It can be a transitional space to move from being merged with, to being separated from (egg), the mother (bird). This is retained throughout life "in the intense experiencing that belongs to the arts and religion, to imaginative living, and to creative scientific work."[35] Through developing a mythopoetic disposition that is inclined towards the symbolic, we can intentionally embody the interior self with self-in the-world without splitting.

Entering other cultivated spaces or activities such as travel, spiritual retreat, prayer and meditation, journal writing, autobiography, expressive arts, and music can also be considered mythopoetic practices, encouraging a different way of seeing that Hillman calls "seeing through events into their mythos."[36] He recommends imaginal responses to human suffering—imaginative literature; film; drama; art; dance; poetry and autobiography—as sources of understanding and holding, which may lead to the development of a transformational space, a mythopoetic space, learning from within one's engagement with the unconscious and its symbols, and embodying these in the arts.

In the transformational spaces created by an imaginal response to life—a symbolic, mythopoetic response—more expansive and inclusive stories (myths) can be discovered "to contain the destructure in the face of a person's narrative."[37] Is there a story that can contain the vast black of blindness and the dis-memberment of transplantation? Symbolic responses to life and suffering such as a mythopoetic sensibility create expressive liminal spaces for the expansive stories we so yearn for. I long for a story that could see my blindness and dismemberment as an extension of Psyche's deeper intent. I want this story to read back to me both the myth I am living as I am living it *and* the larger narrative: the alternate archetypal narrative of the mythopoetic as viewed through the spiral lens. Seeing the blindness as part of a larger whole is implicated through the

35. Winnicott, *Playing and Reality*, 14.
36. Hillman, *Re-visioning Psychology*, 51.
37. MacKay, "Mythopoetic Spaces," 199.

flickers of embodiments (images) cooking in the unconscious, signaling the Klein body. The Klein body feels the future coming in. Is it Psyche's intent, her ulterior motive that I meet the soul of my blindness and those of the transplanted "others" within my own body? Am I back in the bedroom trying to draw a line between her and "me" in the air/flesh? These stories can become the meta-narrative or mythopoeia to contain the wounding and loss in the face of my limited (partially-sighted) heroic-ego (or victimized-ego) narrative.

Figure 21. Second Transplant in Red

As weaver of the images and text of this book and, conversely, its weaving of my own experience—as both heroic and imaginal ego, therapist and client, artist and researcher, healing and wounded (in duo-consciousness)—I have certainly felt a falling away of narratives and images that I have held and that have held me. Autobiographical inquiry, autopoeisis as a form of potentiating one's story into a "larger story," can reflect on personal and professional (mythic) journeys. Through the spiraling and re-visioning of mythopoeia, I become an archetypal activist. As a therapist I understand this as (a) an invitation to the presence of the inherent reflexive nature of consciousness, which takes place within an intimate dialogue with one's soul and (b) to fully enter the dialogical space-in-between therapist and client—the *temenos* where transformation takes place; where intention and extension, literal and symbolic are one complete reflexive gesture. Accepting the invitation and entering the dialogical space of self and "other" has a potentiating effect on everyone's story into the "larger story" of the collective myth we are creating together in the liminality of transformation.

The liminal is the very zone where possibility exists ("emptiness" in Buddhism) where whatever emerges can be given an image. Possibility becomes embodied but not literalized. The symbol-making function of Psyche is activated by crossing the great chasm of the visible/invisible. The liminal figure/body is both the chasm and the bridge that separates/joins the psyche with the ultimate "other" in numinous experience. It is a trans-figure. The combination of will and surrender is the key that opens the lock that would otherwise bar the movement, the transition into the liminal. The practice of deep democracy invites the encounter between will and surrender into a diaphoric relationship which engenders a new possibility: a Presence birthed through the archetypal activist's work with polarities and the ancient knowing of the collective Klein body of humanity—including its death. The ancients know and speak of death.

Figure 22. Liminal Figure inside the Cosmic Egg

Field Notes: Embodying Liminality

As I come to this place, I come to know it. Know it as a place both inside and outside myself. This place holds intention and extension. I am the bridge, the common denominator in this inside/outside di-vision. I join the both. In this manner I embody the liminal space. I take up that space with my being, or that space is taken up, so to speak, with my being. As the liminal persona in this equation, I am the hunter. I am hunting for that place, this place inside, outside. I want to fall into that place, this place, into and out of myself. So I set a trap to catch myself as I prowl in search of this/that space in between what is me and is not me.

Ironically, I must appear to be invisible in this hunt to make visible that which I cannot see because it is me and I am invisible. I must pretend that I am not "me." Like a mask, I hide what is "real" to reveal that which can only be apparent when "reality" disappears. I have disappeared. I am hiding what I am at one level, to reveal a truth I am hiding from at this level—a truth I can see only by hiding the truth I already know so well that it has become invisible to me. My mask shows me, becomes what is lying beneath what I am hiding from/under. It is the actor that best portrays that which I cannot see. This mask is my myth. I see through it. And through the mask I see my myth. I see symbolically. My own myth confronts me at every turn and in turn, I confront it.

Figure 23. The Hunt

As a "hunter," a researcher, artist, educator, art therapist, middle child of an immigrant family, having lived with type I diabetes for almost 5 decades, I have found myself in liminal space over and over again. I would say that this has mostly not been by choice—most profoundly the loss of my vision in 1986. Becoming "dis-abled" at that time, I was certainly a liminal figure in my own eyes, as well as in the invisible gaze of my tribe. I became an "other" to myself. I learned to live in the invisible, to be the invisible; falling into the blackness, into the gap. Who was this invisible being? (Shortly after my first transplant I had a dream that I was a black man in a 60's style suit, a bit like the entertainers in that era. In the dream I was falling and falling with my tie and my lips pulled upwards quivering, fluttering from the force of my descent. There was no bottom).

With the help of a large zoom lens—which had both a telephoto and a macular capacity which my own eyes no longer had—along with wide thick brushes and brightly colored paints I kept beside me, I navigated my way through this darkness while eventually regaining about fifty percent of my vision. With a new identity and a white cane, I tapped my way through thresholds, fingered the lips of abysses, and stumbled on edges of endless despair. Outside of my awareness, Psyche was in the process of creating "soul-eyes" for me.

These delicate instruments let me see what I imagined as a whole. What I did not know at this time was that I was only grasping fractured pieces of the world, a shattered mirror of my self. I could not let go of what I could not grasp! I remember being in a class at the Canadian Institute for the Blind and the instructor writing words in very large print on the flip chart. I almost raised my hand to ask her why she had left out certain letters in the words. Then a wave of nausea went through my body and I realized there were no letters missing. Those invisible letters had fallen into my many blind spots—the gaps of my reality and sense of self.

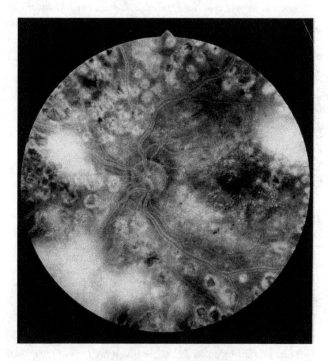

Figure24. Gaps in the Retina

I kept a close eye on what I could not see, checking those impossible places where letters of words fell, where no one or thing existed. Were they not there? Was I not here? I heard disembodied voices around me; I wanted to touch those who owned those voices, pull them close to me so that I could know who was with me. Like a child who thinks that because everything around her is invisible, she too must be invisible. "Where am I? Where are we? Is there even a 'we' here? Am I imagining all of this? Is this a dream?" This blurry brown blood gauze/gaze that was now my "vision," left me feeling as if I was buried in the dark earth alive. I kept asking how, how, how can I dig through this? What kind of outlook can one have with no capacity to look out? "Your body will be somewhere."

I realized this blind, disabled, uninvited and intolerable guest had moved in with me permanently. This shadow sister had taken over my bed, my dreams, my world. So now I was the guest of this dark distorted figure, trapped in her Underworld. No escape, shrunken into a pawn for her dream-ego, a character on her warped inner stage (as what can happen in projective identifications). She was now "me" and I now her in this macabre twist. Much like a complex, colonizing the ego for its own benefit, my blackened sister became the "me" that I was horrified by (I am reminded again of Hillman's statement of images having us versus us having images). This guest had me. Hurt me. She had come to reclaim the life that was foreshadowed in the threshold experience of my diagnosis of diabetes eighteen years earlier.

Depression

Depression holds no currency with the Dead.
Life and Death
are the same. This is our mistake,
to think otherwise.

To be alive we must be
Dead to the world.
To be Dead, we must be
Alive to the world.

Is this not simple
enough to follow?

I was certain that I was dead to the world at the time of my retinal hemorrhaging and detachment. I also knew, however, at some level, that the world was not dead to me. But I had to reach for this, extend well beyond my present grasp or gaze. I had to go beyond my mind—which had previously relied on visual proof in order to "know." Into the imagination, the invisible world of the imaginal, I now travelled the invisible world of being blind. Apparently, I literally needed to go to the dark places, "the depth experiences that lie beyond the conscious visible realm most associated with reality."[38] *From this particular threshold situation, it was imperative that I open myself to "fields of perception . . . become present to them as consciousness in the midst of them, not as an outside observer," as Greene so eloquently writes.*[39] *Moving through self-absence to self-presence, tracking consciousness, and navigating the imaginal mythopoetic landscape takes place in the embodied liminal figure now subject.*

To release my imagination into this bleak nothingness before and in me became my task, my raison d'être, my survival (I had a dream last night that was a series of nightmarish images. In the dream I decided that these would be places I could just be with and explore rather than become engulfed by. The dream maker knew, like the imaginal ego, that this was just a dream).

Radical Liminality

Radical Liminality
releases the next moment
into the receptivity of
unconditional consciousness.

The story of Job holds significance here in the imperative for conscious suffering.

Job's questions [about why he is suffering] have been answered, not rationally but by living experience [*how*]. What he has been seeking, the meaning of his suffering has been found. It is nothing less than the conscious realization of the autonomous archetypal Psyche; and this realization could come to birth only through an ordeal.[40]

The autonomous archetypal Psyche is unconscious. She lives in the realm of myth so her intent can only make sense (like the dream ego within the dream) in her realm. It is only through her images—Psyche's extension in

38. Greene, *Releasing the Imagination*, 72.
39. Greene, *Releasing the Imagination*, 73.
40. Edinger, *Ego and Archetype*, 91.

the form of her affect—that is, through feelings, flickers, flinches, symptoms, symbols, dreams, images, and the stories and myths she generates in her indirect approach—that this intent would make sense. The language of the unconscious was trying to lead me to her intent; to be able to listen to this intent that lies much deeper than my heart can sink. Carrying and caring for what I cannot hold in my mind is to learn the language of symbols so that they can show me my myth, and what it is pointing to. So many myths speak of finding passage to the archetypal realm in the encounters we experience in the liminal—our threshold initiations into the imaginal. Facing the numinous comes at great cost.

What I could not behold was *why* I was being visited by this unbearable guest of blindness and how I was going to face her. She seemed to separate me from everything I loved and more. I was floundering in this liminal space between separation and reunion, dying and being reborn. I no longer knew who or what I was. I was shifting archetypes. New, unfamiliar archetypal energy was now present in my psyche for me to grapple with. A presence. The "outsider" was now inside. What did it want? While I was in this transitional threshold state of "new-found" blindness, the darkness held me tight. It squeezed me. I contracted in fear. Even to this day I feel the constant pressure of its grip. I am queasy. The queasiness has been the tone and texture of the canvas the "flickers" have appeared on—those flickers embodied in the writings and art that have astonished and assisted me in this mythopoetic endeavor, en-abling me to dwell in and see through the liminal moving into the mythopoetic.

What I have discovered is that this darkness—both literal and symbolic—*is* the liminal space of separation and reunion, the dying and being reborn, and the "stuff" myth and story are made of. Entering the dark liminal space as artist, art therapist, and archetypal activist has given me the vision of the mythopoetic.

Inlay: Self and the Imaginal "Other" in Writing (Art)

When I write (or paint or draw) who am I engaging?

When I talk to myself who is the self?

Which self?

My-self.

What lies between this "my" and this "self"?

There is an imaginal space between this "my" and this "self" that I can enter in this moment.

What happens when I enter this space?

Where am I?

Who am I?

What kind of voice do I have?

This space, this imaginal space, might be quiet, holding silence.

Or it might be full of all sorts of creatures to become familiar with, get to know. Even become friends with.

I see the victim here—the hunted, the haunted—crouching in her dark corner, cocooned in the web of her own sorrow and self-banishment. She is enmeshed in her-story, which is her nature after all. A victim must have a story of being victimized; otherwise, she would not be, by nature, the victim.

She has many sad tales to tell and with any given opportunity is happy to tell any of them, hopefully over and over again. You must give her many chances.

There's another figure I see in this imaginal space between "my" and "self." Here is the hero. She is very exuberant, confident, outgoing, and willing to intervene in dangerous situations for the betterment of the whole. She believes in herself and others believe in her too. In this moment, she appears in feminine form with the qualities of being very much in charge of "my" and "self." She sees her-self as in control of the situation. Now what kind of space exists here between the 'her' and 'self'? That is another whole territory to discover. But for the moment I will focus on the dimensions offered in the space between "my" and "self."

Who else is here in the imaginal? I see a family over there pretending to be together; And another one woven into a loose fabric that spreads across oceans and continents, reaching the ancients with their tassels of gold, flickering and tickling these forgotten souls awake.

These families, ironically, are mirrors of each other, trying to tell the same story—the "real" story. Both tales are true. Both are untrue. Each carries its myth, maintaining a mythic process that is inevitably carried forward into the next generation.

Cousin to the victim is the sick one, or at least, sickly. She is lying in a bed, sometimes a hospital bed. She has doctors hovering around her like ghosts of all the possible things that might "go wrong" with her: blindness; kidney failure; loss of a limb; heart disease. Her heart has already been broken by all the words these doctors have been whispering about her over the years, creating layer upon layer of images that have lived inside the sick one since she was diagnosed. She has been sick for a long time. She might say at times she is hopeless. But that would not be entirely true, as glimpses of hope have sustained her presence. Perhaps then, if she became completely hopeless and lost these glimpses, she might disappear altogether. The "my" part of myself is intrigued by this possibility.

Is it possible this sick one could actually vanish? I could only hope for that. But then this hope might travel through and into the imaginal space between "my" and "self," and inadvertently be transferred to the sick self, infusing her again with hope, and therefore prevent her disappearance!

Well I can move along for the moment, as any moment offers the opportunity to move along. I move along into the hospital now. But in the form of a new figure: the BC Cancer Agency art therapist (life offers up these odd chunks of irony now and then). This art therapist is a new member of the imaginal clan and has not yet determined her personality, even though she holds a very particular role which is, however, invisible to her at present. She is back in the cocoon, cuddling with the victim and spinning her-self a fancy silk suit that will match the duties of the new position that will mostly be self-determined.

"Self"-"determined."

The self here moves into a verb, an active mode, determining itself.

It-self. *The myth is a symbol of itself.*

It: something that is identified yet not yet described. I am waiting for its description, its picture of its-self, so that I can base some assumptions upon that picture, that image, that will help me not to have to reinvent "my"-"self" at each moment, exhausting me with this overwhelming constant demand. I cannot know "my"-"self" without some navigational tools, assumptions I can rely on, even though I know these assumptions inevitably only allow me to see a portion of the picture. Or view it from a particular angle that naturally distorts.

Can I come to terms with this predicament of distortion (or partial view), to leave my anguish about this dilemma out of the picture for the time being, so that I can join the populace of the collective psyche and perhaps contribute some special little piece of interest to the world?

Figure 25. This Is My Task

So this is my task. This is the task I set for "my"-"self": to look at my own myth as it looks back at me, to see it as symbolic of itself while collecting all the reflections I see in the mirror of "my"-"self." Through the spiral lens the Klein body has been crafting, I can create a new vision from the many selves I see in the mirrors of my experience, as each is so eager to contribute to *mundus imaginalis*: the world of image. Remembering our histories (the known structures, the old form of *logos* or sense we made of our myth, and even our beliefs—all of which are ostensibly now "dead") and revisioning them from the life of the "divine spark of the individual . . . a more real reality," which engenders a breathing mythopoetic inquiry.[41] Diligently mapping contours and spaces of autobiography, pathography, and mythography through moments of poesies, performance, art, and story brings forth a sense of Presence.

41. Peterson, "Why Are We so Complicated?"

3

The Call

The call is the unlived life. The one that is animating the unconscious.

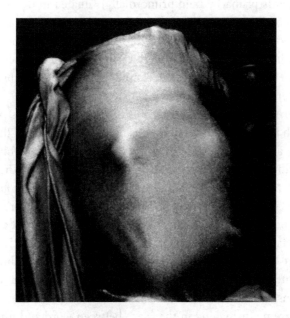

Figure 26. The Call

I am taken into an imaginal journey of how my own illness and consequent loss of vision have acted as a metaphor for lack of conscious-ness. The journey is asking: how do both conditions act as a "call" to deepen consciousness and expand awareness? And how can art making and autobiographical inquiry (in this case partly a path-ography: a narrative of illness) be potent responses to this "call"? The emerging writing and images suggest that (my) health conditions *are* the rendering of a mythography. A mythography is the representation of myths, especially in the plastic arts. *Mourning the Dream / Amor Fati* is such a mythography, an autopoesis (self-creation) that is both autonomous as it is told through the Klein body, as well as intentional, taking Psyche's deeper intent signaled by flickers of embodiment in viscera and imagination. The book has created its own tacit infrastructure, supporting the realization of the mythopoetic dimension of experience, including substantial elements that are the very details of an autobiographical inquiry—particularly the narrative that threads throughout the entirety of the book and the art inhabiting a parallel stream of information and inspiration.

The thread—or threads—of the narrative are braided together with theory and practice, informing and weaving the fabric of a mythopoetic inquiry that is primarily (and primordially) situated in the ongoing relationship between polarities. In the tension of opposites, the imaginal becomes activated, and the practice of listening to Psyche becomes the key factor in the mythopoetic apprenticeship this inquiry offers. The undulation between polarities generates the momentum of a spiral, as the development of psyche is spiralic.

Mourning the Dream / Amor Fati has all the makings of mythopoeia both in its intimate details of hushed secrets, hiding in the corners of rooms, as well as the careful crafting of its aesthetic architecture. It houses stillnesses in movement and momentum in stillness. The dynamic generated through the partnering of art making and autobiographical inquiry—embodiment and reflection—draws the inquirer into the structure of the myth itself, mirroring archetypal patterns of experience in the metaphorical languages of soma, symbol, and narrative. Present experience becomes mythopoetic when it can be seen within its own larger context as part of that which bridges the gap between conscious and unconscious—our myth.

We are myth-making in the space between word and image when we understand that the literal is the ground from which the symbolic arises. Mythopoesis shapes a direction that ironically does not forget the old myth. It takes the familiar patterns, beliefs, and old form of *logos* which defined the sense we made of our myth, now ostensibly "dead," with a discernment of what is useful to carry forward and what needs to be let go of. In this manner, mythopoesis creates a new vision from the raw material of our myth for its own and our own transformation, metamorphosing the old structures from the literal into the literary—where consciousness and the unconscious work together in shaping and being shaped by the unknown.

De-literalizing experience implies the necessity of seeing through the metaphor of the myth by not only viewing it from a conscious egoic level but also to listen to Psyche's autonomous imperative within any given experience, asking: "What story am I telling myself about myself right now? What image am I in that is *having* me?" A symbolic gaze pierces through the liminal space between the conscious and unconscious itself—the "my" and "self" of myself—transcending the restrictions that the myth appears to impose.

The autonomous life of *Mourning the Dream / Amor Fati* has animated a Presence—of the unlived life perhaps—that has accompanied me through its insistent call and recall to the continuous signaling of Psyche through her rich, and sometimes terrifying embodiments. As a process, I understand this Presence to be a form of reflexive listening and actively re-visioning it-self. It is a consciousness that speaks from deep inside the unconscious, an "I" that I cannot know which seems to appear as if out of nowhere. But on reflection, I begin to understand it as being made possible through my willingness to engage the diaphoric imagination (that invites the unconscious aspect of my experience, the unlived life within), while at the same time anchoring myself in the flesh of my Klein body. Through listening reflexively and actively re-visioning itself simultaneously, the personal/collective Klein body both sees and embodies (my) existence *as* metaphor. It knows its telos as the ongoing metabolizing and metamorphosing of my/our experience (*prima materia*) into a spiral lens (consciousness in the presence of the numinous).

One of the most shocking, and enlightening encounters we can have in life is with the autonomous, unconscious assumptions we hold which, in turn, hold us. As I work with the *prima materia* of paint, pain, paper, stories, theories, and the movements of Psyche, everything becomes fluid, nothing is fixed. The wisdom of this imaginal apprenticeship with Psyche presents itself through the realization that my will, if not in accordance with Psyche's timing, is impairing. I have been shaped over the years by this shifting, sometimes drifting teaching that emerged naturally from the many classes and workshops of art making I have facilitated, as well as in my own art practice. I would also include playing with theory, as if concepts were the colors of my palette. Over time, the art making, teaching, and researching have become one and have carved me into who I am becoming today and who I have been becoming for centuries within the archetypal narrative of humanity. It is not my own story I tell. Nor am I telling it on my own. My age, my aging, and my era, are all informants of an alternate story in which the becoming is the way of being: the mythopoetic.

Age

Age carves us
into Who we
really are,
after all
our attempts to
be otherwise.

The poet Rumi's notion that "this being human is a guest house" feels like an appropriate opening for discussing the following questions[1]:

How do my/our health conditions act as a "call" to deepen consciousness and expand awareness?

How can art making and autobiographical inquiry (in this case partly a path-ography, a narrative of illness) be potent responses to this "call" of the unlived life?

This ancient approach of Rumi's being human is a guest house beautifully illustrates the kind of personification that naturally arises in inner work and can arouse unconscious processes in working with images. Epistemologically, this practice is informed by investigating what has been concealed, held secret in the unconscious, and how these hidden forms (archaic patterns from the collective unconscious) reveal themselves symbolically through the actions of personified figures animated through art making. The imaginal performances of these personifications enact the joy, depression, meanness, and dark thoughts that are part of the dialogue of the conscious and unconscious of participants in a body-to-body encounter of flesh and paint. In the liminality of the creative process, in the theater of Psyche, the personifications, like actors in a Shakespearean play, reveal a deeper plot uncovering potent intimacies—essential clues to understanding Psyche's deeper intent. Through the embodiment of the wounded story (tragedy, trauma), comes the way

---

1. Rumi, *Essential Rumi*, 109.

through, exemplified beautifully by Hamlet's words, "Through the indirect, find direction out."[2] The white of the moon. The correct seeing. A soul perspective.

Personification of unconscious contents or the "affects" that arise from these is an aspect of Jung's "active imagination," which facilitates communication between consciousness and the unconscious, ego and shadow, "a method of introspective observing the stream of internal images."[3] Robert Bosnak, a Jungian psychoanalyst, calls this "embodied imagination."[4] Both of these approaches bring to life the inner figures that appear in the psyche; symbols of archetypal processes for us to consider in the midst of facilitating within the "dreamscape" of the inter-relational field—between an individual or group with its many "guests." I consistently ask my students and clients to engage and embody these "inner figures" through the art. This less confrontational, indirect gaze of personification might allow them to come into a more direct relationship with such figures and the feelings they are associated with. In active or embodied imagination, perspectives of the dream ego—as well any "others" that appear in the dreams/dreambody—are brought to life.

Symbolizing archetypal presences as personified "inner figures," we begin to feel ourselves into their resonance (Einfuhlung); we begin to see and feel how they do and gain the perspective of seeing how the images sees—seeing from inside the image, rather than at it (shape-shifting the subjective/objective dialectic). When we come into symbolic relationship with the unconscious through the active, embodied imagination, empathy with the inner figures develops. As we allow ourselves to become more intimate with them and their curious roles in the theater of Psyche, we become highly attuned to collective archetypal patterns that make up the larger picture. We also see and possibly experience the "I" that I think I am as a figure in that vaster narrative and not always as the leading role. As if in a dream, we can explore the polytheism of the psyche by stepping into other roles and view the play from their perspective. And so, as the Greeks demonstrated in their mythology, we become the players of our destiny towards whatever fate has in store for us. In this manner, we begin to feel the contours of the unlived life within, bridging the known and the unknown through image and myth.

2. Shakespeare, *Hamlet*, 41.

3. Jung, *Basic Writings*, 190.

4. See Bosnak, *Embodiment*.

Personifying illuminates the details that are the compilation of the landscape and population of the mythography that, in turn, generates the mythopoeia. This is the intent; Psyche's ulterior motive. Mythopoetic inquiry holds the *telos*—the purpose—of acknowledging the presence of an archetypal story beneath or beyond the conscious, thinking about oneself and the world, and how we can step into the relationship between *anima* and *anima mundi*, between intention and extension, and between consciousness and the unconscious.

Mythopoetic consciousness knows all of the guests that come as guides to further deepen and expand our awareness, recognizing the crucial symbolic, metaphoric, and diaphoric (the unknown aspect of the metaphoric) capacities of these imaginal guests. They bring us the gift of the "unknown."

The method of active/embodied imagination has the conscious mind deliberately invite and invoke unconscious energies, those imaginal figures, guests, teachers, and disturbers which the diaphoric draws into awareness for their transformative potential. The involvement with these guests from the unconscious manifests in dialogues of performative actions, movement, art making, voice, poetry, and storytelling. These are the revelations of aspects of the myth living through me/you which become embodied in the creative process.

Revelations of the myth naturally include societal, gendered, and other cultural mythologies that make up collective myths—the larger narratives the personal myth is embedded in (the unconscious assumptions we have and that have us). Personal myths are not perceived as merely projections or parts of the personality. The "I" in the me-story *is* the most immediate expression of an archetypal pattern present in the morphic field. It offers accessibility, though initially through an identification with archetypal material, that later can be magnified through the lens of personification and amplification through myths, literature, and theater, offering collective embodiments of what might be mistaken as personal, idiosyncratic, and psychic phenomenon. From this perspective of the "I" portraying an archetypal motif, an acting out of a mythic theme, the images (the imaginal figures, the characters of the inner play) have their own autonomy and insights. They are a collection of images together forming another image. A constellation; stars telling a story.

Personification and embodiment in art making and performative actions present an opportunity for seeing how the "I" that takes the central role in a mythic scenario is being played out with other guests of the unconscious. As elements of the dynamic of such imaginal scenes becomes evident in these embodiments, they quite naturally lead to a coherent cultivation of entry points into the liminal, recognizing their familiar patterns or structures. The ability to enter imaginal spaces and meet inner figures that live in the unconscious (and the unlived life) then becomes a skill that can be developed. Refinement of this cultivation enhances the practice of inviting the embodiments of pieces of the myth—the "I's," their stories, and their affects living through me—as they reveal themselves through the body and the body of art materials. In this manner, the discipline of the mythopoetic process becomes an apprenticeship for others to consider.

The activities—or "steps" and "stops" the apprentice uses as guides—bring previously autonomous unconscious forces (secrets or concealments) into conscious play. Through the process of active/embodied imagination, inner figures enter a field of awareness even as this field might seem like a dream. The "dream figures" of the imagination move to the front of the stage, so to speak, and so one can see, hear, and feel them more clearly. One may come to know their smell before they have even arrived. Whiffs of these "guests" inspire an immediate instinctive curiosity about the particular roles the characters enact and what dimension they open us up to in the theater of Psyche—the mythopoetic narrative of the collective. Asking "What story am I in right now?" might prompt an insightful response.

All conscious and unconscious players (myself as therapist and educator, including my invisible unconscious guests, and those of my students and clients) may then be acknowledged as important participants of the inter-relational field of experience. Here the players of the field present us with a mythic mirror in which the actors of the myth play out their characters and roles through and in the body and the environment. What also becomes apparent is how this myth connects to themes and motifs in literature, fairy tales, films, and many forms of cultural expression. In this form of amplification, understanding my/your myth as a reflection of a collective mythological pattern or cultural text, lightens the feeling of being alone or the tendency to pathologize oneself. I have seen how my students and clients have benefited from this contextualization of their own myths as an important thread in the weave of the human narrative rather than thinking of their predicament as isolated, personal stories of failure or sickness. Viewing one's own myth as an essential thread in the cloth of humanity is the kind of vision made possible by looking through the carefully crafted spiral lens. This vision reflexively affects the viewer and what is seen, just as my/your Klein body reveals and *is* both inside and outside, subjective and objective perspectives simultaneously. The Klein body metabolizes archetypal material, thereby accessing that deep consciousness embedded in the unconscious. Individuation is a continuous circular movement often represented by the *ouroboros*, a snake biting its own tail. The powerful undulations of the snake's body propel it into a spiraling motion, catching its own tail and eating it. The symbolism of this mythological image connects to the Klein body's metamorphosing the past (tail) which, through being digested, moves into an inner domain, vanishing from sight, but still a part of the process of self actualizing. Eating our own past experiences—our failures, losses, and dreams already lost except in memory, imagination, trauma and soma—gives sustenance, life out of death, creation out of destruction, a transcendence of duality connecting the ego (as center of consciousness) with the archetypal Self, symbolized by the spiral lens.

Field Notes: Failure

I am interested in this notion of failure as I very much feel this happening randomly throughout creating this large piece of work.

My mind wanders to connections in the past: I failed to be healthy in my life. I failed to live up to the hopes I imagined my family and clan had for me. My lineage; who I was supposed to be in this grand narrative. I weep at this failure buried deep within the heart of the child archetype—the archetype of the past and the future, of possibilities—as I feel the failure my mother and father felt in living up to their own or their parents' hopes.

What does it mean when we contemplate our failures? It means bringing the feelings of those failures into consciousness, not leaving them stuck, not leaving them behind and alone with the oppressive presence of failure with its insidious message of "not good enough."

Learned failure without examination is an important issue in education and therapy.

What is a failure? How do we construct it? Can we deconstruct it? Can we simply see that it might be a misnamed trajectory that has not received any validation from places of authority in our lives: parents, siblings, peers, education? The narcissistic wound.

Can a failure be a creative opportunity, a "stop" that has not yet been considered—a baby yet to be conceived? A liminal space on the threshold of learning? An intention waiting to extend itself? An unlived life so wanting just to be touched?

I'd like to hang out with failure for a while and see what its other face looks like. See what its true nature discloses to me as I turn my back on the internalized voices that have me failing before I have even begun; The heckler, the Komandant, the misogynist. I want to see if I can pass through the narcissistic mirror that is constantly reflecting back the wound. Fixating on this image of self then becomes an act of wounding unless . . .

Maybe I was supposed to begin something else and my sense of failure is simply telling me that because what I want to do does not necessarily fit with what the school, family, the heroic ego, the status quo want. Maybe what my heart of hearts yearns to do sneaks in its request via negativa, by giving me a sense of failure in the face of what is not so important to the soul. Shall I turn around and face this inner figure, Failure, the face in the mirror staring back at me so sternly?

Figure 27. You

An authentic mythopoetic practice holds a place at the table for failure, the wounded narrative. The wounding is the beginning and source of the myth that is the "call" of the Self to be actualized, the unlived life to become animated, ensouled in the imaginal. The re-cognition of the wound—the wounded parts of our story as a central motif to almost any myth, including our/your own—is key to embarking upon a mythopoetic journey. It is the "I" which I identify with that needs to step through the narcissistic mirror (like the Klein bottle maintaining its integrity while passing through its own body and squeezing into a dimension that can realize unconscious experience into conscious embodiment and insight, Psyche's deeper intent).

As the Klein body is morphing soma into lens in this manner, bodily matter transforming into a new way of being and seeing, an entirely different form of consciousness begins to spiral its way towards a perception of experience both deeply inside and beyond present experience of self. We might consider the above as a description of the momentum of the Self-Ego axis that considers the body's role as crucial in one's narrative, as flesh speaks the language of pain so succinctly.

As a focal point, the wounded part of the narrative pulls into itself to hold my attention. It acts as a decoy while the unconscious secretly draws me into a scheme hidden from consciousness. Luring me into the wounded story through the plaintive voice of the victim, I am separated from the constant demands of the heroic-ego. The words and images spiraling in and out of the wounded areas of my story are not detours, as much as they may feel as such. Their callings are crucial in their role as guides through the very symptoms and difficulties they speak of. The symptoms and "issues" are the laments of the wounded story giving me details of the mythography to be mapped through their patterns of expression. As relationship to the wound is central to inner work, it creates soul—soul not as entity, but as spatial being, as a process—a moment of poesis that brings forth a presence. It is the myth of woundedness and its voicing of forbidden secrets that generates embodied relationship with the unconscious, the wound acting as portal. The wound unites us in our humanity and such a radical relationship to it is made possible through the practices of a mythopoetic inquiry: deep democracy, archetypal activism, and an engagement of the diaphoric imagination which summons that which is not yet known.

Figure 28. Wounding

Ethically speaking, it is more important to work *with* the wound instead of *from* it (identifying with it, colonizing it as "me") if we choose to interrupt the ongoing wounding, we will inevitably maintain without this knowing. Here, there is also the possibility of de-colonizing from the images of others (projections and projective identifications). We wound and are wounded out of our own and others' wounds. If I reenact my wounded story without integrity, that is, literally rather than symbolically, and reflexively, the story will maim me and others in its path. If, however, the wounded parts of my myth, long exiled in the buried strata of psyche and soma are "seen through"—mirrored back to me just as my face in the bathroom mirror confronts me with its simultaneous image appearing—then valuable, archetypal motifs and mythic themes appear as reflections of patterns that connect all of humanity. From this perspective, our personal, wounded narratives may in fact create immediate access to the essential creativity of the human spirit. This connecting with soul might be the most potent key to human survival.

In this way, our personal narrative is a place of humanity. In exchange, the collective offers the depth of the archetypal to the personal. This is how the wound leads us into a mythopoesis that is indigenous to ourselves. It is *of* the Self (archetypal). Seeing the wound through the spiral lens that is metamorphosing in the personal and collective Klein body, I experience my myth as necessary—as a visceral and epistemological contribution to the collective mythopoeia of moving from the literal to the symbolic. I have witnessed many times when clients and students come to this knowing and make an archetypal leap from the role of victim into a more deeply human perspective of knowing both faces of the unfolding archetypal dynamic of polarities. This is an archetypal shift from victim to wounded healer.

Here are some suggestions proposed in my work as therapist and educator in groups and individual sessions for working with the wound:

1. Listen to the wounded story as you would the breaths of a maimed animal. You must come gently and close to do this.

2. Acknowledge the wound as crucial, perhaps the deepest part of ourselves as human.

3. Watch when you are operating out of the wound, enacting the wounded part of the story thus continuing the wounding again and again unconsciously.

4. Understand that false selves arise in relation to the wound, the grandiose or limited scripts you adopt to get through the day. Recognize that they are reactive and unconscious—complexes, in Jung's language. If they remain unconscious, they will be autonomous, outside your will or ethics, and will not serve the archetypal Self. Wholeness and self-actualization. These false selves/stories as habitual defenses against the wound are often polarized as inflation or deflation. Superiority/inferiority. The complexes have no ethics. They will kill to survive.

5. The false selves and their tales' original intent was to help or protect you. But now they need to be in service of the Self, not the ego (self interest). This is not altruism but wisdom. The false selves need guidance to grow out of their immaturity and into humanity—they need a broader perspective of what life is. We need to provide this.

6. Work with the relationship to the wound by noting, experiencing the affects (feelings, body states, etc.) and effects (stories we tell ourselves, behaviors, outcomes, etc.) of false selves/stories. What roles do these false selves play in the havoc of your life? See that they interfere with authenticity and self-actualization of yourself and those around you—the world.

7. Soul as process, as a dynamic relationship to the unconscious that can become more spacious the more the relationship to the wound becomes a place of awareness.

Feeling wounded or being a wounder (we are always both) is a clue that this relationship needs tending, deep tending, and that the wound needs to find a place to be in your life so that you can take care of it for yourself and others' sake. The wound is looking for a home or hospice, where all its needs can be provided for, so that its authentic power, its original intent *plus* all the consciousness it has invoked, can be released and/or harnessed. This is how the wounded story has fulfilled its role in our human drama.

In some of the classes I have facilitated, particularly in one course called, "The Authentic Self and the False Selves," we worked on beginnings, perhaps the foundation of building this place, this home for the wound, and invited in all of the "guests" to assist in this process (referring back to Rumi). We had an Open House, inviting all of the collective guests to join us in the group process.

In this wound-work, it is important that the embodied, imaginal ego—the archetypal ego, who lives in dreams and creativity *without* dissociating from consensus reality—becomes the shape-shifter. She is the liminal figure who *is* the subject/object of the archetypal journeying in active embodied imagination. She has been present in the Klein body of human viscera all along. It is the archetypal, imaginal ego who has the capacity to come close to the edge of the wound. She knows instinctively how to fully dwell in the inside/outside of the personal and collective Klein body as it painfully morphs into the spiral lens. It is this archetypal ego, ego as navigator of the subjective and objective Psyche, whose habitat lies between and beyond dualities. Her "twin" vision, like that of the lucid dream ego, does not experience moving towards the wound as if it were tipping on the edge of an abyss.

Without the perspective of the imaginal ego, ego as archetype rather than as complex—who *is* the lucid dreamer in our waking life—it is difficult to see symbolically (and thereby come into relationship with) archetypes/myths other than the heroic-ego or self as victim or split. Not engaging the imaginal "other" is to not consciously partake of the shaping of my destiny, and the destiny of others. Not utilizing the process of active/embodied imagination—the pedagogy of personification—as a means of 'getting to know' the "others" within, I take these "others" instead to be simply mysterious, unexplored, and unexplainable aspects of myself. Or I project them onto other people. I mistake my moods, feelings, thoughts, or images as a secret language my conscious mind cannot read and so miss the mythopoetic dimension these "moods" are pointing to; that is, the implicit archetypal narrative my myth is a mirror of. I don't see through the signals to the underlying story the moods are trying to draw to my attention towards. I overlook the diaphoric moment that might be flickering the light of a thousand mirrors of possibilities. If I miss the "call," I am not taking care of my duties as mythographer and ultimately not taking up the mythopoetic endeavor. As archetypal activist, it is my task to collect important cues from the flickering nature of the theater of the collective psyche. Hearing the "call" through my Klein body as it strains to become the spiral lens brings me closer to trusting the importance of discerning suffering as part of the carving of destiny.

Missing the "call" is not adhering to the ethics of my apprenticeship, making my practice misleading. "To thine own self be true, and it must follow, as the night the day, thou canst not then be false to any man."[5] I will not be a worthy or competent therapist or educator if I do not catch the cues that are available in the intra-psychic and inter-subjective field—that which becomes evident through the diaphoric, that mysterious "other" of the imagination. These cues (the flickers, the smells) then remain undifferentiated blurs of "happenings" in my being; they remain dormant, secrets—concealed information of unborn awarenesses my symptoms are carrying for me. I will know nothing of the unlived life other than an intolerable emptiness.

Isolated, inactive, and impaired by my lack of recognizing important—albeit disturbing—inner figures as archetypal, I am unable to hear the "call" of my destiny; the call of Psyche/soul to express herself, to show her deeper intent, her ulteriority. If I am blind to my own complexes, they lie like stone babies, conceived but not given birth to, incomplete expressions of Psyche's imperative of finding form for the imaginal "other" that engenders those dynamic inter-subjective and intra-psychic relationships necessary for personal and collective evolution. If I have become immune to the presence of a complex—due to its calcification in my unconscious—I remain cut off from the archetype at its core and my own connection to the archetypal realm, the myths living in me, which may contain gifts for myself and others. I will be unable to expand my

5. Shakespeare, *Hamlet*, 25.

vision far enough to see beyond the limited image I have of myself in the narcissistic mirroring of the wound; I will not be able to move from *how I see myself* and *how I think of myself*, to *seeing myself as a way of seeing*, thus seeing the image of myself as the only way of seeing in this moment.

Picking up the cues and embodying them in a living inquiry is the central task of a mythopoetic practice, letting the visceral Klein bottle do its alchemical work. If I cannot engage these cues, they will remain stuck and keep recycling in my system (and that of the collective) until I understand my/their role in this mythopoetic journey. The practice of mythopoetic inquiry guides the soul back to seeing itself in resonant images (art) that hold soul even through the colonization of self by ego (neurosis) or in trauma (psychosis). The resonating soul-images, Psyche's flickerings, lead the practitioner to a sense of Presence through intentional intimacy with other presences on the journey of inquiry. The Presence is the overarching vision (vision-maker) that sees the whole of one's life; it is the spiral lens crafted through the suffering of the personal and collective Klein body in its metamorphosis that brings the perspective and perception of Presence into one's being and the world.

To deepen the resonance of Presence, I must ask myself:

Inlay: How Do I Move through Time?

Do I slice through it, splice it together, chop it up into small, manageable pieces, or sail into it like a graceful schooner?

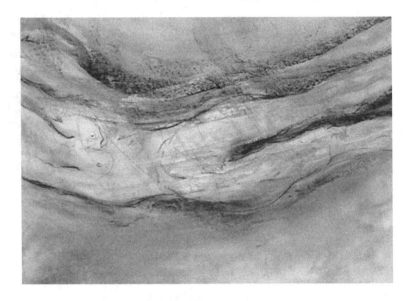

Figure 29. How Do I Move through Time?

Field Notes: Time

I tell the time. I look at my watch when someone asks me, "Do you have the time?" or when I have an appointment. I also tell the time, or rather, can tell the time as it passes only through the shifting of my own experience.

"How do I move through time?" might then be rephrased as: how do I move through my own experience, the many manifold aspects of Psyche the personal psyche, the Psyche of the world, anima mundi, soul?

How do I move through soul?

Do I move "through" it at all? Does the soul know time? I hear my watch ticking on my wrist, resting on this piece of paper. It's almost time to go to class to spend an hour or so on the bus. Spending time with other wet souls I don't know. It's raining. Each drop of wetness holds a moment.

How many moments do I hold, or moments that hold me? And how many do I just let slip by, not acknowledging them, not even noticing them? Like a rude host who takes the time to honor only the prestigious guests who have arrived at Psyche's threshold, ignoring the uninvited visitors and shunning even, the less desirable ones. How does moving through time in this manner influence my experience and the world around me?

And yet, I find myself often doing the tango with these undesirable ones, cemented to these uncomfortable moments I would prefer to avoid. I become locked inside their seeming immobility even though I know that no moment is without its movement, that no moment actually has even the capacity to remain static or singular.

Field Notes: Deep Time

I have come across this interesting sensibility as of late, of time getting deeper as I age, dropping beneath my feet. Often time is thought of so literally, as if it is a line we are attached to throughout life; an umbilical cord left uncut. At first it's a long line, then a medium line, then a short one. It is a thin anorexic line: an unfed perspective. But these days I experience time as deep, unfathomably so, as it drops me into the earth and soars up far beyond my comprehension simultaneously.

Figure 30. Dancing the Time Line

I feel time's verticality, its multidimensionality as if for the first time. Time is intimate, swelling. Outrageous, so how could it possibly fit on this "line" we consider our "time line"?

How is it I come to know this? I know this from the stories I hold within that are holding me. I would like to go back to the sensation of full immersion in deep time, to explore all the minute details of the day, and at the same time know the origins of those details, as does the Klein body, implicitly. These particulars are the pieces that make up the myth. The myth is the story that is then lifted out of the literal and into the literary through the process of mythopoesis:

> Situations where meanings of mythical accounts had been re-visioned, the original literal tellings of myths and stories transformed into symbolically new versions.[6]

Deep time is necessary for the practice of mythopoesis. It is the intention and extension of this mythopoetic inquiry, its center and periphery, content and process. Deep time is when the spiral lens is being caringly crafted.

In my practice as artist, educator, therapist and researcher—where I am engaging the creative process on my own, or with a client in individual sessions, or in a group setting—an immediate intimacy takes hold that is both vast and intricate in nature. This is the sensibility of deep time

6. Doty, *Mythography*, 20.

in which participants enter the liminality or *temenos*, a space of transformation that acts as a dreamscape, a field of possibilities that cannot be anticipated. "Guests" from the unconscious—including the ancestors— show up in this field and become animated participants that generate the energy and dynamics of the story the dialogue of the conscious and unconscious is telling: stories transformed into symbolically new versions through the diaphoric imagination where knowledge comes about in the unknown. Different kinds of stories that are a quantum leap from the original literal tellings emerge. The "guests," now active participants, become embodied in the art, sometimes as personifications of archetypal forces present in the field, surprising clients, students and my-self as facilitator in their diaphoric appearance.

Personification as metaphor relies on its diaphoric aspect, drawing on the automation of the unconscious and its ability to make a creative, archetypal shift, beyond simple mental associations. In this movement from one dimension of consciousness to another, previously unrecognized "guests" become embodied players in the field of possibilities: dreamers in the dreamscape, releasing the true character or nature of the myth being lived *and* the potential for the unlived life to be imagined. Full immersion in deep time naturally stimulates a diaphoric consciousness that is essential to a mythopoeia. That *is* the transformational move from a sense of isolation and irrelevance, the restriction of the old anorectic time-line holds us to. The following performative inquiry assisted me in releasing myself from the literal happenings of the past:

After a long time I finally leave.

I can do this because:

We are never never alone
we are filled with others' ideas, images, genes, genres, dreams
our whole being is based on "other"
we are made up of thousands of pieces of "other"

the thousands of "flickers" specifically arranged to compose "us"
a memory, dream, inspiration is never without
this "other" that amuses, irritates, loves or hates us
we are never without all of these songs of others in our throats
they sing through us in our own particular unique voice, our song

I am born from other and die into other.

I am always in the presence of the unlived life

Without it I know nothing

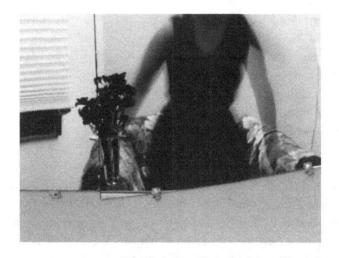

Figure 31. After a Long Time I

Figure 32. After a Long Time II

Figure 33. After a Long Time III

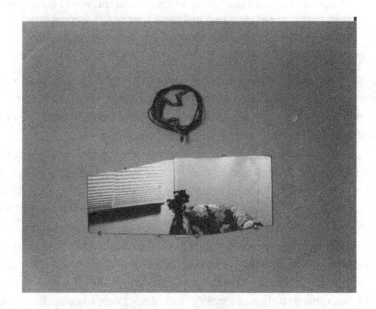

Figure 34. After a Long Time IV

The above photographs were taken at another time, but in the same place. This space between time and place opened a liminal field for my psyche to roam. I had the uncanny opportunity to re-enter the last living quarters I had dwelled in with my partner in Canada before we moved to Japan for several years.

A friend of my sister's was going on a trip. She asked me to water her plants while she was gone. She happened to live in the very same apartment I had left so many years earlier. I took my best friend—the camera—with me as a "let's see what happens" notion, having nothing particular in mind.

I spent many hours over several days listening to the walls, walking the long hallway, standing in doorways I had passed through so many times, so long ago; thresholds I was not conscious of at the time. I let my body become a large ear, big enough to hear the ghosts of time past, their resonances palpable. I was no longer in the partnership, and yet, here, in these rooms, these thresholds of the past, I could feel the remains of the relationship, its old smell asking to be taken in from the past, asking to be brought into the present, asking to be breathed in and exhaled into deep time:

> Many signs indicate that the future enters us in this way in order to be transformed in us, long before it happens . . . We could easily be made to believe that nothing happened, and yet we have changed, as a house that a guest has entered changes.[7]

In my group work I often ask participants "what future might be coming into you through these marks that appear in front of you now after having opened yourself to their significance?" The spiral lens is secretly shaping itself in the Klein body as flesh sharpens into crystal lens.

I put my camera to work. It worked without me. In those inner spaces, it stood on its own, seizing its autonomy, offering its own perspective without me backing it, standing behind it, directing its gaze. So I was free to wander through space, into the liminal in whatever way my Klein body wanted. I entered the past (the liminal knows no past nor future; it lives in deep time, just as the spiral lens sees and offers all time). I stepped in, like Psyche—as soul does, subjectively—embodying now what were just floating memories and silenced wounds. I wanted to see, to be with this past, this old story trying desperately to come to its own conclusion. I wanted to be the guest that changes the house. There was no plan, no direction. No desired outcome. It was only the three of us: the room, the camera, and my movements. The camera shutter opened to the

7. Rilke, *Letters to a Young Poet*, 63.

liminal and I was able to enter the past through the aperture of this space between time and place. And so, I was finally able to enter *and* leave. Stone baby finally birthed. After a Long Time.

The figure in the images, an imaginal figure, knew what I did not. She knew I had to leave this place. And she knew how. The figure entered my body—she was my body in its Klein bottle nature and directed me to complete a process I was unable to struggle my way through. I had been unable to move through these spaces, these thresholds on my own. I needed this guest, this guide, to show me. I needed my own art making process as a vehicle to pass through a void that I could, prior to those moments, not navigate. It was imperative that my "mind" not know what I was doing, otherwise its assumed autonomy would not allow room for the imaginal figures to emerge as guides. The art as liminal here offers an entry into deep time, activating the practices of deep democracy, archetypal activism, and diaphoric imagination—such important steps in a mythopoetic inquiry.

In my own art making process, as well as that of my clients and students, I have witnessed the appearance of these imaginal figures, these "guests" and their strange and wonderful maneuvers. Once they have shown themselves—uncovering their presence under the blanket of unconsciousness, from an unlived life—they can do their work freely. In the practice of active/embodied imagination, I ask my students: "How does this guest affect you? How does your body feel when you are face to face with this "other" entity, as if you are meeting a person for the first time? Where do your eyes/feelings go when you look at each other? Is there something you would like to ask this figure? Is there something it wants from you? Is there something between you, something in the gaze? Who do you become in her/his presence?" The imaginal figure in the above images embodied the archetypal activist who gave me the ability to leave. Move on.

Diagrammatically I see the above performative embodiment as a triangle. It is a triangular relationship or relationality of places and processes:

Figure 35. Diagram

Embodied, unconscious processes have resonance and create presence(s) we can connect with and learn from. Left as dis-membered, undifferentiated forces—wildcards in a sense—these "guests" wander off and become reactive, resistant, or ignorant to the possibility of relationships. The above structure of the alchemical vessel, cooking the future that has already entered us in the form of "guests," shows how we inherently have a dynamic relationship with unacknowledged, unconscious inhabitants of experience as they become manifest through their direct and immediate relating (body-to-body). The body of the art materials and our bodies; flesh and paint trans-formed in the mythopoetic space where symbolic unfolding takes place; the body of the art materials and my body; conceiving a new presence. This is the work-shop, the ritual space of the archetypal activist, who returns again and again to a ceremony of potential transformation, the myth metamorphosing into the mythopoetic. Here is the embodied, imaginal ego who knows herself to be the subject and object of experience where the self becomes a *process*— an alchemical Klein body rather than a fixed center of identity. Intention and extension are symmetrical parts of the same movement of the dynamic capacity of the body. Here the body of the archetypal activist is the Klein bottle morphing into a spiral lens that perceives and reveals inside and outside as one movement. The force of this archetypal dynamic has the power to metabolize experience in an alchemical crystallizing process which crafts (*kraft*, meaning strength in German) experience into the fine glass of the spiral lens . . . which then reflexively bends back and transforms viscera and vision; a lens that bends light and re-shapes its own perspective.

Intuitively, my body (as Klein bottle) was moving through the imaginal space in the above photographs, perceiving and revealing the past as it was now being presented through the spiral lens for a re-viewing. These subtle transitions in the unconscious took me out of a fixed, calcified relationship to an aspect of my past (and myself) left inside, unbirthed. Within the Klein body's invisible potentialities, like the dark body of the camera taking in light, I opened myself to the wounded story that was still entombed within. In that moment, I stepped into the part of my myth which typically presented itself as a repetition, a compulsion that forever eluded me. But this time, through the symbolic act, the spell (the web of the "complex" in the unconscious) suddenly broke and released me from the fixation—like Narcissus staring at his own reflection until the lapping movement of the water dissolved the image. Previous to this particular encounter in my art making, I was unable to perceive the unconscious ritual taking place except through its effects: moods, symptoms, and a certain paralysis that I had no control of. It's re-embodiment in the art making felt as if I was giving birth to the stone baby that had to come out after so many years inside my stiffened viscera.

And so, the imaginal performance of the embodied inner figure in the above photographs marked the entry and extension into the liminal where the symbolic ritual appeared spontaneously from the unconscious. The intimate performance cracked the calcium crust of the stone baby and opened the possibility of seeing into and through the bleakness of the moods that had been stifling me. This mythopoetic performance brought a subtle momentum into the paralysis, a stirring both of the ancients coming into me through the voices of the future and the past. It was as if the ancient ones were lamenting, asking me, pleading with me to tell their stories so that we could move on, morphing together into the future embedded in the moment. The baby entombed in my own body needed to be mourned, cried the old souls. I ask the reader if you might have your own stone baby that the ancients are asking you to mourn: something you have not yet been able to give birth to?

As the extension of the future present in the past was animated in the example above, outlines of a complex deeply buried in unread moods and symptoms were illuminated. Long unopened letters from the archetypal guests of the unborn and the ancestors were now speaking directly from the past into the present from the realm of the dead.

In this imaginal, mythopoetic liminality as imaginal ego, as mythographer and archetypal activist, I can see myself beyond my previous self-inquiry of:

Am I how I see myself?

Am I how I think of myself?

Because the symbolic always implies what is not yet evident (the diaphoric aspect of metaphor), the above questions shifted towards a more fluid, creative, transformative question proposed near the beginning of this chapter. But before I come to this perhaps premature conclusion I must continue a while yet with my inquiry of "Am I How I see Myself?"

Figure 36. Am I How I See Myself?

Moving beyond limited and limiting questions, with the assistance of the now embodied inner figure (body as Klein bottle), I can now dis-identify from oppressive images of myself by seeing them hermeneutically through the spiral lens. The practice of deep democracy allowed me to include the guests of my moods and first say "yes" to their wounding and woundedness. After a while, I asked them to step aside, to make room for a new kind of "yes" to what they are symbolically pointing to: the future coming into me.[8] Only then was I able to leave the relationship whose

8. Rilke, *Letters to a Young Poet*, 63.

remains slept in the walls of the apartment I visited, those left-overs still clinging to my sense of self that was really a self-absence, a blackness.

Now I could take possession of these remains rather than them taking possession of me; to take responsibility for them, mourn them, and care for them like abandoned children. I might now let them grow up and receive new meaning from them, healing their wounded story. Even though there may be repeated regressions/aggressions in this stepping in and out, in and out of awareness (losing this new-found vision), the mythopoetic inquiry continues to ask: *Am I myself simply a way of seeing?* As a mirror, my experience reflects back to me the inside and outside of the Klein body. And so I move through and into myself in mythic time, in mythopoetic space, a timeless traveler in deep time. This way of seeing/being—which emerges in mythopoetic spaces such as art making and psychoanalysis—presents the possibility of transformation. Jungian analyst and author Giuseppe Maffei suggests that:

> time in psychoanalysis has very special characteristics which could be compared to historical time, provided that we conceive of this as mediation between the time of the world (physical and biographical) and the time of the subject who, integrating the legacy of past and present experiences, takes possession of them to give them meaning . . . build their own intermediate time, which unites with the time of the others in the inner rhythm of desire and then is the product of an original creation.[9]

A temporal sense of the unconscious can indeed be what making art invokes through inviting in the traces, the imaginal figures and processes, and allowing them to do their work of taking on tangible form in the body of paint, paper, movement, voice, etc. Similar to dreaming activities, this is what happened for me in my "visit" to my past; the past now visiting me in a new way—fully experienced in the Klein body—with the assistance of the spiral lens bringing a re-visioned, living interpretation into the picture.

The art contains the past, the present, and the future, the conscious and the unconscious. Art making creates an intermediate or liminal time and space in which the concrete piece of artwork morphs itself into the world. At the same time it is taking shape, the image begins to take on conscious meaning (through the spiral lens). "Image and meaning are

9. Maffei, "Experience of Time," 115.

identical. As the first takes shape, so the latter becomes clear."[10] Embodiment is form *and* presence. This presence is often experienced as a call felt through the medium of the imaginal and serves as a symbolic function of resonating something primordial. When such an embodiment occurs in art making, it acts as a bridge between desire and creativity, the ephemeral and the concrete. The inner figure in the above images crossed this bridge and made conscious an unfinished process, an unfulfilled desire. I see the traces Maffei is writing about as moods fogging the underlying intent of Psyche, blurring the spiral lens. I am lost in the moods/symptoms/desires until I am able to personify them, and hence reveal the imaginal figures the moods are both carrying and concealing. The spiral lens crystallizes their purpose to me; I begin to see their ulterior motive of illuminating the archetypal core of the idiosyncratic complex, the primordial cosmic mirror reflecting my personal myth subjectively, temporally.

If these moods are subjected to a lack of the temporal and left aimlessly floating in the unconscious, they exaggerate themselves as symptoms, and so further reinforce the wounded narrative the complex is insisting upon. However, if they are taken as initial sketches, the first traces of embodiment, they can be brought to a mythopoetic field of awareness through the art making. Psyche's flickerings—moods/symptoms now embodied in the art—can be traced back to the signaling of the ancients and colored in, fleshed out and imbued with a consciousness that creates order and meaning. This perspective is the mythopoetic view of transformative learning that the spiral lens facilitates as it is birthed through the Klein body, often a painful birth indeed.

The mythopoetic view relies on images and symbols, the language of poetry. It complements the type of transformation described by Jack Mezirow as a learning in the Klein body which does not take one back to the life of the mind, as might be found with analysis, but to the soul.[11] Here the focus is on images symbolic of powerful motifs that represent, at an unconscious level, deep-seated emotional or spiritual issues and concerns that can initially be detected in the body. Already present in the personal as well as collective body of humanity, these motifs are asking to be embodied in a manner that tells a new story, speaking a language of paradox and *amor fati*. This is an ancient language that takes us past the notion of contra-dictions and well beyond the first two questions posed previously in this chapter:

10. Jung, *Structure and Dynamics*, 204.
11. See Dirkx, et al. "Musings and Reflections."

Am I how I see myself?

Am I how I think of myself?

And into the viscera of:

Am I simply a way of seeing?

Inviting these questions into the *temenos* of the mythopoesis—the alchemical vessel gestating the story that the body is trying to tell—is an act of love.

The motifs presented by personal concerns are often expressions of the collective Zeitgeist, the flickerings of the same story the unborn and the ancients are requesting be seen and heard. Through the *"kraft"* of the Klein body comes the spiral lens that reveals profound significance for both. Becoming visible is a radical act, an archetypal act, and also an act of love.

Field Notes of the Interior:

My body is telling me a sad tale these days. It's a story I know so well, like a familiar fairy tale I was read to as a child. I know every piece and pattern of the dynamic and the tale's tragic end. By heart.

My body knows this story inside out. It thinks it is the story. The symptoms have full paragraphs. The episodes are complete chapters. The cycling and recycling of the themes are like the fairy tale being read over and over again, now memorized. In the body. Even though the story is known by heart, the body is compelled to repeat it. Repeat it like a drum song that uses bones as drum sticks, pounding, beating the rhythm so I will never forget it. Never get it out of my bones.

Can I learn to listen to this song, this story in a new way? Stop its vibrating my being to its beat? It is so painful each time I hear it. I feel it really is me. I think it is me. I believe it to be me. Am I how I see myself?

Am I how I think of myself?

I am a prisoner inside this story/song. I have forgotten all the other stories and songs I learned as a child, as a dreamer, as an investigator of the imaginal, as mythographer.

This strange lullaby tucks me into unconsciousness and, like Sleeping Beauty, I am waiting to be awoken by the kiss of consciousness. Sleeping Beauty remains unconscious for a long time. She is waiting for her own inner Prince in the form of a symbolic performance such as "After a Long Time" above.

The symptoms my body is using as words are wanting to tell my story for me. They are trying, in their own language, to tell the tale to me, as if I were the child listening to the fairy tale again.

I have believed the sad tale the symptoms seem to be telling me on face value, forgetting that they are pointing to something other than themselves. An ancient wound. Like a child rebelling and denying the story the symptoms hold, I have been blind to the underlying mythic tale that is moving through me; I am caught in a spell, heartbroken that I cannot find the way, the secret word, to break this spell. I turn to the autonomous images flickering through my Klein body as they are illuminating, if even for a split second, the powerful motifs of deep-seated emotional and spiritual concerns. I return to the notion that images love me, so am welcomed into their midst in the *temenos* of this mythopoetic inquiry.

Figure 37. P.S. I Love You I

Figure 38. P.S. I Love You II

Figure 39. P.S. I Love You III

Figure 40. P.S. I Love You IV

Figure 41. P.S. I Love You V

I am falling for the images.

The symptoms lie in wait for me. They are relentless and span decades, eons. They are like *coprolites* (fossilized feces) buried inside Psyche,
embedded in the collective unconscious. Because they have become

fossilized, preserved yet no longer alive—similar to the stone baby in its calcification—these symptoms have been prevented from participating in the natural cycle of decay and composting for new life, for the future that is wanting to come in. They are the ancient forms left by the projective identifications that have shaped my myth, the unlived lives/dreams of the ancients. Projective identifications are characterized through a modality that is simultaneously active, unconscious, and discrete. In other words, my symptoms actively—though unconsciously—bring about particular changes in the state of the "other." And in this case, I am proposing the "other" is me. From my conscious awareness, the effect of this type of "communication" from my body is a sudden change in my general state—a sense of passivity and coercion and an alteration in the state of consciousness itself.

Every state of mind has meaning. This altered consciousness ranges from what I believe could be an almost automatic repetition of a relational script (an unconscious relational pattern based on physiological survival reactions), to a moderate or serious contraction of the field of my attention, to full-fledged changes in my sense of self. "We know that altered states of consciousness cause a change in perception, a change in perception [that] results in a change in an individual's reality."[12] Experiencing blindness—no visual cues from the world—pulled me deep into vortices of previously suppressed pre-verbal material of the unconscious. Images with apparently no correspondence in an outer reality swallowed me whole into primordial states of terror, which, ironically, also opened the gates to the archetypal realm of the collective unconscious—the collective Shadow where experience of self lies beyond the personal, and an encounter with the numinous is immanent. No amount of will (ego) could protect me from this deeply mythic landscape where a new kind of navigating was waiting to become embodied in me.

Cristiana Cimino and Anonrllo Correale, psychoanalysts and researchers, propose the theory that this type of communication from the body—a communication from "other" than self, archetypal in nature—can come about through the emergence of traumatic contents of experiences from the non-conscious (non-declarative, implicit) memory, a communication not based on will.[13] These contents belong to a pre-symbolic and pre-representative area of the mind. They are made of

---

12. Bancroft, "History and Psychology," 112.
13. Cimino and Correale, "Projective Identification."

inert fragments (*coprolites*) of psychic material that are felt rather than thought, which can be viewed as a kind of *writing to be completed*.

These pieces of psychic material are the expression of traumatic experiences—not just of my own, but those of the dead as well (my transplant donors). Such fractured pieces of the collective carry the archetype of trauma itself; in turn, exercising a traumatic effect on me in the form of altered states of perception and consciousness. Such personal and archetypal material should be understood as belonging to an unrepressed unconscious, a "morphic resonance":

> Morphic resonance is a process whereby self-organizing systems inherit a memory from previous similar systems. In its most general formulation, morphic resonance means that the so-called laws of nature are more like habits. The hypothesis of morphic resonance also leads to a radically new interpretation of memory storage in the brain and of biological inheritance. Memory need not be stored in material traces inside brains, which are more like TV receivers than video recorders, tuning into influences from the past. And biological inheritance need not all be coded in the genes, or in epigenetic modifications of the genes; much of it depends on morphic resonance from previous members of the species. Thus, each individual inherits a collective memory from past members of the species, and also contributes to the collective memory, affecting other members of the species in the future.[14]

In his intriguing book, *The Presence of the Past*, Cambridge biologist Rupert Sheldrake lays out the evidence and research in support of his controversial theory of morphic resonance, exploring its far-reaching implications in the fields of biology, chemistry, physics, psychology, and sociology. Sheldrake explains how self-organizing systems, from crystals to human societies, share collective memories that influence their form and behavior. In his research, he proposes that nature is not ruled by fixed laws, but rather by habits and collective memories: "The morphic fields of mental activity are not confined to the insides of our heads. They extend far beyond our brain through intention and attention."[15] And I would like to add through extension, in the sense of how extension is presented in this book: the momentum of Psyche's ulterior motive towards full and conscious embodiment in intimate relationship with the unconscious:

14. Sheldrake, *Presence of the Past*, 108.
15. Sheldrake, *Presence of the Past*, 108.

We are already familiar with the idea of fields extending beyond
the material objects in which they are rooted: magnetic fields
extend beyond the surfaces of magnets; the earth's gravitational
field extends far beyond the surface of the earth, keeping the
moon in its orbit. Likewise, the fields of our minds extend far
beyond our brains.[16]

Sheldrake's findings are significant for mythopoetic inquiry as they invite
an understanding that personal and archetypal material from an unrepressed unconscious may in fact be transmitted through morphic resonances, extending into personal and collective experience—thus being a
part of shaping the world and how we live in it.

In *Mourning the Dream / Amor Fati*, I am suggesting that the pieces
of psychic material that are expressions of traumatic experiences—the
archetype of trauma—are morphic resonances that have become fragmented and fossilized. They are inherited memory from previous similar self-organizing systems, calcified so as not to threaten the life of the
mother. These fragments have, in this particular autobiographical inquiry, been experienced as a sense of something having been taken away,
lost, or surrendered. And this sense of loss is stuck, fixed, and calcified
refusing to be metabolized in any manner. It does, however, register in
soma and presents itself through the Klein body when acknowledged
as mythopoetic raw material to be properly remembered, mourned,
and metamorphosed. In the natural rhythms offered by Mother Nature,
the cycles of death and elimination towards new life are asking to be
respected.

The presences behind the morphic resonances are asking to be
given new form through the creative process. In the liminal space of the
creative, these fragments/resonances can be transformed through the
birth-death-rebirth cycle and, in turn, transform me/you in order that the
future that has entered through them—as seeds—can now be re-seeded;
re-embodied in the ground of the alchemical process of mythopoetic
inquiry. As *temenos* or archetypal vessel, the mythopoetic inquiry itself
becomes the *coniunctio* of *anima* (life force) and *anima mundi* (inherent
interconnectivity), allowing for the restoration of what has been lost to
take place in mythic time.

Like cooking soup on the low burner all day, filling the home with
the smell of carefully cut ingredients, the act of restoring is an act of love

---

16. Sheldrake, *Presence of the Past*, 108.

(*eros*) and respect (*ethos*). If I understand that the *coprolites* were uncannily preserved until such time as whatever spell they were cast under so long ago has been broken, then *anima* and *anima mundi* can together contribute to the collective memory affecting other members of the species in the future. A mythopoetic endeavor that recognizes the future entering us in order to be transformed and transform us can bring about such a time—deep time—allowing the *coprolites* to become transparent, like amber, revealing the old story in a new, symbolic, and precious light.

Field Notes: P.S. I Love you I–V

I was not aware of the words "P.S. I Love you" in fluorescent tubing on the back wall until after I had taken the photos (which were not digital). Did Psyche whisper their presence to me?

I am imagining my nausea as the toxins of the coprolites *beginning to release into my system; that this might be the start of their dissolution, however long this takes. My task is to support this painful dissolution towards a greater love that perhaps cannot be touched in any other way. The dissolution of the* coprolites *indicates to me that they may actually have a chance of returning to the original intent of nature's cycle of elimination in the birth-death-rebirth cycle.*

Understanding this offers a change in perception, and the reality of my body feeling under threat in the face of a constant, nagging reminder of death: An interruption of life; Images of life dying; Images of death living within me. Developing the capacity for "choiceless awareness" as Jiddu Krishnamurti called it, conjures the notion that true freedom lies in having no choice, no duality.[17] No split. Unanimous.

In the liminal performance of the above images I found myself in, I am sitting to the side of my-self, almost like a ghost. I am beside myself. I am under the spell of a story of the complexes. I change positions in relation to the original posture the symptom places me in. I have to slip, slide, and fall in order to re-place my very presence outside the automatic repetition of the relational script my symptom is re-enacting (a repetition compulsion). I want to actively, dynamically, and yet discretely slip into the liminal, becoming invisible, to visit the ancients where the projective identification lives without form—lost and trying to express itself

17. See Krishnamurti, *Choiceless Awareness*.

in whatever way it can (no longer fragments that have been taken away or surrendered). Stone babies lost to life. Dead inside the womb. Let the guests move freely throughout the house not as ghosts who frighten but as guides who enlighten. They are teachers, seeds of the future, the new life the stone baby was meant to live.

A misreading of unconscious, autonomous, relational scripts—hauntings not based on will or recall, performances of the complexes emphatically repeating themselves through physical and emotional symptoms—is risking taking on the form of the projective identifications literally instead of receiving them as "flickers," the guests/gifts of Psyche. Without the discernment between the literal and the symbolic, I may believe the sad tale about being under continuous threat and remain in that state of dissociation brought on by trauma. Working with projective identification phenomena symbolically, however, with particular atten-tion to altered consciousness, can offer access to very primitive levels and modalities of experience that need to be treated within the context of their own language—the language of symptom as story or song—so that I do not misinterpret the symptoms as "something wrong with me," a denial of life. A denial of Self.

The mythopoetic sensibility instead suggests seeing experience, in-cluding symptoms, as a mirror.

My response to the "call" of the unlived life, the one animating the unconscious through the Klein body as it is morphing into the spiral lens, is to take the risk of being touched by the consciousness which lives in the unconscious—the archetypal Self of Depth Psychology, the wisdom of Psyche from mythology, and the cosmic mirror of primordial wisdom of the Tibetan Buddhist tradition, to bring forth its Presence. How I in-tend to do this is to engage my direct experience within the alchemical container of the embodied creative process with its inherent *Einfuhlung* (feeling myself into the aesthetic object/process non-dualistically). By willingly stepping into the unpredictable, uncharted landscape of the liminal—which my blindness has insisted upon—I might feel the seed in the wound instead of the stone, the seed that wants to sprout, grow, and express itself through the ongoing dialogue of the conscious and uncon-scious; the "me" and "not me." This kind of response is a practice of being in the presence of whatever shows up in a mythopoetic inquiry similarly to the notion Rumi proposes in the "The Guest House."[18] A symbolic po-

18. Rumi, *Essential Rumi*, 109.

etic response helps me feel into what the story behind the symptoms is, and to see what is at work here in service of generativity and good faith; to see the tethering of intention and extension as the full breath so that I move from a sense of interruption to a sense of flow; to move ontologically and teleologically towards *amor fati*.

In his writing, David G. Smith, scholar of hermeneutics, looks at the way interpretation attempts to show us what is at work in different disciplines: "How I will be transformed depends on my orientation and attitude toward what comes to meet as new, whether I simply try to subsume . . . or whether I engage it creatively in an effort to create a new common, shared reality."[19] I extrapolate from Smith's provocation towards creative engagement here as an invitation to take a mythopoetic attitude towards what is at work in the story of symptoms. And, like Smith, I challenge myself and you, reader, to bring my/your experience into a hermeneutic endeavor—the practice of interpretation that reads the mediation of meaning as a third space. A different opportunity arises simply from a shift in attitude.

This third, as liminal, draws on the imaginal imagination that sees the way the image sees. It sees what is going on as pointing to something beyond this going on: the original story's impulse to morph into a mythopoetic inquiry (much like the imperative of the eyes to see is unaffected by blindness). Seeing symbolically, mythopoetic inquiry has the capacity to look through the spiral lens and understand metaphorically what the mirror of my experience is reflecting back to me. Gazing into the unconditioned mirror of the primordial, I see mythopoetically. "By primordial mirror we mean unconditioned . . .This unconditioned state is likened to a mirror . . . is willing to reflect anything . . . and it remains as it is . . . free from bias: kill or cure, hope or fear."[20] The aperture of the spiral lens brings into focus pre-existing familial, cultural, or normative texts of self (the unconscious myth) as the raw material to be looked at reflexively. Metamorphosing through the act of "seeing through" the repetition compulsion, the ghosts of past certainties lose their very substantiality.[21] They no longer hold sway in their old biases. They no longer hold me.

Looking through the spiral lens in this manner places me in that liminal third space. As liminal figure—the Klein body is both space

19. Smith, "Hermeneutic Inquiry," 193.

20. Trungpa, *Cutting Through Spiritual Materialism*, 100.

21. Hillman, *Revisioning Psychology*, 83–84.

and who/what is in that third—I am re-positioned in relation to "what comes to meet": more stories, more images, the unconscious material, the "guests" from Psyche. I can feel and give words to them now as they move through the Klein body and see them clearly through the spiral lens. In the reading of mediation of meaning as third space, I am actively tethering the intention and extension of Psyche, openly admitting the possibility that something exists beneath what is at work in "what comes to meet": that which the symbolic is pointing to; that which is coming into existence through its own possibility; that which exists or is said to exist; "that which has no boundary, no center and no fringe . . . the wisdom of vast and deep perception beyond conflict . . . the wisdom of the cosmic mirror."[22] From a Depth Psychological perspective, this is the mythopoetic realm, the *both/and* non-dualistic symbolically embodied way of seeing what "comes to meet" in deep time.

I often say to students and clients that if they have achieved or become something new in the art (that is, symbolically), then they have fundamentally embodied this. The action or being now exists in the body. The Klein body has been awakened and the possibility—hence, the existence—of what is new is made present. Even if it remained only a possibility, its pattern has now been introduced and thus it becomes part of what is happening; it is part of the field. Mythopoesis is about acting on this faith, engaging that which outlives the categorical identifications of:

How I see myself.

How I think of myself.

Beyond these limited and limiting perspectives—largely based on cultural scripts—emerges the "becoming," the presence of something/ someone "other" that the "guests" have been indicating all along, requesting over and over that I ask:

Am I simply a way of seeing?

I find myself once again in the imaginal, back in the studio of the unconscious . . .

22. Trungpa, *Cutting Through Spiritual Materialism*, 101.

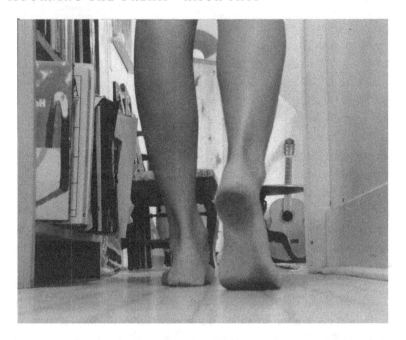

Figure 42. Into the Studio

Part 2.

Falling into Context

4

Black

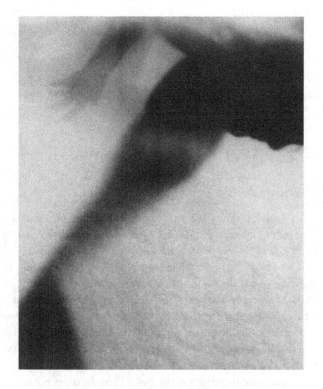

Figure 43. Black

Black is the mark on the paper.
Absence speaks.
What does black intend to achieve?[1]

1. Irigaray, *To Speak is Never Neutral*, 139.

Opaque Blackness

Opaque blackness
no image
no entry
blank
blind

Black
empty
dark
full
Black Sun

Wounding
wandering
in the darkness
wondering
as I step into
blackness

Field Notes: Memory

In February 1969,

I awake smelling the sheets of a hospital bed. These sheets bind me like a baby swaddled too tightly. I pull myself free, letting limbs extend beyond this white cocoon.

My legs swing in unison to the right side of the bed. I look at them, thin and pale, not sure if they are even mine. I am wearing a mustard yellow hospital gown tied only at the neck. The gown sails out behind me as I step onto the cold linoleum floor and slowly make my way to the mirror. I need to see. I feel weightless as each step carries me towards the hope of finding some clue to who the ghost in this austere alien environment is.

I gaze into the mirror above the sink in the room not recognizing what I see.

Figure 44. Mirror

I say out-loud: "Nothing is ever going to be the same."
I am 15 years old.

Serious Journeys

Serious journeys, these visits with death. Can we, in all seriousness, think of them, feel them as only visits? In the moment mostly no, we cannot, because the nature of death is so absolute. Its presence does not allow any other presence to be known. Death is so complete, so utterly filled with itself, so expansive in its fullness that there is no room for anything else. Or is there?

In images of death, particularly those of the body and its processes, what is really going on is a dying of the images of life. Ironically, these images of death are living images. They live within us, thrive in our imagination, hoping perhaps that we will heed the offering of their strange fullness, their awkward sense of completion towards another kind of completeness we cannot yet imagine. I am stuck in one of those dense images of death at present, that melancholic deadness that has its own life within.

I imagine now, in this moment, these living images of death are calling me, leading me in a direction I think I wouldn't possibly want to go. But when I ponder for a moment the aliveness of these images, their gravitational pull and the range in movement they afford me in their implication, I cannot be anything other than deeply curious. In this liminal space, these living images of death and dying images of life conjure, I wonder at the toying with life and death that is coming to meet here in my imagination. The whole process is very much alive, like a lake teeming with endless schools of fish, darting split second in any direction, creating a myriad of invisible currents I will inevitably be swept along with.

As I am swept, I swim. If I swim with the current, I have learned, it will be easier, even if the destination is seemingly unfavorable, undesired. If my desire goes against the desire of the current, there is a death; there is the death of a moment opportunity presents itself—completely naked, utterly without knowledge of before and after, unclothed of the presence of any living images of death or dying images of life. No image of image.

I am swept along in the current of the river, destination unknown. Like an immigrant, a liminal figure, I am transported from one reality to another. I made this journey from image to No-Image in my own body.

A Word about Image and No-Image

As I am suspended in the mythopoetic, I am destined to navigate the distance—or rather, movement—between image and No-Image. As I enter into this dialectic, I become less entangled in the notion of a "problem" and increasingly more enchanted with the dance that occurs in this "in-between." I hear the tones and nuances in the image and No-Image as a variation of the dialogue of the conscious and the unconscious. Conscious and unconscious, image and No-Image, archetypal image and archetype per se, all forming the same movement. They are of the same pattern, mirroring each other in a mutual kind of witnessing of the primordial Nothing. In this *pas de deux*, or duet, I discover how the tension between image and No-Image need not be particularly problematic and could indeed be the deepest of conversations my being can experience. This dance for me embodies an image of the soul's dialogue with its own existence. Soul. Its echo is heard in the space between conscious and unconscious, in deep time that moves me towards experiencing how images emerge out of their ultimate source, which is the No-Image. How sound sings out of silence and vice versa. How each creates the other in the endless dance of life and death. *Mourning the Dream / Amor Fati.*

In this profound conversation, I hear the story of how images actually serve as guides into the realm of No-Image, just as sound holds deep silence at its core. I can see and hear how images and sounds are vehicles, so to speak, which carry us to and from our given destination: No-Image, Silence. As an orienting device of the psyche, the image/sound could actually be a function acting on behalf of No-Image. Like the God-image, the archetypal Self connects with the Divine which has/is No-Image, Silence. This is the method of a mythopoetic inquiry whose pedagogy is in alignment with the symbolic function of image *as* the soul's dialogue with its own existence—as the mirror of my experience being reflected in the primordial wisdom of the cosmic mirror.

Figure 45. Images and Sounds Are Vehicles

Seeing image as the soul's dialogue with its own existence, I recognize the "flickers" I experience as stars charting my path. I want to follow these stars, those "flickers," the images that move me. I feel desire pulling me into the black sky of No-Image, the only place I can see stars. In the desire to chart the stars, I can hear a call—the voice of my own being telling me which way to turn, which seas to set out on, and which to avoid. This voice orients me in the vast oceans of my experience, the sound of its embodiment providing both vessel and language with which to sustain the intense intimacy of the soul's dialogue with No-Image. No-Image, whose Silence I know I couldn't possibly bear without the accompaniment of the trustworthy image and the voice that resonates my existence.

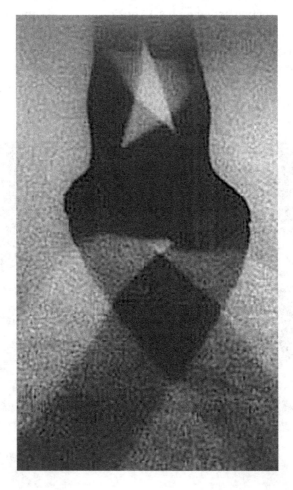

Figure 46. Star

The life of your imagination swings on the rusty hinge of your commitment to your inward life. The wellspring of your creativity depends on the presence of Eros, the god of love, the archetypal force that brings forth meaning, wisdom and beauty.[2]

With these words in mind I am able to enter the following doorways and passages.

The Black Doors of Destiny

The door closes. I am outside, or so I perceive the situation. "Which side of the door is outside?" I ask myself, in this sudden feeling of bewilderment and destitution. Silenced de-sire; it's dark. I notice the absence of stars. The door is large, much bigger than me, looming in fact. I cower in the shadow it casts. I am like a child or lover that has been ousted. Standing there on the "outside," I experience an unbearable sense of exile, separated from my beloved. My lost lover, the creative process itself, has shunned me. I feel a great shame and unfulfilled desire. I lose sight of my star and, as a consequence, begin a grand narrative of self-pity. I feel the piercing of a kind of humiliation that only that inner sharp-shooter Apollo, god of archery, could master with such exactitude. This personified, archetypal figure instinctively knows the enemy's weakness. He aims the arrow precisely at the old wounds he knows will bleed easily, profusely.

So I have become the enemy, the one standing outside in the dark, being attacked by the archetypal figure of Apollo, god of *logos*, who perceives me as weak, the one to be killed off. I prepare for my execution. But not without a long lament of the loss of what stands on the other side of the door, the inside. The lament is the first sounding of transformation.

James Hollis, writer and Jungian analyst, describes this kind of psychological phenomena of feeling threatened and under attack from within as an enslavement to the protective adaptations we have made in the past, spectral presences of the past. Exterior definitions projected onto us that become internalized have a similar effect. I ask myself how these phenomena are part of my myth and what truth or untruth they speak of and to.

2. Cousineau, *Stroking the Creative Fires*, 55.

Donald Kalsched offers a provocative perspective, characterizing the melancholic world of fantasy in the "self-care system" as defensive.[3] There is a hermeneutic function of the system in how it provides a meaningful "story" of sorts amidst experiences of chaos, even as this "story" casts the person into an equally untenable role that perpetuates splitting: victim/persecutor. The archetypal scene unfolds in the unconscious and is embodied in obsessive replays—unless one can see through it, meeting the archetypal image beneath the narrative rather than acting it out, as does the complex of the personal unconscious.

Archetypally and ecologically speaking, within the practice of deep democracy, Apollo may have his shot. But how I perceive this action hermeneutically opens the scene of attack into a wider field of perception into the third space that is the mediator of meaning (that space between conscious and unconscious, the soul's dialogue with its own existence). The soul offers its perspective of the situation indirectly in the liminality of the body, dreams, and art, whose images then act as mirrors reflecting the symbolic, imaginal core of experience: the archetypal dynamics taking place. This fluid, liminal space, where liminal figures travel, has no fixed script. Players can improvise their performance to create a different outcome. Such an opportunity to improvise arises each time the scene is repeated and the expected—the usual pattern that presents itself habitually, unconsciously—is potentially interrupted if one "stops" and watches the play, intently, in the mirror of one's perception. This time, the conscious act of re-considering (*sider*, the same root as desire) the mythic scenario, repeating itself in the complex, imbues it with the desire to see through it. Or consciousness may spiral around and around the scene like a hawk, looking for signs of movement below, indications of a change in the pattern.

3. See Kalsched, *Inner World of Trauma*.

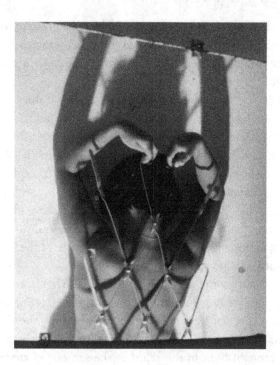

Figure 47. Preparation

I know this felt-sense of being on the "wrong" side of the door is an image in which I become trapped. Being on the "outside" of the door could just as easily imply a freedom, a being set free, albeit unconsciously, from a set of limitations. So I engage the image of the door this feeling of shame and exile conjures. I turn to Jung's notion of the image as a doorway into another reality. If an image is taken as a symbol and not literally, as Jung suggests, then my door paradoxically symbolizes both the trap holding me prisoner in the concrete—the narrow reality I experienced—*and* what I imagined was on the other side. Self/Other. Desire and the desired.

An image as doorway into an "other" reality here presents a paradoxical situation in which the image is me and is not me. I am on one side of the door *and* on the other side in my imagination, albeit in the shadow. A necessary duality has been created. Necessary because all creation depends on this perceived duality; the tension between the two opposing forces that *is* relationship. A oneness has been torn asunder and yet is secretly implied, waiting to be born out of the tension of opposites within the situation. It is in the liminal space in-between that new life can be born. In the context of self-reflection, this new life can bring new insight, the possibility of a new pattern of experience.

I wonder what new pattern of experience this feeling of being shut out—the door having been slammed in my face—might lead to. So I follow the associations this feeling-image-charge holds for me. I begin a process of active/embodied imagination. I feel a subtle "flickering," a visceral signal from the Klein body, suggesting that the experience of being on either side of the door is actually leading me to the potent symbol of the door itself as portal—to the imaginal, the presence of "both/and."

Preceding the flowering of this awareness, several stories unfolded through experiencing myself on the "wrong" side of the door, be that inside or outside. These are dark stories. Black.

In these stories, the door has been shut. The light cannot come in. I am hoping that telling and writing these stories now will let the door open to let a sliver of light sneak through, revealing the shadows that have remained silent in these rooms of body and melancholy.

I am brought back to the chant of the sad tale of chapter 2: "As I listen to the voice of my body, I hear the old story I know so well, like the familiar fairy tale I listened to as a child." This is the longest of the stories, the most sustaining, and has many chapters. But has no sustaining note.

I have lost the melody.

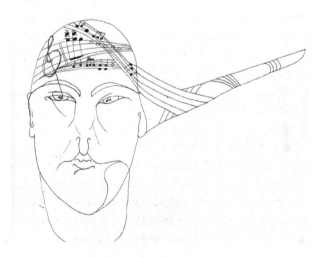

Figure 48. Sustaining Note

Field Notes: Dream Time

Near the time of writing this chapter, I had a dream that my brother's girl-friend had inadvertently killed herself by walking into a pitchfork she had not seen. Her name was Melody.

I keep hoping that I might hear this particular note that hangs in the air between connections of the heart. I think it is a note of inheritance, a note that creates the mark of the pack, the tribe, the song of the family. I have lost this song. I am constantly bending my ear towards the melody it belongs to (my brother's love). Am I singing in the wrong pitch, preventing me from recognizing the familial songscape? The loss of the tribe, the loss of the song, voices not heard from the other side of the door, the wrong side, the outside—being "outside," having a visit with death, while the family is eating dinner without me. I am emigrating from the homeland. I have lost the fire of the hearth.

It is the death archetype that resounds through life and creates what Krishnamurti calls an awakening to eternity; the resounding asking us not to leave out the middle, the crucial centerpiece of the birth-death-rebirth archetype, lest the cycle be forever interrupted.[4] Leaving out the middle; leaving out the middle child.

Figure 49. Moonlight at Midnight at the Halifax Burial Ground in 1978 I

---

4. See Krishnamurti, *Choiceless Awareness*.

Figure 50. Moonlight at Midnight at the Halifax Burial Ground in 1978 II

Melancholia is a state of sustaining a minor chord, a B flat reality. I try to stop running away from my melancholic melody by thinking I can change it, to adapt the tune by not pathologizing it, but rather to start accepting it as an important song of my being—a beautiful melody about being human, loving, and knowing suffering: the leitmotif, the guiding motif/myth.

> For those who are racked by melancholia [bewitched by the surrounding songscape of their inner melody], writing about it would be having meaning only if writing sprang out of that very melancholia.[5]

Sustaining through that very bewitchment.

5. Kristeva, *Black Sun*, 3.

"Within depression, if my existence is on the verge of collapsing, its lack of meaning is not tragic—[this lack of meaning] appears obvious to me, glaring and inescapable."[6]

This script is the wounded part of the narrative the body is wanting to heal.

Our bodies can help heal the wounded parts of our self-narrative, the story we keep telling ourselves about our lives. The body is inherently creative in its generative capacity, but there are also destructive forces, those living images of death. The unborn and the ancients live in these images and are beckoning us not to forget them in their crucial part in the birth-death-rebirth cycle. I remind myself of the inherent creativity in my being human so that I might be able to face coming into full dialogue with the dead, with my-self as dead, having passed away, yet not.

The approach to art making and writing in a mythopoetic inquiry is not an ego approach. It is not "me" who draws, paints or writes, or even teaches or facilitates . . . I leave that for the "guests." I let them guide me, move in the direction of their stirrings as I follow their "flickerings." One of these "guests" beckoned me to move closer to the future entering my mother's body near her time of death.

What Moves Her

What moves her
forward
inward
upward
outward

out word

the words want to get out
and move around

her hand is shaking
she tries to still it

she lies down
forever

6. Kristeva, *Black Sun*, 3.

gets up after
a thousand years
after a thousand pangs
have passed
talking in centuries

has she passed?

no

she is still here
lying beside another mountain
they speak to each other
in voices so low
decibel deep
inaudible to senses

what moves her through
this thick sonic of soul

(2 weeks before my mother's death)

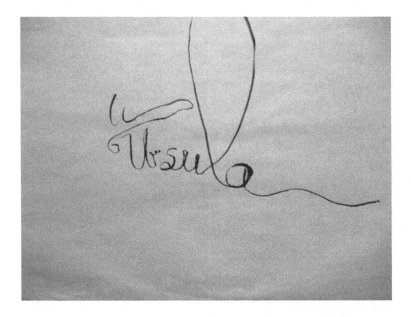

Figure 51. Ursula

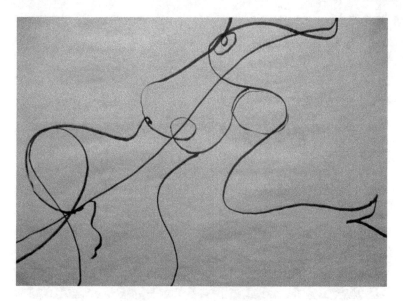

Figure 52. "Your Body Will Be Somewhere" I

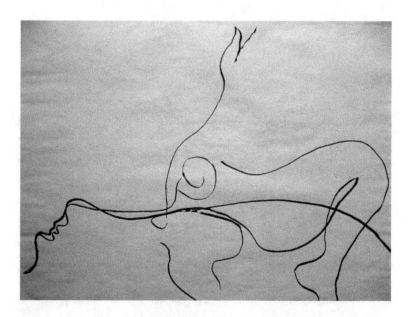

Figure 53. "Your Body Will Be Somewhere" II

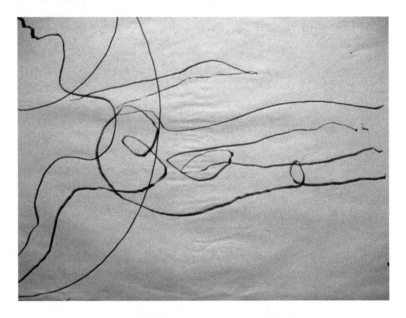

Figure 54. "Your Body Will Be Somewhere" III

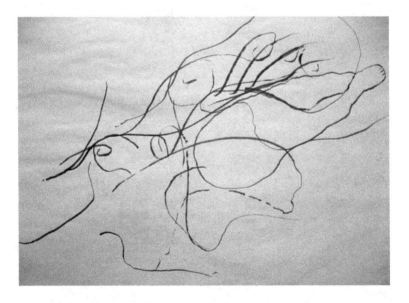

Figure 55. "Your Body Will Be Somewhere" IV

"The past isn't dead. It isn't even past."[7] I am the embodiment of presence and absence. Impulses and affects driven by archetypal, ancestral patterns are the resonances of unconscious material from familial, cultural, and archaic scripts which manifest in the present through disturbances, symptoms, issues, and compulsive urges I am not aware of. The unfinished business of the past, likely generational, is carried in the body and psyche. As archetypal material, it is morphing into the present through the embodiment of old scripts. Mythopoetic sensibilities welcome the *past in the present* as moments that initiate the Klein body's ability to metabolize archetypal essence through and into another dimension.[8] The pre-reflexive aspect of the Klein body (experiencing inside/outside simultaneously), presents an implicit, ongoing, and more primary self-consciousness, which creates the subjective feel of the "I" in the human experience. Explicit, reflective self-consciousness is possible only because of this pre-reflective self-awareness. As a contiguous dialogue between implicit and explicit forms of self-consciousness develops, each mirrors the other flickering archetypal pattern that may now be engaged mythopoetically.

The patterns of the past that are present as morphic resonances are not illusions. They are alive and, if not seen through the spiral lens, can create disturbing, distorted assumptions about self and other. They could be experienced as a kind of "spell" I am under: a complex, an old mythic scenario left floating in the collective and looking for embodiment in my being. I imagine this is what may be happening through the presence of the DNA of the donors' cells in my body. These cells are agitated, wanting to tell their stories through my flesh, pushing for their life-line to be enacted and extended through me. Without any mythopoetic imagination, this morphic phenomenon can be overwhelming and disorienting.

Living images of death and dying images of life are vestiges of trauma still flickering through my body as fragments of incomplete stories of the unborn and the ancients' narrative trying to speak through my myth. It is up to me to catch those flickers and inquire into what they are asking for: connecting the dots of light they are sending in hopes that I might catch and chart them like stars in my black sky; to draw them together into a new pattern of seeing in *their* dark; creating something new out of the raw material of the old autonomous self-story that is asking to be released

7. Faulkner, *Requiem for a Nun*, 275.
8. See Sheldrake, *The Presence of the Past*.

through a generative embodiment (art, poetic enactments), including the contribution of the dead in this dance of the creative/destructive polarity in the birth-death-rebirth archetype.

As Jung writes in his autobiography, *Memories, Dreams, and Reflections*:

> When I was working on the stone tablets, I became aware of the fateful links between me and my ancestors. I feel very strongly that I am under the influence of things or questions which were left incomplete and unanswered by my parents, grandparents, and more distant ancestors.[9]

Through Jung's words, I was able to contextualize the recurring voicing of "the ancients are lamenting," from what seemed to me a bizarre statement from some unknown "guest," to an understanding of the role of the lamenting. I now see this phrase mythopoetically—my ancestors asking for acknowledgement in the living inquiry as it spirals into the past-present-future. Jung continues:

> It has always seemed to me that I had to answer questions which fate had posed to my forefathers, and which had not yet been answered, or as if I had to complete, or perhaps continue things which previous ages had left unfinished. It is difficult to determine whether these questions are more of a personal or more of a general (collective) nature. It seems to me that the latter is the case. A collective problem, if not recognized as such, always appears as a personal problem, and in individual cases may give the impression that something is out of order in the realm of the personal psyche . . . The cause of disturbance is therefore, not to be sought in the personal surroundings, but rather in the collective situation.[10]

Is this quote a "flicker" of another sort, something that has come to meet through the synchronicity of my reading it now in the midst of this mythopoetic inquiry? The synchronistic reading of Jung's words at this later stage in writing here tells me why "the ancients" insisted on inserting and asserting themselves in the research; that the work is not just about me, but about humanity. The presence of the ancients and the unborn appear in my individual path through the subjective as it speaks

9. Jung, *Memories, Dreams, Reflections*, 233.

10. Jung, *Memories, Dreams, Reflections*, 234.

to the general, the collective, for the soul of the world; *anima* is reaching for *anima mundi* and vice versa.

Jung's insight into the importance of completing or continuing things which previous ages had left unfinished became all the more pronounced for me after receiving the DNA of two other human beings through transplants. Was I being asked to complete or continue the unfinished lives of the two people who had travelled past the end of life through their DNA continuing to live in my body? These living cells of the dead were offering living images of death/dying images of life for my psyche to experience. This "transplantation" of images and body parts left me with a profound sense that I have intersected with two "other" blood lines. Biologically and symbolically, these blood lines are alternate tributaries of the flow of a timeless life force. I see myself now as a confluence of at least two more alternate myths, stepping into a river of possibilities.

Others have written about this. One book in particular stands out which was published more recently, but after the emphatic statement "the ancients are lamenting" arrived through my unconscious. James Hillman and Sonu Shamdasani's *Lament of the Dead* is a discussion between two scholars about our relationship with the dead and to the inner figures of the unconscious; the nature of creative expression; the relation of psychology to art, narrative, and storytelling; the significance of depth psychology as a cultural form; and our relation to the past.[11] The book examines the implications these relations have for our thinking today. Coming across this book by "accident" shocked me as well as reinforced a deep respect for what is happening in the collective Psyche through my subjective experience.

The discovery of *Lament of the Dead* felt like another circling of the spiral revealing more about my subjective experience of the Klein body as a confluence of morphic resonances. The literal embodiment of the life force of these "others" in my veins, offered an immediate intimacy of how alternate stories flow into and through the personal and collective psyche. Stories of the life force are the myths we live by. They are expressions of how the archetypal narrative lives in the Klein body and twists through the subjective into an "other" dimension: the mythopoetic. Clearly amplified by the presence of "others" in "my" bloodstream, I know I feel those who have passed and are still coming, the dead and the unborn, through the "flickers" in the Klein body. I see the ancient ones,

11. See Hillman and Shamdasani, *Lament of the Dead.*

the souls living through *anima mundi*, becoming transparent to me as I look through the spiral lens. Sensation, symptom, synchronicity, and tensions of the opposites transform into powerful symbols, pointing to that which was never born and thus can never die: the archetypal. I am initiated into the third space with the accompaniment of the ancients, the dead, and my donors' whose DNA continue to live in "me."

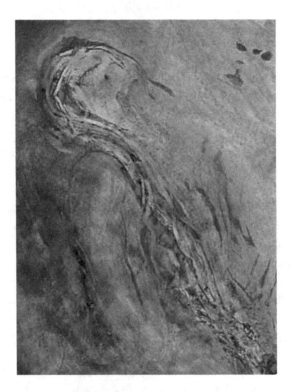

Figure 56. Scorched Blue Flat Minor

I must point out how a relationship with the dead activates archetypal forces which the "I" (that I think I am) is terrified of. The body resists death. The ego also resists any experience of relationship with the dead as it cannot distinguish the difference between this and actual dying. However, if the imaginal ego can link trauma with transformation, a metamorphosis can take shape through the Klein body, burning through in the process of firing the spiral lens.

"Scorched Blue Flat Minor" is an embodied, poetic enactment of such profound metamorphosis. The figure in this painting is trying not to look at death (my dog Taana had died). Even looking at it now hurts me, reminding me of how I turn intolerable experiences against myself, and then turn the unbearable image of the experience into a self-image. This figure *is* and is experiencing the intolerable; a fathomless symbiosis is taking place in the unconscious. "All this suddenly gives me another life. A life that is unlivable, heavy with daily sorrows, tears held back or shed, a total despair, scorching at times, then wan and empty."[12] Inside this intolerable self-image, I cannot hear the soul's dialogue with its own existence; its melody has been silenced and desire stranded without the beloved. I can no longer discern what feels so deeply personal from what is in the collective situation—as Jung suggests above—so that the intolerable is being experienced in the collective through me. I return to the notion of the Klein body in its inside/outside metabolizing of the raw material of life in the crafting of the spiral lens.

The Spiral lens sees the contents of the intolerable and then sees it through. As it is continuously revealing and embodying inside and outside simultaneously, the Klein body takes the life that is unlivable into itself. As it is ingesting and digesting the abject, the horrific, it maintains the archetypal intention of a metamorphosis of "seeing myself as a way of seeing." Such an epic task requires the presence of the archetypal activist who can bear such terror; to see the unbearable No-Image (No self), symbolically, reflexively, and archetypally. "The reflection is now presented in another tone, another mindset."[13] And so, as archetypal activist, I am mythopoetically situated to encompass what has been rejected, and, by extension, what has been rejected by humankind: death.

"To be with the fullness of life, including what is most horrific in it . . . is a realization that if you rejected part of existence then you [have] rejected all of it," including yourself.[14] Self-absence. Suppression of the Underworld is released when we come into relationship with the dead. Something in the collective leans into this relationship. We see how it is consistently expressed in the personal. Suicide. Here is the need for validation of personal, subjective experience as one side of the mirror, the other side being the collective which contains the shadow we cannot see. The validation of the subjective here is a search for meaning—finding in

12. Kristeva, *The Black Sun*, 4.
13. Hillman and Shamdasani, *Lament of the Dead*, 20.
14. Hillman and Shamdasani, *Lament of the Dead*, 20.

the subjective that which reflexively shapes the collective: "What's happening in the collective shapes us."[15]

As it is being shaped and fired in the mythopoetic dimension, the spiral is showing me how to become an archetypal activist. Without its presence, I become meaningless, lost, swimming in a sea of negative narcissism and absence. I forget the necessity of encompassing the defensive self-image for what it is: the ego's protective strategy in the face of the collective archetype of trauma. The ego mistakenly identifies with the trauma, colonizing it, in hopes that this might contain or control it. In this process, a false union with the trauma is created. A heroic stance against it; a splitting apart; an interruption of Self/Other.

> *I can't stop singing that song I learned before I was born.*

> Indeed, sadness reconstitutes an affective cohesion of the self, which restores its unity within the framework of the affect. The depressive mood constitutes itself as a narcissistic support, negative to be sure, but nevertheless presenting the self with integrity, nonverbal though it might be. Because of that, the depressive effect makes up for symbolic invalidation and interruption (the depressive's "that's meaningless") and at the same time protects it against proceeding to the suicidal act.[16]

Instead of hanging myself:

I Hang Galleries from My Lungs

I hang galleries from my lungs

lost my sonic resonance with *anima mundi*
because of a broken instrument

a string has snapped
a reed splintered
one key gone flat

I am afraid to get up
once again to
stumble into the day
falling into pieces of brokenness

---

15. Hillman and Shamdasani, *Lament of the Dead*, 24.
16. Kristeva, *The Black Sun*, 19.

a leg lies crying
under the bed
an arm flailing madly in
the air above
eyes like marbles
across the bedroom floor

how do I gather these
broken pieces
to make a whole note

The constant "interruption" by the depressive mood and its resulting symbolic invalidation of the self is reflected in a negative narcissistic self-image. The negative self-image was originally generated by unbearable experience—disintegration (trauma)—and acts as a mirror constructed to block my view. Its persistent presence at the core of the melancholic mood will not allow me to "see through this image to its myth."[17] Without the spiral lens, this self-image cannot see the collective influence on my myth. The identification with the black mood blocks the diaphoric imagination that could re-embody this myth into a mythopoetic process which sees my-self on both sides of the closed door.

While endlessly fixating on this false sense of union and cohesion within the melancholic cloud, what I am missing is that the "sustaining note" of this, the longest of stories, has sadly been the same one that my body has been repeating to me for decades. This note carries the leitmotif that *is* the lament of the ancients. It lives in my body but does not *belong* to me.

I can't see through the image in the mirror as it keeps bouncing back the same "me." It has captured my gaze and frozen it. Calcified, I am fixated in this image in the mirror that is a disguise, a mask of trauma. A fossil from an old life passed. To protect myself against dissolution— which facing this betrayal directly might bring—I stare blindly at this intolerable image of myself. I cannot take my eyes off it; I keep looking for what I cannot see. I cannot see through the charade that is pantomiming the deeper story: the archetypal narrative asking to be released into a living mythopoeia. I cannot bear looking. My darkened eyes can only make out that I am on the wrong side of the door: I am on the side of the mirror that only reflects back the same frozen self-image, that does not see the door as a symbol of passage. Thus, transparency to the larger story, one

17. Hillman, *Revisioning Psychology*, 15.

that might act as a container for me, is lost. I am locked out because of my fossilized vision, my dead myth that cannot see through.

Seeing through the mirror of my experience is not possible unless I have a spiral lens. Without this mythopoetic lens—twisting through itself and me into the dimension the ancestors live in their one-sided predicament—I cannot make sense of this unconscious suffering. I am left alone in this other-side-of-the door situation. I am unable to build bridges through a symbol formation of my myth, to unblock the dammed up ancestral energy, so that I might mourn that traumatized self and those of the ancients and unborn within and amongst me. To be actively engaged in my destiny, allowing the love of images and my fate—*amor fati*—to unfold, I need my spiral lens. So I begin to craft it through the aches, the cries and desperations life presents me with:

> The mythic thread . . . is different for everyone, but I believe it provides us with an image for what is constant and continuous in life. Don't ever let go of the thread. The thread is the link, the connection, the continuity of life. You can't stop time, but you can hold onto the thread that ties together your past, present and future . . . The thread might be inspiration, love, desperation, or passion.[18]

If the love affair with death is the only story that can sustain direct contact with the ancients . . . am I living a death that is not only my own?

I reach above my head and pluck one single sparkling strand of silver hair out of the air: a ray of starlight. The thread is the mythopoetic inquiry and through its activism for Self, becomes a golden thread, the gold of alchemy.

One either retreats from one's destiny—the path of agency towards one's fate—or enters creatively into it. As I keep myself "locked out" of the larger narrative through my negative narcissism—staring at the intolerable image in the silver mirror, fixing it in the dye bath of my wound blood—I maintain my position on the "wrong" side of the door:

> I live a living death, my flesh is wounded, bleeding, my rhythm . . . interrupted, time has been erased or bloated, absorbed into sorrow . . . the disenchantment that I experience here and now . . . appears . . . to awaken echoes of old traumas, to which . . . I have never been able to resign myself. I can thus discover antecedents to my current breakdown in a loss, death, or grief over

---

18. Cousineau, *Stroking the Creative Fires*, 73.

someone or something that I once loved. This disappearance . . .
continues to deprive me of what is most worthwhile in me. I live
it as a wound or deprivation, discovering just the same that my
grief is but the deferment of the hatred or desire for ascendency
that I nurture with respect to the one who betrayed me or abandoned me.[19]

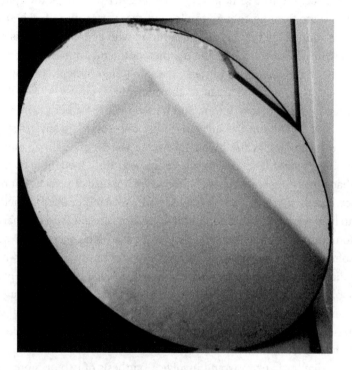

Figure 57. Mirroring

Under the mood, inside the melancholia, lies an inner liminal figure, speaking the language of the heart, the heart in pain. The heart betrayed: the one that is caught as if in a spell of a loss, death, or grief over
someone or something she once loved. The inner figure is embodying the
drama of having lost that essential being Kristeva writes of. The fantasy
or spell of having lost this being continues to deprive me of what is most
worthwhile in me. In this scenario, I myself become the wound, depraved
by having abandoned myself, the very being I feel betrayed and was abandoned by—my absence. This is what I have become in the face of trauma.

19. Kristeva, *The Black Sun*, 4.

"I am alone so I dream of the being who has cured my solitude, who would be cured by solitudes. With its life, it brought me the idealizations of life, all the idealizations which give life a double, which lead life toward its summits, which make the dreamer too live by splitting."[20] Here, the wounded becomes the wounded healer of the Self—that liminal figure the spiral lens both brings into focus and brings focus to.

If I feel the tear of flesh fully and succinctly, perhaps the splitting separates me for long enough to pick out that very being I feel betrayed and abandoned by: that figure in the mood who embodies what is most worthwhile. In the shock of the dis-memberment, I finally discern her from the fog of feeling and listen earnestly to her lament. Through her song—as she sings the lament of the ancients so clearly—I am able to hear her suffering, move into it, and have empathy for her (*Einfuhlung*), rather than becoming the suffering itself, the wound, in my resistance. Now, the bleeding is life-blood to release the wound: "That moment when things are still not completely congealed, dead. It ought to be seized so that something can happen."[21] The inseparability of presence and absence equals mystery. In the paradox of absence/presence something entirely new emerges: the diaphoric. Metaphors are always a comparison to something, diaphors are not. They are that which create the presence of something not previously experienced consciously. Like a newborn, the diaphoric is birthed by metaphor in the force of the exchange of metaphoric comparisons (the tension of opposites). In art making, the imaginal triangle of guests from the unconscious, the body of the art materials, and my body lead to the third space, the *temenos* where this birth takes place.

"A diaphoric myth would involve a synthesis of two or more forms charged with presentness."[22] *I think of the DNA of the two human beings whose blood-lines continue to flow through my flesh.* The "synthesis" of two forms as "presentness" (absence/presence) creates an intervening space in the same nature of Irigaray's statement: "An encounter between self and other becomes an interstice, an invitation, and an improvisation."[23] In this encounter, there is self, "other," and the space/relationship between them—the third. The third is the liminal; something primordial, uncon-

20. Bachelard, *The Poetics of Space*, 77.
21. Irigaray, *To Speak is Never Neutral*, 9.
22. Wheelwright, *Metaphor & Reality*, 74.
23. Irigaray, *To Speak is Never Neutral*, 22.

ditioned by circumstances. In the same way, just as a symbol reveals the familiar (a resonance), its power also lies in bringing "something which . . . is less known or more obscurely known" into play.[24]

The act of "stopping" and noticing something that is "obscurely known" requires hearing an invitation to something of importance. The symbolic inner figure of the wounded one is here to tell me about what she is carrying for me, even though I don't like the voice she is speaking in: the voice of pain, the words of the wound in its initial stages of lament. It takes courage to hear this inner figure, to touch her, or to ask her a question. She frightens me. But I can also see her as a messenger the ancients have sent to offer me a secret. I have not been able to decipher the coded message she is sending me over and over again—through sounds of the body of melancholia. The difficulties I perceive I am having are having me. I am caught in the narcissistic spell of the unrelenting repetition of these soundings. Tap tap tap goes the blind girl who cannot see where she is going. She can only feel her way through the extension of her sight that her Klein body offers.

If I could set the inner figure free from my steel wool mood so that she might speak her language in a manner that is truer to her origins, her essence, soul—she might help me look back and see that it is my longing for what I perceive I can no longer have that destroys my connection to life. She helps me read the patterns phenomenologically anew in the spiral inquiry. The essence of this inner figure, by virtue of her being connected to a vaster dimension than what my limited story encompasses, reconnects me to a mythopoetic sensibility I can only discover through meeting her in the Underworld, spiraling through the mirror into a dimensionless space of possibility.

24. Wheelwright, *Metaphor & Reality*, 73.

Figure 58. Inner Figure of the Underworld

Being in the Underworld would immerse me in that diaphoric narrative of polarities in which I might catch glimpses of an alternate story than the dominant one I am telling myself about myself—the one that cultural, societal, familial, and gendered scripts reinforce. How do I enter this alternate story that secretly but persistently parallels my habitual way of seeing myself?

Am I how I see myself?

Am I how I think of myself?

Or am I simply a way of seeing?

I am reminded that hermetic actions involve the qualities of "art and spirit in making one's way in life"; the *temenos* that is the liminal space where art and spirit gather light in the dark.[25]

Hunger

hunger
emptiness
wanting

hunger   emptiness   wanting

25. Paris, *Wisdom of Psyche*, 69.

hunger pulls
emptiness gathers in
wanting reaches

how my belly pulls
how my soul gathers
.how my heart reaches

belly
soul
heart

belly   soul   heart

each one pulls
each one gathers
each one reaches

pulls what
gathers what
reaches what

pulls air
gathers seeds
reaches heights

air
seeds
heights

air   seeds   heights

the seeds are blown
high into the air
their flights necessary
before their important descent

dropping
landing in the place
they might settle
nestle in

see if earth tugs them
pulls them

gathers their force
reaches for them
to grow down
so that they might also
grow up into

air

into the heights
gathering light

"The soul's answer of time is the experience of timeless being. There is no other answer."[26] The life of Psyche marks no time. Timelessness is available in the Underworld when/where consciousness is non-dominant, made dormant. After descent comes the possibility for re-embodiment, bringing flesh and blood back to soul, even as flesh hurts, holds wounds, and carries secrets. Scars as scripts. Letting consciousness sleep for a while awakens secrets that are voiced through the dreambody. There the leitmotif of the unspoken myth is called out while coming to life in dreams and the imaginal.

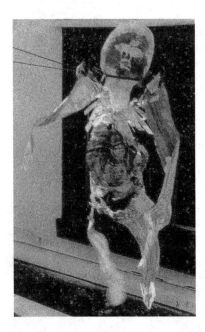

Figure 59. Remember Me? I Still Think I Would Be Fun to Be in a Relationship With

26. Needleman, *Time and the Soul*, 112.

Rilke's words in *Letters to a Young Poet* have so often reminded me of the excruciating necessity of the Klein body's metamorphosing into the spiral lens. The following is a response to an excerpt which expresses certain sensibilities of surviving the ongoing ordeal.[27] The words here also offer a poetic description of the perhaps less familiar term, diaphoric, used throughout the book.

> *Something new has entered me in the writing and image making, something unknown. I can sense astonished presences living in me and me in them. I imagine that many things inside me have been transformed perhaps somewhere, someplace deep inside my being; I have undergone important changes while I was sad. I know I am standing in the midst of a transition where I cannot remain standing.*
>
> *I think I under-stand a little now why the sadness passes: that the new presence inside me—that I cannot name but can some-times paint or dream of—has emerged and entered my heart, has gone into its innermost chamber and is no longer even there, but already in my bloodstream. And I don't know what it was. I could easily be made to believe that nothing happened, and yet I have changed, as a house that a guest has entered changes.*
>
> *I cannot say who has come. Perhaps I will never know. But many signs indicate that the future enters me in this way in order to be transformed in me, long before it happens. And that is why it is so important to be solitary and attentive when I am sad. The quieter I am, the more patient and open I am in my sadnesses, the more deeply and serenely the new Presence can enter me, and the more I can make it my own, the more it becomes my fate; and later on, when it "happens" (that is, steps forth out of me to other people), I will feel related and close to it in my innermost being (adapted from Rilke).[28] The new Presence becomes the healer, the "knower" in me.*

Something is nibbling at my fate.

Someone.

I am searching in for that deep Presence I am catching glimps-es of in quiet chambers of my body. I can feel subtle stirrings in those places that quickly become still as soon as my awareness touches them; like sighting a wild animal that disappears the moment she senses "my" presence.

27. Rilke, *Letters to a Young Poet*, 12.

28. Rilke, *Letters to a Young Poet*, 63–68.

I must continue as if I do not know of this Presence, and yet move deeply into its path, following its invisible footsteps that are only indicated by feel.

This "following by feel" replaces another ordinary, habitual movement that does not in fact move at all; Just stays in the same place, creating the same stale out-breath, that same flat note of resignation.

Who?

When I step into places I have wounded myself, thinking it is others who are doing the wounding, I know I am visiting the ancients in the land of the dead. I can feel the wetness of the wound as if it were a fresh slay. Its moisture seeps into caverns of forgotten feelings, watering the emotions of those long dead souls who quicken and quiver at these stirrings; they agitate and ache.

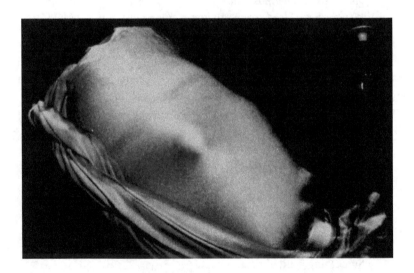

Figure 60. Caverns of Forgotten Feelings

I want to go now to those who agitate and ache, not leave them behind, abandoned to their own absence—these ancient ones and the unborn, who, because of their own plight, are unable to close the wounds themselves. I want to bend to them and begin the work of stitching together the split of their absence/presence living in my own gestures, those invisible visibles, those "archaic forces that are present in the here and now through disturbances, symptoms, issues, and impulses that one is not aware of; unfinished business of the past possibly generational that is carried in the body and psyche; archetypal material that is pushing to be embodied creatively rather than destructively."[29] These figures are trying to come into consciousness but generally remain in the form of undifferentiated anxiety. Through our embodied gestures, we invite their laments, their wounded story, their attempts at transfiguration through transforming their "absence" into a presence in our consciousness. We then join the circle of the ancients, the web of humanity.

Figure 61. The Ancient Ones

Then we may be able to tell them our story of mourning their dream, about *amor fati*. We could do this by inviting the future to come into the ancient and unborn ones through our flesh, through conscious and creative embodiments of the songs they sang so long ago. Our body

29. Hollis, "Hauntings: Dispelling the Ghosts."

carries the tune after all, the lament of their absence (and the melody of their presence). The calling is to bring this absence into presence in full song. *Mourning the Dream / Amor Fati* itself has been the invitation, the interstice through which the wounded story of the ancients/unborn has come into a mythopoetic field of awareness. Suturing the split between the two forms of presentness (absence/presence) through symbolic practices such as art making and mythopoetic inquiry, an embodied and reflexive practice is birthed.

"Surely all art is the result of one's having been in danger, of having gone through an experience all the way to the end, where no one can go any further."[30] Writing "once upon a time. . ." with group art therapy participants invites the working with words as images to act as portals for the ancients/unborn to visit. The combination of drawing words and writing with art materials (drawing the words, writing the images) often results in a space-in-between word/image through which the ancestors and the unborn feel comfortable enough to reveal themselves. They can speak in this liminal space where past, present, and future live together as one moment (deep time). Here they can roam the mythopoetic landscape generated by the diaphoric imagination and be released from the spell of the habitual. Having been set free, my/your myth is now the messenger that carries the symbol pointing to the future within, that form of consciousness that lives in the unconscious. The Klein body, while embodying the laments of the unborn/ancients, is becoming the spiral lens that sees this consciousness Jung called the archetypal Self. The Self has the capacity to heal the split of absence/presence in the wounded parts of our narrative by not rejecting it. Through the hermetic movement into this central archetype, we are letting the ancient/unborn ones know we have seen and heard them and are heeding their call, not leaving them behind in forgetfulness or denial. Joining the attempts at receiving their "absence," allowing this very act to become a transformation into presence, becomes the living mythopoeia.

Mythopoetic inquiry can turn to collective archetypal themes and figures of mythology, literature, and other cultural expressions. These mythologems amplify the personal myth, revealing the gifts of the ancients as invitations to mourning personal and collective dreams, thereby creating the possibility of *amor fati*. In recognizing and relating to how others throughout millennia have travelled to and from the Underworld,

30. Rilke, *Letters on Cézanne*, 4.

practitioners of a mythopoetic approach have a symbolic map to guide them through this treacherous territory between life and death. Travelling this in-between consciously becomes the mythopoeia as we join the great journey of humanity and are no longer solitary in our attempts at seeing ourselves as a way of seeing.

Inlay: Pausing for Images

As concern about suffering increases—the more we perceive ourselves to be suffering—we might also consider heeding a call to play. Creating space to play is as important as relieving symptoms or solving problems. These very symptoms may in fact be drawing us into this play in the first place, in order to create a different kind of consciousness. As a hermetic space marked off within which the mystery of transformation can proceed, "play" can create an entirely different relationship to the original symptom/problem at hand. This space to play has thus opened the mind of the player to the unexpected, the unknown, creating a symbolic place to gather a new kind of energy. This kind of symbolic engagement always leaves room for the unconscious. I see the diaphoric imagination here as key to learning the mythopoetic approach:

> Play may be the root metaphor of an emergent mythology...We may be witnessing a mythological revolution, turning toward a new frontier in which leisure, meditation, and contemplation are potentially dominant. Instead of work being our model for both work and play, play may be the model for both our games of leisure and our games of vocation. Play may be the mythology of the new frontier.[31]

It is important to consider this emergent mythology in the form of play where the symbolic engagement of the unconscious generates energy—energy that comes directly from Psyche.

31. Miller, *Gods and Games*, 213.

Figure 62. Breath of Psyche

The psyche, being the most immediate experience we can have, creates symbols that are always grounded in the unconscious. The forms of these symbols, however, are molded by the ideas acquired by the conscious mind. The unconscious does not simply act contrary to the conscious mind, but rather acts much like a challenging opponent or collaborating partner in its relations to the conscious mind. Jung stated that he tried to help his patients understand all the things that the unconscious produces during conflict. He believed that the mask the unconscious presents to us in its opacity is not rigid, but rather reflects the face we turn towards it.[32] If the face we turn to the unconscious is playful *and* "real" (as opposed to notional), the response we get will be the same. It is not simply a matter of reflecting the same back, but rather that of the unconscious meeting its own needs in relation with the conscious mind. Thus, the collaboration between the two sets up a space for the "real" and for play. A mythopoetic inquiry holds the intention of and pays attention to this reflexive mirroring of facing the unconscious and its facing back. Through play, it creates the third space of meaning.

32. See Jung, *Psychology of the Unconscious.*

Through this playful reflexivity, we can both access symbols that are grounded in the unconscious and give them form with the information of the conscious mind. These symbols express meanings that are already present but perhaps unrecognized by our frantic attempts at making meaning. Oskar Doering writes that symbols are metaphors for the eternal in the forms of the transient; in them the two are "thrown together," fused into a unity of meaning.[33] The throwing together of the transient and the eternal, where the conscious and unconscious meet, is a symbolic, diaphoric engagement inherent to art making. The union of these polarities takes us into the heart of the imaginal. This is a place where it is all play and all "real." The imaginal is a world between sense and intellect where the mythopoetic dimension of experience lives. It is a plane of awareness that is different from our usual day-to-day, practical, and oftentimes linear, awareness. When we enter the imaginal, we are coming into the world of image—where play and reality become our experience and a lateral move into an alternate way of being/seeing is opened.

When we allow ourselves to be drawn into or even taken by this play/reality of the image, the imaginal, we enter into a different form of consciousness—the diaphoric. Diaphoric consciousness: the symbol-making realm of Psyche, where the known and unknown can surreptitiously meet to enact the mysteries of transformation. Within the immediate experience of Psyche, caught up in the unexpected mysteries of her images, we may discover that the pictures of suffering we had previously been trying to solve or alleviate have become rich symbols expressing the challenge and/or collaboration of the unconscious with the conscious; the eternal and the transient.

Jung describes this consciousness as an eye that contains in itself the most distant spaces; yet it is the psychic non-ego that fills these spaces non-spatially.[34] The essence of the hermeneutic imagination "throws open the challenge to inquire into what we mean when we use words like curriculum, research, and pedagogy. We are challenged to ask what makes it possible for us to speak, think, and act in the ways we do from the perspective of postmodern hermeneutics."[35]

Gadamer expresses a similar perspective in his statement: "Nothing that is said has its truth simply in itself, but refers instead backward and

33. See Doering, *Christliche Symbole.*

34. See Jung, *Man and His Symbols.*

35. Smith, "Hermeneutic Inquiry," 188.

forward to what is unsaid."[36] A myth is always just as much about what is present (said) as it is about what is missing (unsaid). A mythopoetic inquiry includes absence and presence, relying heavily on both the hermeneutic imagination and the diaphoric imagination, challenging the inquirer to unveil and re-embody meaning—that is, to engage experience with a form of consciousness that is both a kind of "eye," which contains in itself the most distant spaces, and also the psychic non-ego, filling these spaces non-spatially. This "eye" sees beyond one's present interpretation, its gaze creating those further possibilities to be offered presence through the mythopoetic aperture embedded in the spiral lens. A playful, imaginative gaze holds the depth of field that the spiral lens offers, apprehending the possibility of something beyond existing notions:

> The aim of interpretation . . . is not just another interpretation but human freedom, which finds its light, identity and dignity in those few brief moments when one's lived burdens can be shown to have their source in too limited a view of things.[37]

36. Walhof, *Democratic Theory*, 67.
37. Smith, "Hermeneutic Inquiry," 189.

Part 3.

The Hermeneutic Imagination:
The Spiral Lens Crystallizes

5

Learning How to See Again

Figure 63. The Work of Seeing

The Work of Seeing

The work of seeing is done.
Now do heart work
Upon the images within you.[1]

---

1. Adapted from Rilke's *Ahead of All Parting*, 129.

I ask you, the reader, to kindly consider the space in between intention and extension, inviting you to walk your imagination with me into this uncanny adventure.

Intention/Extension I

We usually suppose that the intention of a concept determines its extension. Consider: the intention of mind; intention of body; intention of heart; intention of psyche/soul.

Fully experiencing the extension of implicit impulses—intentions of mind, body, heart, and psyche—offers these intentions form. Engaging direct experience of sensation, feeling, and intuition animates them, like seeds called by the earth to sprout. The earth (*anima mundi*) calls and the seeds come to life. This sprouting activity is literally an extension of the seed, an inner energy or intent (*anima*) that expands and grows. Feeling into the dirt and finding new form, trans-forming in the dark earth, is an organic mode of embodiment:

> The plant world owes its life to the fact that it clings to the soil in which the forms of life express themselves.[2]

The expression of different forms of life *is* the intention that grows towards its own extension: Self-actualization, the embodiment of intention through extension. The enactment of intention towards its own extension is both the essence and synthetic capacity of the practice of mythopoetic inquiry. It is the creative dialogue of implicit and explicit forms of self-consciousness. Intention embodied in art is brought into the world as the implicit moves towards the explicit. Because extension involves things in the world it is called synthetic.

Furthermore, in the reflexive dialogue embodied in the process of viewing and being viewed by the archetypal presences in the art, the liminal space between the art and the viewer creates a resonance of potential meaning waiting to be actualized. A third space is implicit in this resonance, or gaze, a space of potentiality offering glimpses of alternative actualizations of self.

The generative force of the inner intent, *anima*/Psyche, pushes up into the atmosphere and begins to explore an expansiveness within which these intentions (seeds) can move freely, express themselves, and

2. Baynes, *I Ching*, 536.

be seen. They travel from the invisible to the visible. Could the seeds of my blindness also extend themselves like this, towards their expression, making their intentions visible to me? As a shadow intention to the seeds of sight's imperative to see, are these dark alternatives asking for a deeper inquiry into the difference between sight and vision beyond the semantic?

Could the energy they hold still be pushing towards the kind of actualization that continues to carry the inherited message coded in their DNA to see, even as they cannot in their present condition? How so can the seeds of the blindness fulfill their own way of seeing in a different way without sacrificing themselves in the endeavor to do so? They must find an alternative route, a different narrative than the one so far in effect.

In the midst of navigating this mythography of *Mourning the Dream / Amor Fati* as a discipline of love, I have discovered that the ontological extension—the nature of the being of these seeds of blindness—is looking for a new foundation from which to practice seeing. Building this foundation requires the practice of (1) deep democracy (which is inclusive of blindness), (2) archetypal activism (bringing black and white, dark and light, and blindness and sightedness together), and taking up the energy generated in these steps towards (3) the diaphoric imagination that creates presence (resonance, the gaze, the third space). These practices are important in mythopoetic inquiry so that the diaphoric imagination can act as the dirt of the dark earth, pulling intention into a different kind of extension in the form of an alternate story. The original story is only the symbol, pointing "backward and forward to what is unsaid."[3] I would translate Gadamer's "unsaid" here as the narrative of the imagination that engenders an alternate myth—creating the story as I am living it, writing the narrative at the same time as I am reading it to myself and the world, including the unlived life. I am creating vision through an imaginal seeing of what is and is not and what can be. A spiral lens crafting vision.

3. Walhof, *Democratic Theory*, 67.

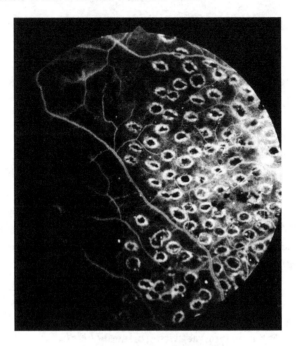

Figure 64. Seeds of Blindness

The intention (seed/*anima*) has gone through a metamorphosis of its own extension—the sprouting process—as an awakening of awareness activated by the pull of the earth: *anima mundi* (soul of/in the world, inherent interconnectivity). It is the relationship between the two:

a) *intention*: seed/*anima*/soul, implicit.

b) *extension*: budding thoughts, sensations, feelings, and intuitions pulled by the animating power of *anima mundi*—earth and all her forms; the explicit.

In this relationship, creativity is spawned. Consider the word "unanimous"—being of one mind or one soul.[4]

My blind eyes leave the world invisible to me. But they still want to reach—like phantom limbs, full of their original desire—into that world, to show its contours and colors to me; they want to embody this world for me so that I too can extend and express myself.

Dwelling in the interiority of this very intimate relationship between intention and extension, implicit and explicit, opens me to a new

4. See Abram, *Spell of the Sensuous.*

dimension in which both form and the creation of an environment for that form emerge simultaneously. This is necessary as the road between inner and outer, figure and ground, is less distinguishable when light has been dimmed in sleeping retinas. But I can feel something pushing for wakefulness, something in the process of birthing itself. A moment is unfolding into and beyond itself, beyond what has been said. Living in this moment, directly experiencing its subtle but powerful movements in the Klein body, I acknowledge this deepest of relationships. It is a relationship that has the potency to bring about that level of awareness I equate with a symbolic way of seeing. Seeing the invisible—the spiral lens morphing through the Klein body, including my retinas—has commenced, even as I am not sure what is going on. I am trusting that the seed/*anima* instinctively knows how to extend into the unknown just as naturally as light travels into dark. I begin to have a relationship with what has not yet been said, a story untold.

How Can I Find an Image in the Dark?

As the seed starts to stir, I can feel contractions in the black earth beneath me, first gently, then making larger and bolder movements, as it digs its way both down, deeper into the earth, and, simultaneously, reaching up, to break through the surface towards the sun. This is like the sun within that moves closer to the sun without that alchemy speaks of. How the small "s" self is pulled towards the large "S" Self in individuation. Implicit/explicit, demonstrating to me once again how as an image "takes shape, meaning becomes clear."[5]

The first small movement is straining, painful, cracking the husk of the seed; *anima* must break her shell, leave home, and travel in the dark for a while. Her extension pulls on every muscle in her being, but is also full of intention, yearning, desire, and necessity. The Klein body is woken up by the call of the mythopoeia. It cries out in pain.

To feel these first gestures from the unconscious—those subtle signals from the ancient and unborn ones, flickerings of the morphic resonances in the field—is the initial inclination towards image: finding an image in the dark, finding meaning in the blackness, *Nigredo*, the first phase of alchemy. These first tremors of the unconscious are the oscillations between polarized energy systems, pushing against each other. The

5. Jung, *Structure and Dynamics*, 204.

tension of these involuntary tremblings are an expression indicating an inner encounter, a fracturing or discontinuity of the tectonic plates of the self-structure. If not consciously *attended* to, such encounters can lead to the activation of a trauma response. However, when its resonance is given form in the alchemical container of the creative process, this pushing force is transferred from the unconscious into the imagination. Here the impulses of body, mind, heart, and soul are baked, shaped, and formed into gesture, notion, inquiry, and depth in what Merleau-Ponty described as a subject-object dialogue. To comprehend this dialogue, we first need to grasp the idea of the lived body, a concept Merleau-Ponty brought to phenomenology: "I am not in space and time, nor do I conceive space and time; I belong to them, my body combines with them and includes them . . . My body has its world, or understands its world, without having to make use of my . . . 'objectifying function.'"[6] Merleau-Ponty clearly understood that form and the existence of an environment for that form are inseparable, coining the term "body-subject."[7]

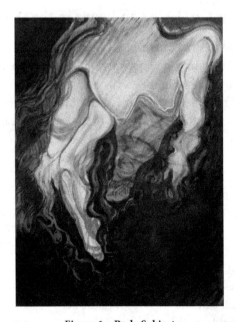

Figure 65. Body Subject

6. Merleau-Ponty, *Primacy of Perception*, 140–41.
7. Merleau-Ponty, *Primacy of Perception*, 406.

"My" lived body understands her world, without having to make use of my "objectifying function." "We are nothing but a view of the world."[8] *I am simply a way of seeing.* "Inside and outside are inseparable."[9] This is the body as alchemical Klein bottle, which extends viscerally into the diaphoric imagination through the archetypal imperative of the seeds of blindness, creating a new working definition of vision found and developed within the *temenos* of this mythopoetic inquiry. My flesh is my living Klein body, its stirrings and strainings are the beginnings of the metamorphosis of viscera shaping into the spiral lens. There is a formidable ache in this process of transformation.

Having experienced the entire spectrum of vision—from being fully sighted to almost completely blind, landing in the in-between place of living with a visual impairment—is with great irony, now opening a way for me to see again. Living in the invisible and learning how to trust the seed's animation towards . . . the deeper intent or soul of my blindness. This is my "living inquiry":

> What is living inquiry? It constitutes a practice of inquiry whose horizons are our everydayness and immediate participation in daily life . . . seeing my world with a fresh eye . . . intended to inquire qualitatively into the structure, content, and movement of daily life.[10]

The "living inquiry" of my journey with blindness, my "fresh" though wounded eye, is part of the "call" to embark on this mythopoetic voyage. It is my way through the shadowed chapters of the wounded narrative, honoring the dark—where the ancients live amongst us, calling me.

8. Merleau-Ponty, *Primacy of Perception*, 406.

9. Merleau-Ponty, *Primacy of Perception*, 407.

10. Mayes, *Inside Education*, 165.

Figure 66. Blindness Calling Me

Mourning the Dream / Amor Fati invites unfinished business of the past—generational business, carried forward as archetypal material—to be symbolically embodied into a full spiral of the birth-death-rebirth cycle. The gesturing of the ancient ones flickers invisible presences; they agitate and ache in their self-absence as they are unable to tell the whole story without my intention to be present to those stories. My absence, my turning a blind eye to these old souls, *is* the suffering I feel in the gaze of the abyss. My desire to tell these ancient ones of their embodiment in my story of mourning their dream intensifies. In this suffering, I feel empathy (*Einfuhlung*) with these invisible/visible ones. I wonder if they are the seeds of an implicit intention of the lived body to grow towards *amor fati*: loving the gifts of this living inquiry as they shape themselves into mythopoeia. *Anima*, the seed, still yearns to sprout and reach into *anima mundi*, the intrinsic connection between all living things. This is her nature. And the nature and desire of stories/myths is to extend beyond the habitual by moving *through* it. In this manner, my very myth becomes the symbol that is pointing to something beyond itself, activating the vision making function that asks *am I simply a way of seeing?*

This is *Amor Fati*, the love affair with fate.

Mourning the Dream / Amor Fati is the living inquiry that emerged from my response to the call of *anima mundi* to the lived-body of this "not-me" that has been hidden in the dark for so long. The "not-me" is a soul-figure, animating the intentional body that is lived through in relation to possibilities in the world. This intentional body carries the archetypal force (*anima*, the archetype of life itself) that pushes the indomitable insistence of my phantom sight to find another way of seeing/extending. This archetypal vision-making function is pulling me into *anima mundi*, calling me to do the impossible. It demands that I invite this "other," this "not-me" to be present. It breaks the taboo of inquiring into the soul of blindness and reminds me of my intrinsic interconnectedness. Who do I become in the presence of blindness? Through the practice of deep democracy, the presence of the soul of blindness is seen and heard as she whispers: "*Let me speak from the dark so that you might find the image you are looking for: the image that is living in the body of the darkness that is your experience.*"

Does this voice of the soul of blindness speak of something deeper than my knowing? Does it speak the unspeakable? Is it whispering blasphemies? Am I to recoil at its presence? The practice of archetypal activism, bringing the polarities of blindness and sightedness together, challenges an oppositional relationship. Instead, a liminal space of initiation, inviting an encounter, and possibly an embodied shift in perspective. Through the work of the Klein body, I experience the voice from the dark viscerally; I feel something from beneath or beyond *am I how I think of myself* or *am I how I see myself*? Both have been important questions pointing me to *am I seeing myself as a way of seeing*. Through the spiral lens—feeling its metamorphosis in the twisting through of the Klein body into another dimension—I see the mysterious "otherness" of the symbolic. For a moment, I see the mirror of my experience being reflected in the cosmic mirror of primordial wisdom and hear the autonomous voice of the soul of blindness, sounding from the archetypal dimension the conscious mind is most often deaf to.

The archetypal soul of blindness resists my knowing it in its entirety even as I always experience it in relation to my own body—the wounded body, the feminine body, the body-subject with diminished vision. This personal and collective body (*anima* and *anima mundi*) and the wounded story it is telling is calling for something else, an alternative. The Klein body, my body, is the instrument that resonates the patterns of the ancients, the soundings of soul—essences, presented to me through morphic resonances, asking to be re-sounded, re-imaged, re-embodied. It does this through finding images living in the darkness I experience. *Living images of death. Dying images of life*. Is this the birth-death-rebirth cycle pushing through the "not-me," this "other" I experience as having stepped in and taken my place—the archetypal Shadow? Is this the image that, even though living in me, is resisting my knowing it? Is this how the soul of my blindness claims its own autonomy?

We cannot integrate the archetypal shadow (or any archetype) directly for it is too dangerous. We can only engage the archetypal Shadow through its connection and expression in our own stories, myths, bodies, and pathologies—all embodiments of the Shadow asking to be attended to symbolically. I invite the reader to gaze into the mirror of your experience, to attend to Shadow chapters of your own and that of your culture's narrative as calls to an alternate story living in you, a story that has yet to become conscious. The future coming into you.

"Seeing through" our wounded narrative and our often unattended identification with it invites us to break the habitual (unconscious) repetitions of the myth it is being constellated through. The reflexive relationship between concrete (literal) embodiments of an archetypal pattern and its symbolic reinterpretation (mythopoesis, living inquiry) is made possible through the workings of the hermeneutic imagination. In the dialectical component of seeing, the creation of meaning holds the possibility of an alternate story, secretly embedded in the flesh and the world recognizable to consciousness. Herein lies yet another perspective of the practice and purpose of mythopoetic inquiry. In the act of extension, synthesis is actualized. I often suggest to clients and students that if they have done something symbolically (such as overcoming a challenge in the art), then the seed of that ability is present for them. Its possibility (extension) already exists in the imaginal.

An Unexpected Turn. Psyche as Studio

Where does the inquiry go when it is torn apart by what it uncovers? What dangerous discoveries does the inquiry rip open? I am dying, yet I am alive. I am blind yet strangely I see. Split. Egg cracking, letting in such an enormous light that it is blinding. Fingering in the dark, I discover the fine details of veins that carry cells as they travel through tunnels of perception undetected by the naked eye. I have moved in, back into the pre-verbal cellular experience of the intentional body, *anima*. I can feel her warm placenta bathing us. Washing us clean of everything we have assumed.

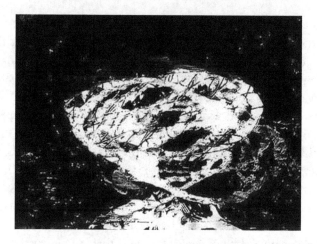

Figure 67. Blindness Speaking from the Abyss

Stepping through the doorway into the imaginal—to the light that illuminates images from within its own darkness, like the black sun—is a new/ancient way of seeing. It can happen simply with a gaze.

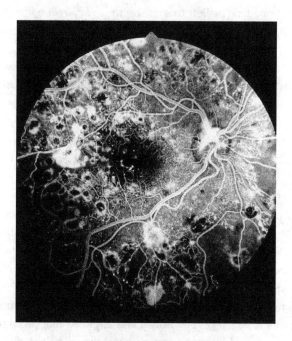

Figure 68. Wounded Retina Illuminating Darkness

I had equated literal vision with *the* legitimate form of extension, just as the heroic-ego in consensus reality sees its envisioning as the only justifiable one. I considered the more literal narrative I was telling myself about myself as my "reality." I could not yet see how this habituated narrative was a long prepared alchemical container in which an alternate story would be cooked. I came to understand how shadow experiences disrupt our sense of self, assuming a kind of authority over us, threatening us through scripts of trauma, holding us hostage through the powerful belief of their right to proclaim their truth about us. So persuasive are these autonomous stories that they reinforce the insistence of such dark versions of ourselves, overshadowing those as-of-yet unembodied stories trying to make their way through the Klein body.

Held captive by these invisible scripts that are never read outloud, the taboo of mentioning anything about what must lie beneath their distorted messages leaves our future a fallow field in which nothing can grow. In this unsown state, our myth lacks the inspiration to engender an imaginary act of interpretation of itself, that is, a hermeneutic imagination that can see and work with things as they are as the prima materia of transformation. This insight that my myth is exactly the way it is, tailor-made, so that I can enter it without resistance, invites me to consider that, from there, inside its image, I can work with it symbolically, mythopoetically, as if it were my studio; that place which welcomes the unknown at the same time as it keeps me in-the-world. Through touching all the paper, canvas, paint, and brushes I need to work with my wounded narrative, it works reflexively on me. Like my Klein body—which does not differentiate between inside and outside—my myth, the story I carry, is transforming itself and me through its own intention and extension, embodied in the art making.

The art making shows me what working mythopoetically is, providing an initially non-threatening way to come into relationship with "other," the "not-me," so polarized from whatever and whomever I am identified with. Before writing the mythopoetic inquiry, *Mourning the Dream / Amor Fati*, I had yet to break the taboo of inquiring into the soul of my blindness. I was too afraid to see it as anything but "other." It didn't belong to me. It hurt me. I could not identify with it, but felt forced to be with it all the time. Never get away. I was appalled that this dark "guest" refused to leave. I did not yet comprehend that this "not-me" was simply that which was showing itself in my perception; a deeply embodied perspective that was actually hidden inside and from itself. Hidden from me. Death is hiding from us in fear of our rejection of it.

Dying images of life and living images of death, flickering throughout the Klein body through my own unconscious postures and gestures, became a method of tuning into morphic resonances to respond to mythopoetically. Tracking these flickers and the images they generated charted a path into the reflexive nature of the relationship between the conscious and unconscious, the living and the dead, right to the heart of the deepest of conversations of the soul with its own existence. Such is the practice of deep democracy and archetypal activism, leading the inquirer toward a diaphoric perspective, that which requires the unknown, the "not-me," in order to create Presence. Through the view offered by the spiral lens—having been carefully crafted through the inside/outside non-dualistic embodiment of the liminal Klein body—I have come to know trauma as a potential vision-making function of Psyche, the transcendent function that takes us into the third space, the imaginal, the function which mediates opposites. Expressing itself by way of the symbol, it facilitates a transition from one psychological attitude or condition to another. "The transcendent function represents a linkage between real and imaginary, between rational and irrational data, thus bridging the gulf between consciousness and the unconscious. It is a natural process, a manifestation of the energy that springs from the tension of opposites."[11]

In Jungian terms, the transcendent is where one is no longer plagued by duality. From a mythopoetic perspective, this offers a different way of experiencing the inherent reflexive nature of interconnectedness—and with it, a new respect for a sensibility that intuitively and instinctively grasps a symbolic way of living. Admittedly, my conceptualizing mind and habitual body often pull me back into painful dualities I experience at those levels. In order to shed more light on how the conceptual mind and habitual body are being lived out in the world, I return to posing my inquiries to the unconscious to assist me in the central task of crafting my spiral lens through the Klein body. In this endeavor, I invite the transcendent function through fully living the opposites so that I might find myself in that place-in-between that is neither here nor there—the third space—the imaginal where I am both blind *and* sighted; where the blind one takes on her role of vision-maker in the mythopoetic.

Again, I ask:

11. Samuels, *Critical Dictionary*, 150.

How can I find an image in the dark?

Having had the orientation of a sighted person almost half of my life, I have now, through this living mythopoetic inquiry, become alerted to the capacity—necessity, even—of the existential extension of the creative psyche. Here, the vision-maker who has made herself known understands that most often an existential extension paradoxically presents itself in the invisible. It is held secretly in the unconscious intention, Psyche's ulterior motive, and remains in the shadow until such time as certain kinds of experiences have taken place, to then reveal/embody this existential intention/extension (such as my blindness). The intension/ extension is the soul-dialogue of *anima* and *anima mundi*, that place in-between, where the relationship and dynamic between the two becomes three—the third space of resonance and the imaginal gaze.

The concept of the liminal (third space) as transformational brings us into the realm of the symbolic. The symbol points to what lies beyond it. Like the diaphoric, reaching beyond the given of the metaphor, the mythopoetic provides a matrix for the unknown and, in turn, the soul's dialogue with its own existence, its indwelling in the mysterious third of psychic or imaginal reality.

The creative process steps into the imaginal to find out which direction the symbolic is pointing, a direction that might lead to truths that lie beneath ego consciousness or consensus reality and into the "stratum of the psyche that mediates experience that is perceived as spiritual."[12] The art and writing of *Mourning the Dream / Amor Fati* is an inquiry into the dark, between worlds: the Shadow, the collective layer of the unconscious where blindness is necessitated. If glimpsed, this shadow world is simply avoided or denied. Beautifully illustrated in alchemy as the first stage of individuation, *nigredo* is the symbol of the black sun. Paradoxically, the black sun illuminates from within its own darkness. A mythopoetic inquiry is often a search for the tools to begin without knowing what one is beginning. We are in the dark, so to speak. "If we imagine the outcome of these attempts, we will see that empirical observation finally ceases, inner beholding of what develops begins, and the idea can be brought to expression."[13]

The blind seed, like an inward eye is expressing itself through its own embodiment. It then shows the seed what its intention is reaching

12. Kalsched, *Trauma and the Soul*, 316.

13. Goethe, *Scientific Studies*, 16.

for. What is the seed/soul of my blindness intending in its embodiment of blackness? How do I heed its longing to find an image in the dark, an image of itself? I suspect generating the steps of a mythopoetic inquiry is what Psyche's ulterior motive is here. From within the dark earth of the unconscious, the steps and "stops" of the mythopoetic inquiry emerge. Activating the vision-making function of Psyche—re-cognizing "flickers" as clues to one's own mythopoetic journey—leads one to the crafting of a spiral lens.

The Klein body is an embodiment-through-extension into the world *and* the deeper intention of Psyche. *Mourning the Dream / Amor Fati* offers a practice that invites us to enter the unknown. The inquiry itself is diaphoric, intentionally reaching into the unconscious, trusting that the symbols of our experience are guiding us to an "other" point of view (another dimension of consciousness/unconsciousness), and spiraling us into an alternate myth—part of the collective mythology.

Mythopoetic inquiry becomes a practice which bends back on itself, reflexively finding more and more invisible passageways, connecting the conscious and the unconscious. In an uncanny footstep-by footstep dance in the liminal, the inquiry enters the inside/outside metamorphosing through the Klein body and a spiral lens emerges out of the dark.

The Inward and Outward Eye/I

Consciousness likes to believe that it has the order of things in place and that it is its job to define what reality is. The heroic ego, or outward-eye, always wants to know where it is, to maintain a hold on how it defines itself within its own reality—most often the sensate material-flesh world. The dream-ego does this as well, through its assumption that its perspective defines the meaning of the dream. I myself am a dream. To practice deep democracy in earnest, the imperative of the ego towards wanting to "know" must be regarded as an honorable part of mythopoetic project. Ignoring its particular call to consciousness (which is its nature) would be antithetical to the practice and would result in a lopsided perspective—perhaps to the other extreme—thus lacking the kind of containment and directionality the ego generously offers as the navigating and orienting function of Psyche.

A broader perspective would not exclude the will of ego-consciousness and would realize that this knowledge is not only "in our heads" but

also very much related to the intentional body in the world. A mythopoetic sensibility feels into the space-in-between different kinds of consciousness and the unconscious and sees the dance that takes place here
in the listening and movement of the inside/outside of the Klein body as
it is metamorphosing in the third space of the liminal. "Dance is needed
as we recover what it means to be adults in the world learning with mind,
body and soul."[14] The dance of the mind (thinking), body (sensing), and
soul (intuiting and seeing through) takes place in the space-in-between.

The intentional dance of the Klein body *is* the practice of seeing, feeling, and sensing through the mythopoetic inquiry, leading to a diaphoric
way of experience that draws on all of the aspects of Psyche—thinking,
feeling, sensing, intuiting, and seeing through—by the very nature of its
inherent non-duality. This form of experiencing is not restricted to (but
still somehow addresses) what often seems like fundamental questions—
those which logic alone attempts to answer, but never quite in a satisfying
manner.

The body-subject knows the world by moving into it—I am the "seeing body." I am the vision-maker becoming the spiral lens.

The dance of the body-subject—the Klein body metamorphosing
its inside/outside into the spiral lens—has the ability to move the object of perception of existence to in-sight. This ability comes from the
diaphoric imagination, which Sandra Gilbert, professor of English, and
Susan Gubar, American author and professor of English and Women's
Studies, describe as follows:

> The diaphoric acts not so much as a comfortable "bridge" be-
> tween the real and the intangible, [but] as a disturbing presence
> that validates the real and forces us to apprehend "things in their
> thingness," including the person of the artist and by that means
> to approach what hiddeness active within them.[15]

The diaphoric impulse, moving from metaphor to diaphor, demands an
existential confrontation. The "disturbing presence" that "lies behind"
the artist, is what the body senses and knows beyond an over-thinking
mind. This disturbance is bodying-forth new meaning, engendering a
new presence. The "existential confrontation" is the acknowledgment
and embodiment of these hiddenesses so that they can become conscious through the body itself. In this manner, the generative intentional

14. Snowber, "Dance as a Way of Knowing," 73.
15. Gilbert and Gubar, *Shakespeare's Sisters*, 164.

energies of the body can meet with equal force this potentially danger-ous "disturbing presence" symbolically. In the doubling of the trigrams of hexagram 29, "The Abysmal (Water)" in the *I Ching* reads, "Properly used, danger can have an important meaning as a protective measure . . . Thus the rulers make use of danger to protect themselves against attacks from without and against turmoil within."[16] Ironically, the danger or "dis-turbing presence" (blindness, illness) acts as a vehicle, the third space in between the "attacks from without and turmoil within."[17] In this sense, it is a kind of autonomous entity within itself that the ego is not responsible for. Realizing this makes way for what is bodying-forth with new mean-ing, a new presence not to be blocked. This is, however, an enormous ask of the ego, who uses identification with the disturbance as a mechanism to maintain its sense of continuity and control. To ask it to step aside in its most fearful state is nothing less than an archetypal shift into an alternate narrative where something other than one's sense of identity is at hand. What is it that is pushing through here? Ego as center of consciousness and place of identity is left bewildered.

Archetypal action allows for such a confrontation, from which the sense of a new "presence" is allowed to make itself known. It is the Klein body that implicitly carries knowledge of this presence *a priori* to the thinking mind. The practitioner of archetypal activism understands and brings this pre-reflexive form of consciousness into the mythopoetic project. Here, the creative/destructive dialectic potentiates a momentum towards living beyond present perceived or assumed limitations, the construct of my-self, *am I how I see myself*—the now old myth. Engaging such powerful archetypal processes asks the practitioner to be "wide-awake" to the subtle and profound astuteness of mind, body, and soul which mythopoetic inquiry potentiates.

New forms of being and unborn awarenesses are birthed within the mythopoeia as extensions of Psyche manifesting through the Klein body to be taken up by the archetypal activist. The archetypal activist sees the invisibles offered through the Klein body and takes this pre-reflexive knowledge to help her craft the spiral lens. The artist as archetypal activist and teacher of her craft takes the plastic forms of the imagination and art materials and makes the invisible visible through the dance she does on the canvas or with a group of students before her, inviting us to see and

16. Baynes, *I Ching*, 114.
17. Baynes, *I Ching*, 114.

live mythopoetically. As imaginal ego, she sees myth in form, formed and trans-formed in the art, and the psyches of clients and students in their art making. Within the academy, the archetypal activist can engage the diaphoric possibilities of theory to embody the presence created therein into a living inquiry—whose intention is manifested as an extension of deep time—and in the development of a living apprenticeship for others. Through the mythopoetic inquiry she creates a method with the practices of (1) deep democracy, (2) archetypal activism, and (3) diaphoric imagination, shifting from an egoic perspective to that of the vision making capacity of the imaginal ego.

Figure 69. Archetypal Activist I

Informed of the material of myth, the archetypal activist re-sources the *logos*, *ethos*, and *mythos* of the deeper intention of Psyche, the soul, *anima mundi*. She has a key role in re-mythologizing life because she has the ability to live symbolically while immersed in her mythography, the land she tills. Within the landscape of the mythopoetic, the archetypal activist invites the wounded narrative and its strange *telos* to guide her while ethically attending to the woundedness through her understanding of the reflexive nature of Psyche. In this sense, education can be a *temenos* that is strong enough to both contain and amplify the encounter with the numinous through flickers as texts. Following the footprints of her trekking through *logos, ethos, mythos, pathos,* and *eros* in this manner *is* the practice illustrated in this book, including *telos,* the goal and purpose of mythopoesis towards *amor fati.* As we work with it symbolically, Rilke's statement that "the future enters into us, in order to transform itself in us, long before it happens," poetically elaborates the significance of both the wounded narrative and where its details are taking us.[18] The reflexive capacity of Psyche discloses images of the future through the "flickers" she offers which, like seeds, will sprout and reach the surface of consciousness long after their initial emergence in the unconscious.

The future enters into us . . .

As therapists and educators, we are naturally involved in the dynamic of how the future enters our clients, our students, and ourselves, long before it "happens out there." As a soul-practice of Psyche's deeper intent, a mythopoetic inquiry generates an environment of "wide-awakeness"—an awakening of what has happened before through a resonance with our past and the past of our species; those morphic resonances that live across space and time as like upon like, carried by morphic fields that order self-organizing organisms. "These fields are souls updated."[19]

Mythopoeia engages a kind of history (myth) that allows the researcher to locate herself in intersubjectivity, reaching backwards and forwards in time. Merleau-Ponty wrote of the kind of awareness this locating of oneself produces: "My life must have a significance which I do not constitute; there must be, strictly speaking, intersubjectivity."[20] I am proposing that this intersubjectivity is inclusive of Sheldrake's updated souls. Merleau-Ponty's emphasis on the significance that we (the ego) do not constitute suggests to me a "wide-awakeness" (imaginal ego, ego as archetype) which holds awareness of "other"—including that of the ancients—in the same manner that the archetypal activist works with polar-

18. Rilke, *Letters to a Young Poet,* 63.
19. Sheldrake, *Presence of the Past,* 98.
20. Merleau-Ponty, *Primacy of Perception,* 448.

ities. The tensions of such polarities generate the diaphoric imagination towards Presence, the polarization of the living and the dead, and an underlying dynamic asking to be brought into another kind of awakeness. A mythopoetic sensibility.

The social philosopher Alfred Schutz talked of wide-awakeness as a type of awareness, "a plane of consciousness of highest tension originating in an attitude of full attention to life and its requirements."[21] The tensions of living and dead, self and "other," conscious and unconscious, and illness and health offer the greatest opportunities for developing a symbolic sensibility. In the practices outlined in the mythopoetic endeavor of this book, one comes into Presence—that is, being present to the numinous. This is the approach I am offering clients, students, therapists, and art therapy trainees.

Figure 70. Bearing Witness

21. Schutz, *Problem of Social Reality*, 213.

A mythopoeia, as *temenos*, protects, supports, and contains the presence of inner figures in their process of being "re-membered" in a new way that the family of origin could not. The death archetype lived in silence in post-war immigrants. In the imaginal space of art making in art therapy, updated souls are offered a safe place/process that provides direction and insight towards the emancipation from the chaos of psychosis and illness—the illness as both the chaos and the messenger—in that enfleshed post-war psychosis. As a place of paradoxical yet authentic embodiment of death, I turn to the words of David Abram:

> If this body is my very presence in the world, if it is the body that alone enables me to enter into relations with other presences, if without these eyes, this voice, or these hands I would be unable to see, to taste, and to touch things, or to be touched by them—if without this body, in other words, there would be no possibility of experience—then the body itself is the true subject of experience.[22]

It is in "this body" that I know the imaging of Psyche who holds all forms of experience and expression: love—*amor fati*. I would ask the reader to return to the archetypal activist as a turning back into image, into the fleshiness of image as this body holds heart and soul and reconnects to *anima mundi*.

---

22. Abram, *Spell of the Sensuous*, 45.

Figure 71. Archetypal Activist II

6

Vision-Making

Eye-Sight and In-Sight

Darkness within darkness
The gateway to all understanding[1]

Not long after my vision loss, I went on a trip to an unfamiliar city. My Klein body sensed that stepping this far "outside" would bring me equally as far "inside," creating a longer continuum between the outside (as unfamiliar) and this intense sense of interiority my blindness maintained. Somehow my body knew that this extreme move to the opposite pole of my predominant present reality (blindness) would stimulate the transcendent function in the psyche, engendering a third middle path. It felt almost like a trick the unconscious was letting me in on as I really didn't know how else to pass through to any kind of understanding of what was happening.

Where was I inside or outside of my-self? Which side of the door was I on in the darkness? Was this blackness surrounding me or in me? What was it leaving me out of? Or, what was it leading me out of? I was terrified I was on the wrong side of the door once again, be it the darkest abyss of this black interiority or the experience of an endless Nothing around me. Or worse still, was I the darkness? This "inside/outside" dilemma kept me occupied for some time. It was hypnotizing in fact, with strange repetitive sounds like a chant or mantra. The inherent liminalality of inside/outside, me/not-me initially became the space for the ritual

1. Lao-tzu, *Tao Te Ching*, 3.

of the complex to be re-enacted, the same story of abandonment being told over and over again. Lost between my and self. I fell into a trance much like a spell in a fairy tale. A spell "I" could not break, feeling both paralyzed and extremely agitated. I wanted to move, to introduce a different beat to the one the chanting was sounding out. I needed to extend my dark interiority in a manner I had never done before so that I might discover its seed, the deep intention Psyche held for me. I wanted to twist into the inside/outside polarization itself. So I waited on images feeling into the subtle flickers in my Klein body.

Figure 72. Psyche's Seeds

I had previously taken for granted my ability to stride into the land-scape in front of me so blindly, yet fully sighted. I did not know of this gap between intention and extension, this mythopoetic landscape I now needed to leap into in order to bring these two together. The extension needed to move closer to the intention, just as the intention wanted to move closer to the extension. In this intimate dance, I might step in tune with the beat of Psyche's dynamism in a mythopoetic matrix of the union of divine spirit with embodied soul.

I was the dancer, the liminal figure, my body the alchemical Klein bottle taking up the call for archetypal activism to craft the spiral lens that sees beyond seeing, crystallizing images into insight. Wanting to shape symbolic processes into embodied images I could see, I felt for my camera. The camera is a small symbolic version of the Klein body, its lens a perfect metaphor for the spiral lens. The camera operates much like a mythopoetic inquiry, holding images inside its dark body and transform-ing them into pictures. The inquiry itself is the "future coming into us" through the body of writing and art making that is taking shape in the alchemical vessel of invisible images birthing words and words giving voice and place to images. I knew the camera would surely be the trusty friend it had been for so long while I was fully sighted, acting as the ex-tension part of this budding new relationship of intention and extension.

My hand was shaking as I took my old friend into my arms and headed out the door. I was on my way to the wedding of *anima* and *anima mundi*: inner and outer, intention and extension. The ceremony took place in the liminal.

What was Psyche's intention in this survival mode I found myself in? My intention was to see, even if my eyes could no longer do this in a manner I was accustomed to. I couldn't rely on those eyes any more. They were damaged beyond repair and left me facing the unbearable image of no image, eyes literally bleeding inside. Retinas hemorrhaging. I plunged into the abyss of blur and gray with no distinct outlines to map out my path.

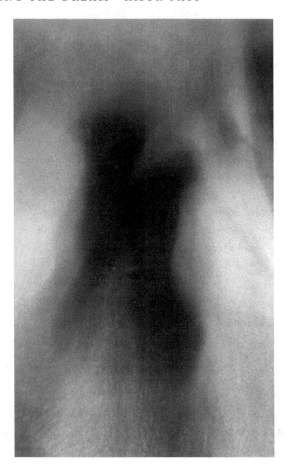

Figure 73. In the Abyss and Blur

The intention of the blindness, its ulterior motive, was to create new pathways "inside." Intuitively, I knew this would be done by extension, as the story of my trip to an unfamiliar city above illustrates. Through extending my blindness into a world I no longer knew, I was testing this intention, its seed, that was life flickering inside darkness. The seed of blindness was straining to sprout, to shine like the black sun illuminating everything around it while maintaining its inherent darkness. In the interiority of the Klein body—this black place of No-Image much like the inside of a camera—the spiral lens was being conceived.

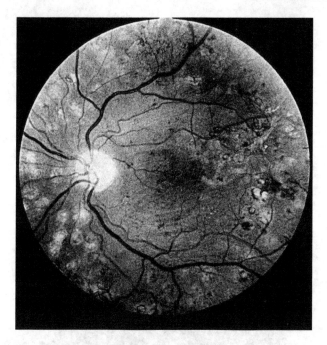

Figure 74. Wounded Retina as Black Sun

How did my mind miraculously bend all those things I could no longer see into shapes to play with, to become the space of creativity that I inserted myself into? The seed of blindness began sprouting images within the very gaps my eyes presented to me as Nothing. Without my knowing, these gaps were morphing into possibilities, no longer just holding the deadness I was so terrified of. Here the ancient ones offered their dwelling in death as a thread Psyche was following in her secret ulterior motive of vision making, moving from eyesight to insight, from the literal to the symbolic. A mythopoetic eye.

So with my friend the camera and my love of image, I played. I flew into the gaps the intention of my blindness had created for me. I entered the uncanny. I could not know then what mysterious intention my body and intuition were speaking of through this blindness. I hadn't heard this language before. I wanted to know of its wisdom, far, far away from my immediate experience of being blind. I had no idea what might reach into those traumatized places my retina now held like shocked babies.

Figure 75. Baby

I did not know how my mind bent light and shapes for this soul-play, but my body knew something. I had to stride into those gaps, into those uncanny spaces of nothing/anything, not knowing where or even if my leg would reach a spot for my foot to land, some solid ground. I had overwhelming fear that this leg extension would simply throw off my balance completely, finding no horizon line to orient me. No horizon.

Figure 76. No Horizon

I am still unsure of my footing. A friend once confided in me that she could not "see" my blindness until one day she noticed me pausing briefly upon entering or exiting. In. Out. A "stop" my blindness offered. A pause as each step entered into or out of a house, a room, from light to darkness, or dark to light, she observed an ever so slight hesitation: a pause for . . . an image, a feeling, a sense of where I am going, where I am; mapping out new territory with footprints that vanished into an invisible horizon, a new notion of myself without horizons; assessing the intention of body, heart, mind, psyche, and my extension into/out of . . . the next step in life:

> I am always situated in the present, on the way somewhere as having been somewhere. Thus, experience is always in the process of becoming. Just when I am aware of things as determinate and thematic, new possibilities emerge on the horizon and the past fades away as more ambiguous.[2]

This stepping, toes edging surfaces of . . . "Your body will be somewhere," my mother used to tell me.

---

2. Robbins, "Maurice Merleau-Ponty."

I, too, could not "see" my blindness, though I knew all too well that my sighted life had faded to black. The leitmotif of my being was now something I would find in an entirely different context. Darkness. I had entered the Shadow where no horizon is determinate. What world was I looking to that was looking back at me, that might hold the structure of a horizon? I think of my friend the camera. Was this unfamiliar world looking back at me that I might re-create its structure? I could not know until I stepped in/out, entering/leaving this dark enclosed cocoon my blindness had spun.

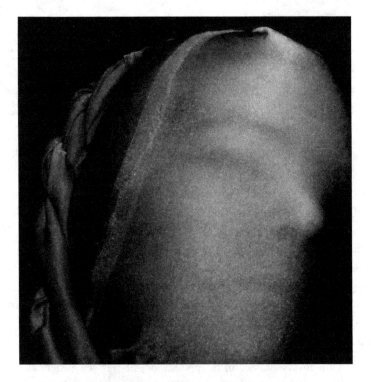

Figure 77 . Cocoon of Blindness

I wanted to reach out as I reached in, to trust that the two would meet somewhere in the imaginal, in the mythopoetic my spiral lens would eventually bring into view. But first comes the embodiment, the gnosis of the Klein body. I was sniffing out a route into the mythopoetic even though I did not "know" that this is what I was doing. I turned my head slightly in the direction of the truth of fourteenth-century German theologian Meister Eckhart's words: "When the soul wants to experience something she throws out an image in front of her and then steps into it."[3]

Figure 78. Sniffing and Listening

Was this what my liminal Klein body was doing? Throwing out an image in front of her-self and then stepping into it—in her desire and imperative to experience something? I turned towards the essence of Eckhart's image of soul/Psyche performing such an act so that I might hear the soul's desire (intent) and extend into an image I could then be (in). I wanted to know the truth of the intention of my blindness, to feel it in my Klein body, so that I could extend my leg towards some stepping stone in place of the horizon I had lost. My phantom vision knew it was the precursor or seed of the vision-maker living in the mythopoetic, reaching back for me to fulfill the intention of my blindness in this imaginal maneuver. This archetypal action, this radical imagination, would re-turn my vision of my world by entering it, moving into the gaps, and embodying Psyche's deeper intention, step by precarious step.

"In the movement of my gaze from one thing to the other, I do not drop into the invisible."[4] Yet I *did* drop into the invisible—into those gaps in my vision that seemed like Nothing but absence.

3. Eckhart, *Complete Mystical Works*, 31.

4. Ozeri, "Merleau-Ponty on Seeing."

Figure 79. What Blindness Feels Like

But I am now beginning to enter these gaps subjectively, to fill them with myself in the manner Meister Eckhart suggests, by throwing and then stepping into an image of herself (soul of blindness). As I enter the space in front of me which I cannot "see," I drop into a part of myself that was previously invisible; it only becomes apparent to me the moment I step into it. I become an embodied image of myself in deep time, an experience in which the present is not lost in itself. For a moment, I am not lost in an absence because I cannot see myself. Because I am embodied in Psyche's intension/extension, an embodied image that *is* Psyche's intent, I am an embodiment of the imaginal world that I can now enter. I have always been a part of this world. A deep re-membering is taking hold here.

I step into this image just in time for me to land. I am in an image I experience as "me." I am no longer lost. From inside this threshold of Psyche's image, the horizon is nothing other than myself/Psyche, imaging/embodying the future entering me in order to be transformed, and in turn transform my image of myself as separate, invisible, absent. Rather than experiencing nothing but emptiness in the gaps—the absence of my vision and the absence *from* myself—I can feel some other form of consciousness coming into being. *Einfuhlung.* This offers me a sense of an alternate selfing emerging. It feels as if a connection to the future, the seeds of which have already been present in my myth, are waiting to sprout through the mythopoetic inquiry itself.

The myth I have been living unconsciously follows the same patterns of inner activity as my ancestors (and certainly my family), but now is perhaps challenged by those of the DNA of the two human stories that have been implanted into my life through the transplants. "The collective memory of form, pattern and organization is accessed through morphic resonances that carry a collective memory of previous organizing systems: humans, animals, plants as well as culture, society, family."[5] If my myth is an extension (or the myth of my clients, my students, and you, reader), carrying forward the same patterns of the organizing system or field I have inherited, I feel even more the pull of continuing this mythopoetic voyage. Mythopoetic inquiry takes the very imaging of my myth into a selfing process that is creative rather than habitual, drawing on the transformative potentiality of the diaphoric sleeping in the myth. The diaphoric aspect of the metaphor of myth becomes animated, creating the appropriate ground for the seeds of a different future to take hold.

A new horizon appears for me to orient myself in the inner and outer landscapes of experience. This mythopoetic horizon now looks back at me and so teaches me its knowing of the future already inside my being, morphing reflexively through the Klein Body into a spiral lens that sees past-present-future in a moment of deep time—the "immortal present."[6] The resonance between this mutually transformative knowing that the horizon holds and the seeds of this future in my body in the present creates a field of meaning that is revolutionary to me. It is nothing less than learning how to see again. Sheldrake proposes that the "kind of learning that happens through re-engaging pre-existing patterns" (the ancients, the ancestors, the myth, DNA) that are present now, affects learning all over the world.[7] This is the kind of learning where re-engaging and re-embodying the pre-existing patterns of personal and collective myths—archetypal DNA so to speak—can take place in a mythopoetic inquiry; a reparative imagination that, for me, has been essential to survival. I believe it is a form of learning from the ancients, our own inner wisdom tradition so to speak, indigenous to the Self.

5. Sheldrake, *Presence of the Past*, 99.

6. See Jung, *Red Book*.

7. Sheldrake, *Presence of the Past*, 208–10.

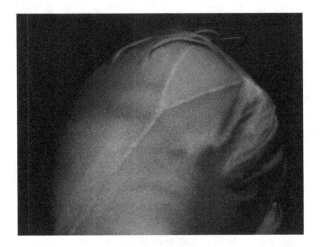

Figure 80. Morphing through the Klein Body

Through the mythopoetic practices of (1) deep democracy, (2) archetypal activism, and (3) diaphoric imagination, comes the increasing ability to sense pre-existing patterns now present in the Klein body, patterns which invoke new dimensions of meaning through the hermeneutics of the spiral lens. These new dimensions of meaning offer the revelatory understanding that the images and stories we hold, who hold us, are more than mere data. Instead, they become a new vision of imaging as a creation, a transformative power located within the human condition. They are the symbols pointing us to Psyche's deeper intent—which holds alternate selves, alternate self stories, and alternate self images—and speak of the multidimensionality of perception; an active perception that is looking through the spiral lens. *Mourning the Dream / Amor Fati* is the mythopoetic space and process in which the Klein body morphs into the spiral lens. This book is an embodiment of the crafting of the spiral lens which looks backwards and forwards reflexively in the vision-making of the living mythopoeia.

"Attention and focus require some things to be out of the field of vision, to remain in the dark."[8] This is the alchemical *nigredo*, the darkening, and the beginning of the opus of transformation. Here is the gap I needed to enter into and experience what my terror was bringing to light, to follow the glimpses of its trail through sensations in my body, a body

---

8. Abrams and Zweig, "Noticing, Naming, and Embracing," 3.

of fear, knowing the trembling to be an ancestral terror flickering with information.

I still have this trembling, often without knowing the letters this Morse code is tapping out within/for me. I can be tricked easily and clamp down with the notion that something is wrong! My body is warning me of something. Alarm bells ringing, alerting me, reminding me of something else going on. I am taking lessons in some animal language through the breaths of my dog, hearing her breaths in and out as they expand and contract her little body. She speaks to me in this language and, when I listen to these animal sounds (the instinctual, morphic), I catch a different tune in the air, settling into a new smell. I stop trying to see and start to "sniff." The heart stops fluttering and fingers cease their shaky search for something solid.

Intention/Extension II

> Seeing's invisibility to itself is what makes it approximate to thought, to transform itself into "insight," to capture itself as "reflection." We are always seeing; seeing can stand for consciousness as a whole. Our seeing reaches into sleep. We see even in our dreams. We need to pay careful attention to all the different kinds of seeing—staring, glaring, looking, glancing, gazing, inspecting [sniffing, hearing animal breaths, touching, the leaning of plants towards the sun, psyche yearning, soma aching]. There is a rich plurality to the practice of seeing.[9]

Merleau-Ponty's quote is key to the development of a mythopoetic sensibility, listening to the polyphonic texture of perception. To listen to two or more simultaneous lines of independent consciousness—as opposed to just one voice/seeing myself only through the lens of the wounded narrative (duo-consciousness of the myth and the alternate story, speaking and heard through the practice of deep democracy). *Am I how I see myself?* I can't see myself because I am blind.

9. Ozeri, "Merleau-Ponty on Seeing."

Field Notes December 2013

Lately I have noticed the subtle forthcoming of another way for finding an image in the dark. On several recent occasions, I lost a small object while at home in my apartment. Previously when this happened, I would either search endlessly for this object or not even bother, due to my diminished eyesight. Now, unexpectedly, Psyche has offered me an alternate means of finding what I lost through a seemingly imperceptible sound memory. It could be days after the loss (the split) when the tiny sound of the impact (trauma) of the lost object hitting the hard floor would spontaneously come to the forefront of my memory (complex). In that moment of "hearing," I could "see" where my body was ("your body will be somewhere") when the earring, for example, dropped. I then went to that space my body had previously occupied and quickly found the precious item (the Self that had been lost in trauma).

The first time this happened, I was intrigued, as I had never had this experience before. When these "sightings/hearings" from the reservoir of my spontaneous memory (Klein body) continued to guide me to the desired outcome of finding what I had lost, I was truly amazed. An alternate "self" (the archetypal activist), who was not reliant on literal seeing, and had the resilience to move beyond the fear of having No-Image (blindness), was now fully animated by Psyche (imaginal ego). I believe that this animation is the expression and extension of Psyche as she holds the archetypal polarities of image and No-Image, sightedness and blindness, even with the enormous tension between them—in deep time (stepping into the mythopoetic)—like the "soul throwing out an image in front of her and stepping into it"?[10]

Meister Eckhart's image of the soul opens a kind of interiority beneath that of the complex, that place of identification with the wounded story. In this manner, stepping into the mythopoetic realm illuminates the archetype the complex is symbolically pointing to while, paradoxically, blinding us to its presence. Though experienced very literally in the here-and-now when trauma is triggered, the complex—if seen through the spiral lens—can be recognized more and more as a morphic echo. Listening for the "presence of the past," a deeper resonance of the collective call for mourning and dreaming is inspired:

I remember my mother having this uncanny ability to find things in the house that I could not. Whenever I could not find something I had

---

10. Eckhart, *Complete Mystical Works*, 31.

misplaced, I would ask her about it. The Field Note above seems to be an illustration of finding images in the dark through morphic resonances (my mother in me, the past in the presnt).

When I suggest to clients/students that they close their eyes and use both hands to draw—so that they might sense these morphic resonances through their own Klein body—they seem to enter a universe of presences of the imaginal, revealing themselves in their own bodies and the body of the art. As if by magic, clients/students feel into (*Einfuhlung*) their own archaic resonances and their presence in space—both interiorly and exteriorly—as they share the collective dreamspace with others (internal and external others in the field).

A kind of deep listening occurs in this space: timeless moments, the sounds of one's own breathing and heartbeat, the breath of other beings, the shuffling and shifts in body movement and posture, the sound of the pastel touching paper, creating a totality of experience—a polyphony of the deep democracy of perception.

I did not realize until almost two decades after my loss of vision that this practice of closing the eyes was actually a maneuver on Psyche's part. Through her uncanny craft of secretly guiding me to throw my blindness in front of me—the blindness now leading—Psyche indirectly created a seamless extension of my dark interiority into a journey of finding images in the dark. I found myself no longer alone in this blackness. I was beginning to learn how to take the soul of the blindness into the world and let it lead others. Unconsciously, I was already using the spiral lens. When I finally became aware of what seems so obvious to me now, I had a similar feeling to when the "sound memories" described in the field notes above had woken me up to the multidimensional capacity of perception.

Figure 81. Psyche Throwing an Image

Merleau-Ponty says, "To see is to enter a universe of beings that display themselves . . . in other words to look at an object is to inhabit it."[11] To feel into it is *Einfuhlung*. Seeing, entering, and inhabiting with empathy. Psyche throws an image out in front of herself and steps into it—with compassion *and* curiosity. She envisions and feels into the extension of deeper impulses/intentions of mind, body, heart, and psyche, displaying themselves and offering these intentions form, embodiment, and a connection to the numinous. Even though seeing seems to be detached from the other senses, it is, in fact, folded in with them. It is the act of entering, the act of perception. The spiral lens (perception) emerges from the Klein body (viscera) and touches light.

The soul of my blindness touched sight.

11. Merleau-Ponty, *Phenomenology of Perception*, 79.

Sniffing, animal breaths, sprouts reaching, plants leaning, psyche yearning, and soma aching all localize me in the world in a way that seeing does not. We can only see because we can touch, which is the root of all perception. Eyes touch and are touched by light and other beings in light creating light-forms. The body touches and is touched by inner and outer forces which are the "flickers" signaling invisible presences and events, the morphic resonances we are tuned into (entering and being entered by). The soul touches and is touched by its own nature, which animates being: *anima* (life force) and *anima mundi* (inherent connectedness). And so we are in intimate dialogue with our own existence. We are looking into our very nature. "If we want to reach a living perception of nature, we must become as living and flexible as nature herself."[12] The presence of Nature. The nature of presence:

> As the experiential source of both psyche and spirit, it would seem that the air was once felt to be the very matter of awareness, the subtle body of the mind. And hence that awareness, far from being experienced as a quality that distinguished humans from the rest of nature, was originally felt as that which invisibly joined human beings to the other animals and to the plants, to the forests and to the mountains. For it was the unseen but common medium of their existence.[13]

Anima mundi.

Mourning the Dream / Amor Fati is an inquiry into the presence of nature (the nature of being) and the nature of Presence. Its crafting has taken many deep breaths into quiet chambers of body, where subtle stirrings quickly become still as soon as awareness touches them. I continue, however, as if I do not know of the presence of these stirrings—just as Psyche offering the technique of closing the eyes while drawing. And so I move deeply into their morphic path, following their invisible footsteps indicated only by feel. I ask: what presence entered me when I lost my vision? I was alone, I felt. Everything I was familiar with had vanished. No horizon line; I stood in the midst of a transition where I could not remain standing . . . How could it not be difficult for me?[14] Was it a moment when something new entered me, a pause for something unknown, the breath of an unlived life? The "not-me" autonomously takes her rightful place

12. Goethe, *Scientific Studies*, 64.

13. Abram, *Spell of the Sensuous*, 237.

14. Adapted from Rilke, *Letters to a Young Poet*, 151.

in my-self, entering the soul's intimate dialogue in an alternate manner. This time the "not-me," this shadow-self, cleverly disguised as blindness, brought a softening—an openness and compassion towards the one who mythopoetically incorporates the horror *and* the beauty of being oneself, being human. "A silence arose, and the new experience, which I did not know, stood in the midst of it all and said nothing."[15]

I was trying to navigate through a liminal landscape and I desperately needed to hold the paradox of seeing/not seeing, visible/invisible, but I did not know how. I kept slipping away into the unconscious, let loose without a container, falling deeply into the complex of not being seen. Annihilation anxiety.

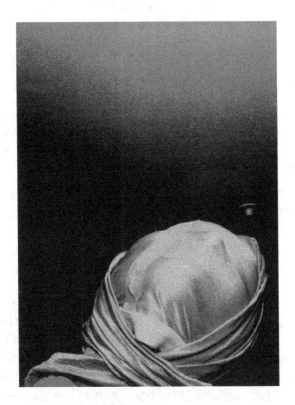

Figure 82. I Cannot See So How Can I Be Seen?

The unconscious was spilling out in unbearable images that I needed to call home in order to not be depleted in the process of releasing

15. Rilke, *Letters to a Young Poet*, 151.

them. If left to run rogue, they might devour me. I needed a new relationship to the images—to help them find their home in their initial intent of survival. Their rogueness needed guidance and direction, offering them a process whereby they would act as reminders for what their intent was (the archetypal core of the highly charged complex of invisibility that is annihilation). Mythopoetic inquiry is such a process *and* container for living images of death and dying images of life to do their transformative work. As an extension into the flesh-world through art making, the images that emerged from the dark unconscious flicker somatically, then symbolically and diaphorically, taking the metaphor of life experiences beyond the known or the literal. Beyond the self.

A re-directing of psychic energy occurs in the decontextualisation of the literal to the literary, the mythic to the mythopoetic. Bending back on thoughts, sensations, emotions, or intuitions reflexively invites extensions of Psyche to become raw material for moving from the literal to the symbolic, understanding that these extensions are the symbolic mirrors of Psyche's deeper intent: a performance of her ulteriority, the alternate mythopoetic narrative taking place.

Recognizing symbols moving into consciousness through the flickering of the Klein body offers glimpses into a deeper story that is affecting me, nudging me towards participating more consciously with the logic of "otherness." From this mythopoetic perspective, Persephone shows me a way of bringing polarities together through her seasonal descents and ascents to and from the Underworld. Just as Persephone has been snatched away from her mother and the upper world, there is a tearing apart from life into death that is necessary for something new to happen (a new pattern of experience, a shift in consciousness). This dynamic sets up the conditions for the archetypal activist, as liminal figure, to enter that space in-between life/death (creative/destructive) a *coniunctio*, "the alchemical operation consisting essentially in separating the *prima materia*, the so-called chaos, into the active principle, the soul, and the passive principle, the body, which were then reunited in the personified form in the *coniunctio*, or chemical marriage."[16] It is the union of unlike substances in alchemy. It is the marrying of the opposites whose fruition is the birth of a new element often symbolized as the child. "The Child

16. Jung, *Structure and Dynamics*, 122–23.

archetype symbolizes potential for greater wholeness by combining attributes of both."[17]

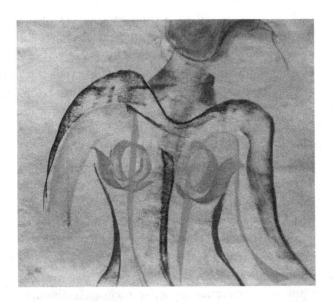

Figure 83. Persephone

To bring about the *coniunctio* in my psyche and my practice, the vision of the mythopoetic asks that I *be* that liminal space for the archetypal Persephone to traverse the space-in-between the upper and under worlds, visiting the ancestors and the dead, so that we might develop a living relationship. By becoming the mythography itself—my body the mountains and lakes and trees—what I discover is that the open wound (mourning openly) becomes the place of inquiry, the rite of passage into the open field of experience. I am embarking on serious journeys of living images of death and dying images of life.

Such a voyage means breaking the binding agreement with the old myth. This is done by re-placing myself into the text through the very writing of this book. In the con-text of mythopoesis, being the open wound *and* mourning this wound is one complete breath. Each breath draws in the opportunity for the diaphoric imagination to re-embody the old myth. The re-imagining, re-visioning requires a serious practice of archetypal activism in which unbearable images are tended to gently and nourished back to health so that they do not eat me but, instead, feed

17. Samuels, *Critical Dictionary of Jungian Analysis*, 135.

me. If I step out of the war zone, as the ancients have already done, facing the images of my own mortality—those living images of death and dying images of life—to consciously make the decision to be where I already am, I will be with the presences of the old souls.

Through preventing my way of extending in the usual unconscious manner that I had previously functioned, the soul of my blindness pushed me into a more intimate reflexive capacity, animating each avenue of perception: sensation, thought, feeling, intuition—each a jewel in Indra's web, each reflecting in all of the other jewels.

The nature of consciousness and what we know about it *is* a matter of epistemology. As the study of knowledge, epistemology is concerned with questions, some of which have been identified and pursued in this mythopoetic journey:

Am I how I see myself?

Am I how I think of myself?

Or am I simply a way of seeing?

Epistemology holds the underpinnings of beliefs and their justifications. Its intent is to answer questions such as those above. Knowledge implies two facts: the nature of that which is known—that is, that we exist—and the nature of that which knows. Each notion also inherently suggests its opposite, non-existence and ignorance, respectively.

I can only be aware of consciousness subjectively and by introspection. The research lies in-between the seeing and being seen reflexively. The inquiry addresses the complex of not being seen (annihilation anxiety) and not seeing (being unconscious, ignorant, "blind"). *Mourning the Dream / Amor Fati* attempts to reveal the ulterior mythopoetic motive of not falling victim to either of these wounded parts of the human story. Mirrored symbolically by the complex, Psyche's deeper intent of metamorphosing the fear of death into a rapprochement with the ancient ones asks me again: *am I simply a way of seeing?*

Given the above statement, self-awareness in a mythopoetic capacity is amplified by the use of a reflexive journal ("field notes") which mirrors the nature of archetypal participants (ego, complexes, inner figures: the inner "guests"). My "field notes" are a part of my data that reveal previously hidden contextual information, which is then transformed through the mythopoetic endeavor. From this "data," an inherent structure underlying the entire mythopoetic project emerges. With the guidance of Psyche as midwife and the practices of the steps outlined above—as mythopoetic inquiry—a reflexive living hermeneutic takes its informative place in the intention and extension of *Mourning the Dream / Amor Fati*. These "field notes" continue to emerge from actual teaching, and so generate more method towards a pedagogy of the imagination.

The intent of bringing a reflexive hermetical lens to a mythopoetic inquiry is to envision the inherent structure, method, and integrity of a practice that "turns back on itself," each turn of the spiraling motion a step in the sharpening through crystallizing of the spiral lens. The application of the findings of the research involves asking living questions while dwelling in the everyday, listening to the call, and feeling into the "flickers" as clues to the direction the inquiry is both led by and leading into the symbolic. The insights that emerge through the application of the research provide another mirror through which the inquirer—artist, art therapist, and educator—can more deeply consider her own assumptions, values, motivations, and relationship to her myth and the unconscious, applying these to her practice and everyday life.

The truth of one's myth and what its mythopoetic purpose is un-veils and animates a new, alternate narrative which imagines my story reflected in your story, building a depth dialogue: dreaming together. In this dreaming together, big, universal, as well as highly personal questions and motifs can be explored. Through inquiry (quest) we can discern what kinds of conditions we are creating within ourselves and the world, to then address personal and collective issues. While the reflecting form of hermeneutics is to obtain insight, a reflexive hermeneutics is an active vital part of organizing both the inner and outer world: intention/extension. It is not a passive reception of information, but an engaging form of perception that automatically positions the inquirer ethically and aesthetically in relation to the very phenomenon that activates a mythopoetic response; reflexivity.

Our individual story is part of a larger narrative to which we contribute our particular perspective, our way of seeing, our unique fragments of the whole. Such fragments, like pieces of a mosaic or stained glass window, form a structure that holds meaning. Building this structure of meaning through images and stories becomes the day-to-day that evolves into soul-work. This daily practice creates an orientation in a landscape that has lost its previous landmarks. Its tending finds interior passages that extend beyond skin, into those hills and valleys, those mountains and lakes that are made of shivers, sighs, sobs, insights, and deaths.

Momentary sensations—feelings and thoughts within the magnetic field of intentions of mind, body, heart, psyche/soul—become extensions of deeper impulses that embody themselves in the form of sensation, feeling, thought and intuition, the foundations and raw material our stories and images are made of. Like a braid, they plait our myth, lived out until the ultimate extension—where we join the dead.

Figure 84. Death

7

Embodied Reflections in the Diaphoric Mirror of Experience

Mourning the Dream / Amor Fati

Field Notes from the Dark Presence

I look through my bedroom door into the dark. I am lying in my bed but I am not sleeping. I bend my eyes around the corner to the right and travel into the kitchen. I feel the graininess of this dark as the rough skin of an ancient animal rubbing along the length of my turn. I keep moving even while I am still lying in bed. I follow the eyes swallowed so many years ago and trusted they were guiding me towards something; something necessary that could only happen in this moment, the moment I went to bed to let my eyes rest after having worked so hard at trying to see. In the bed of the symbolic, the metaphoric—the diaphoric imagination conceives Presence.

Figure 85. Image as a Door

I look through the image in the dark. I am lying in my bed but I am not dreaming. I bend my imagination around the corner to the left and journey into a new pattern of being. I feel the rasp of going against the grain of the old dark myth I have been travelling for so long. My flesh is scratched and cut as I make this uncanny turn, the characters of the old narrative using their tongues as knives to cut into me as I pass. But I keep moving even while I am still lying in bed, following a Presence that had come into me long before this moment: a Presence that spoke to me long ago, but I had not yet grown the ears to hear it, the mythopoetic eyes to see it, the empathy to touch it.

I am travelling across this invisible threshold of self by throwing an image of soul in front of me, and embodying this image even while my body is quietly lying alone in bed in the dark.

Traversing my own mythopoetic inquiry and discovering the practices it revealed (the footsteps Psyche showed me), I offer students, clients, and other inquirers the opportunity to consider the following:

The Work of Wording Is Done

The work of wording is done.
Now do soul work
Upon the cells within your dreambody

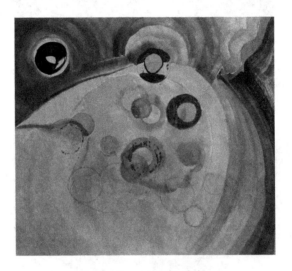

Figure 86. After First Transplant: Whose Cells?

Something/Someone Has Come In

Something/someone has come into being.
Something/someone has trans-formed into another Presence.

This Presence comes into being through the diaphoric imagination, opening to hiddenesses which usual ways of seeing cannot apprehend. Sometimes this opening first reveals a disturbing presence (or presences) that lies just around the corner of perception. It hangs there, suspended in the unconscious, yet asking to be known. The presence(s) is sometimes disturbingly known to the Klein body, experiencing an existential confrontation consciousness itself cannot acknowledge.

The presence of these hiddenesses, these invisibles—their embodiment starting with the flickers—makes possible an encounter with the numinous through the body itself. Through a direct experiencing of these presences and a welcoming of them within the mythopoetic framework, a full-on meeting of the creative/destructive dialectic is presented as a potential opportunity to re-myth and re-embody ancient wounds, traumas: to hear the laments of the ancients and the unborn and invite them to finally sing their long silenced song without the devastation the memory of its tune has continued to carry forward.

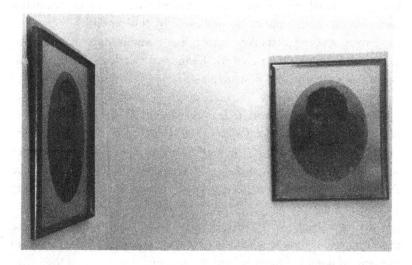

Figure 87. Silenced Presences

The Presence comes into view after having been asleep in the body before this body knew itself as Klein body, working its entire being into crafting the spiral lens, the vision-maker.

Field Notes: Voices of the Ancients

Who is it that is left hanging here, darkened by decades of silenced disturbances in the corners of experience left untraveled/ unravelled? Old portraits of forgotten or denied embodiments suspended in shadowy moments. If I look closely at these images, these presences, they might act as a door for me to see through to a resemblance, a pattern, which, now re-cognized, is released of its imperative to repeat itself; an archetypal pattern whose presence lies beyond consciousness; morphic resonances that echo back and forth, back and forth, through past and future generations in the timeless chambers of forgotten or hidden trauma.

Yet the images here, as I gaze at them, body-to-body, re-mind me of deep forces my flesh knows only too well; the same forces carried in the bodies of my siblings, my parents, their parents, and all who have since come from their flesh. Flesh both carrying and hiding those dark stories that are pleading to be told in a different voice, a mythopoetic voice.

To pause and fully experience the profound impact of such multi-intergenerational intersubjectivity is possible when one has prepared a vessel strong enough not to be swallowed by this powerful, potentially dangerous, archetypal shadow vortex. The body as place of liminality, as the inside/outside, non-dualistic Klein body that lives in the space in between the creative and destructive—life and death, the living and the dead, divine and incarnate. The body has this capacity. As my Klein body is doing the alchemical work of transforming itself into a spiral lens, the body itself is viscerally reminded of the lament of the ancients, having deep empathy for those still living *and* dying in the present moment of selfing. The Klein body aches in this painful dissolution, much like the body of a larvae first dissolving before its new structure as butterfly emerges.

I take up this task of dissolving/dying so that I might become a vision-maker, a spiral lens who can see the ancients. To be born and go to them, to not leave them behind, buried and abandoned to their own absence—these old, lamenting souls who, because of their own circumstances, were unable to close the wounds for themselves. I bend to them through the reflexive contortions that the Klein body is able to make, to begin the work of the archetypal activist, stitching together their absence/presence living in my own gestures, those invisible visibles. Through embodied gestures, I invite their laments, their attempts at transfiguration taking place in my Klein body, for the sake of the spiral lens: to see the ancients, the unborn, and myself non-dualistically—as one Self.

To do this, I need to mourn openly. Dream fully. Love fate. *Amor fati.* Love the images, those mirrors of my experience that offer me the possibility of embodying living moments diaphorically, creating a new sense of Presence the Klein body and spiral lens have offered up as the fruits of their hard work. As I re-cognize that the core of mythopoesis, living mythopoetically, includes this love of dying images of life and living images of death—having a relationship with the dead directly in my body—I know that these images (and the dead) are loving me back, each moment a caress, even if it is the caress of death. Through this radical mythopoetic love, the diaphoric creates Presence through the metaphors engendered by my myth, transfigured into a new living mythopoetic Presence. This Presence knows *amor fati* as it breathes life (and death) into the old narrative. The old myth dies. Having served with its entire being in preparation for this death, its dissolution leaves a space, a void into which the Presence of the dead, having waited for so long, watching, can step forward and speak their truth.

Mythopoetic Presence is a dimension that transcends both time and space and includes the pooled memories of our ancestors from the collective imagination. Mythopoetic sensibility knows life *and* death, as does the body, and can carry the grief of the ancient ones—those intergenerationally traumatized ones that tried to emigrate to un-bloodied lands and bodies unmaimed by war, albeit unsuccessfully. The mythopoetic voyage returns the traveler to the waters that separated the old from the new: the waters of war, dis-memberment, a crippled symmetry, and loss of the dream of a vision of a life to live. Mythopoeia is a place in between self and other, the living and the dead, a human container that is both the Self and knows how to grieve. By not rejecting but rather healing the split of absence/presence in the wounded parts of our narrative, the Self has the capacity to contain our "absence" and proclaim this very capacity to be a transformation into presence. From the mythopoetic perspective, my-Self is the passage of mourning deeply the trauma transported through generations across great lands and oceans.

Mythopoetic practices of (1) deep democracy, (2) archetypal activism, and (3) diaphoric imagination trans-form lament into song and absence into presence, spiraling through this archetypal dynamic back into absence and so on . . . the transfiguration of loss back into love (which was its origin) and *amor fati* includes the love of death, to love our spiraling destiny. Deeply conflicted love births images that love bodies, just as the light/life force needs bodies to be reflected in; it is catching the reflexive light of the flickering moon—true seeing, a true embodiment. The con-figuration of conflicted love is a dialectic of fear and desire, all of which the Klein body feels and the spiral lens sees. All of one's fate. Our fate.

Field Notes: Braga, Portugal

I am sitting here in an office down the hall from my host who is a professor of education, specializing in "bullying," at the Universiado do Minho. I stayed with her and her family in their home and we spent a lot of time touring the local castles, churches, cafes, and other historical sites—in particular, the renowned beginning of Portugal: the town of Guimarães.

It has been interesting not being able to understand this unusual language, not having the language to communicate. Having wandered well beyond my comfort zone in terms of my sight, I found myself having to rely on other, less obvious forms of navigating the unfamiliar. I have had some startling experiences regarding this, coming face-to-face with how little I actually see. I didn't expect to meet the blind one here in a far-away country, across a continent and an ocean. I thought I had left her behind in my brave stepping out to present at an international conference here.

Here I am, here she is, lost in those dark wombs of the churches; unable to find the edge of steps in castle passageways, walking from one enormous stone room to another with—to me—invisible artifacts all around the ancient chambers. Large expanses of tapestries, illustrating historical kings and wars, remain secret from me; just whispers that might slip through the small peek-holes my perception offers up here and there.

I feel my way along the stone floors to detect possible ends and beginnings of descending or ascending steps into the next invisible display.

My body is tight. I am contracting yet moving forward slowly so not to lose the semi-discernable heads of the group I am with. My host sees my hesitancies in the thresholds between the different spaces we are travelling through and tells the group, her Brazilian students, in Portuguese that they must help me. I only know this as I feel a soft touch or voice at my shoulder as we encounter another step: "Up," "Down."

I feel vulnerable, terrified, and dependent in an awkward kind of way. But also grateful, softening this familiar harshness towards myself when I cannot do something because of my vision: the hatred towards this blind one who blocks my view. But I allow myself to receive the help of the Brazilian students, so full of life and generosity; I let myself experience this dependency and I feel a double pang inside my body: both a brittleness and a softening simultaneously. This is so odd. It confuses me. I feel this great fear and enormous desire coming face to face inside these interiorities of body and history.

My desire to move forward into and through the dark chambers of those historical passages has me meet my fear head on.

Face to face; body to body; the body of the fear and the body of the desire.

What happens when these two meet in a new place, without the usual defensive maneuvers, without the ever so habitual avoidance tactics, so that neither have the chance to live out their full lives?

Here I am. Feeling for the edge of another step, inching my toe along the cool stone floor, tightening, pulling in to avoid a fall. Yet en-couraged by my desire to open into those dark places inside my-self, inside the vestibules of the chapels where the Madonnas sit high above me holding the child: the hope.

I feel this meeting place of fear and desire viscerally. I don't need to see the tapestries of the battle scenes inside the castles. I can feel them in my own flesh as the fear and desire come to meet me, the outcome yet unknown; hanging in the liminal just as the tapestries covering the castle walls so silently, their grand narratives stilled.

Desire and fear. What is their relationship? Why is it even important to want to know this? Where can this pair rendezvous for the first time in the light of day; in the light of a consciousness of their simultaneous mutual presence; so potent, each.

Could I revisit this fresh meeting place, the little cafe on the street corner of a small town—the origin of Portugal no less—with a full view of the church nearby?

Figure 88. Simply a Way of Seeing through the Eye of the Chapel (Braga, Portugal)

Where is this new meeting place that has come in, this Presence from so long ago that has little interest in how I see myself, or what I even think of myself? I didn't expect to meet the blind one here in a far-away country. Did she cross the great ocean and feel her body as a ship—as she had longed to do with her older brother, sister, and father? This time, she was not left at the shore waiting. She dove into the water and was swept deeply into the currents of the unconscious; so powerful in their capacity to have carried her here now, into the dark womb of mother church, and the ancient chambers of her myth. Here she was, naked as a baby.

Here the blind one was dead center in the archetypal vortex of the relationship between fear/desire and *Mourning the Dream / Amor Fati*. This was the destination of her voyage, back to the continent of her tribe, though still far enough away from their country of origin. This seemed somehow appropriate, a mirror image whose reflected light would not burn through the heart. This geographical, metaphorical gap created the space-in-between, necessary for the dismembered body-memories that were not included in the myth, memory being selective as it is. Ancestral guests were invited in and a *coniunctio*, a re-union, of the memorized and the forgotten held comm-union in the body of the church.

To be able to mourn such great losses, the wounds of *anima mundi*, I want to know the gaze of the ancients—to see what they have seen and lived, to listen to their murmurs in my throat, to feel their pullings and aches in my viscera. I yearn to receive their messages, reading their flickers of light in the darkness of my vision. I want to open up the blackness as spaces for them/me to enter—entering into those gaps in my vision, gaps in my understanding—bringing my voice to the song of the tribe. To be touched by the mythopoetic melody streaming through me. This melody helps me. I know now that I am not how I see myself or think of myself, as these old ways of seeing did not include the essential Presences of Psyche's deepest intent: Psyche's polyphonic nature knows and addresses the death archetype. How can "I" know my death if I cannot conceive of it?

Visiting with the old souls, including everything I cannot remember, helps me to come out of the narcissistic wound and disidentify with the melancholia that has replaced my sense of cohesion: the trauma having become the self-image, the false self-presence, and the self-absence my body has been grieving so terribly. To truly begin mourning, the death of the self-image in the mirror of narcissism needs to take place. This dying is already taking place in the body, asking to be held in a *temenos* of empathy, tended to by the collective souls of *anima mundi*.

There is great fear in pulling myself away from the mirror of who I think I am. And yet, there is a profound ache my body speaks, asking me to hear the very bottom of its desire, to move out of this fixated state of identification with the wounded narrative—wounded because it was incomplete, left constantly waiting and wanting. The broken-language of the ancients is stuttering the request to re-compassion the body. I desire to reconnect with those voices and presences who can replace my false sense of cohesion through the narcissistic wound by offering their laments as the missing notes of the song of the tribe I lost so long ago. Joining their lament now connects me to my own grief.

The lament is the first sounding of transfiguration.

In the company of the ancient ones, in this mythopoetic place, I cannot continue to gaze at the image in the narcissistic mirror. The unbearable image of trauma has become the intolerable self-image, generated by a loss of connection—a loss of self-presence in the absence of "other" and a betrayal of the love between *anima* and *anima mundi*. In the dark womb of the interiority of fear/desire and *Mourning the Dream / Amor Fati*, the diaphoric imagination can re-embody the myth of the blind one into a mythopoetic process of "turning the light around."[1] The world of the imagination is fully embodied; all senses are involved. Psyche's imaging and seeing is a clear phenomenological eye, a cultivated inner eye/I. I know I can touch the inaccessible through the body and the diaphoric imagination to let the invisible come into me through the door of image. This is self-healing in which the liminal limbs (eyes) return, pulled back from the shadow vortex they were sucked into. Now re-membered, my eyes are recalling their inherent desire to see, even as vision had been swallowed up in trauma.

I wait for meaning to unfold by attending to the images this remembering spontaneously ignites. *Pausing*; taking the risk of being in the invisible, trusting that my body will find its way. "Your body will be somewhere." Waiting on images; waiting for the diaphoric, discovering/uncovering how the body works/lives with conflicts of love. I think the work is about these deep conflicts of love that have buried themselves in flesh. Wounds that tell wounded stories . . .

1. Cleary, *Secret of the Golden Flower*, 28.

The relationship to the wound is central to this mythopoetic inquiry. It is what creates soul—soul not as entity, but as a space, a movement, a process; a relationship to the unconscious. It is the wound that eventually generates a more conscious relationship with the unconscious, the wound acting as a portal. The wound unites us in our humanity through the telling of its tale.

Ethically speaking, if we choose to interrupt this ongoing wounding—which, without the conscious choice to engage and re-embody it, we will inevitably maintain—it seems imperative to work with the wound, through the telling of its narrative.

I wound and am wounded out of my own and others' wounds. Let me instead go to the wound as portal to the numinous. The wound is in direct relationship to the authentic self (archetypal Self) as well as to the many false selves that are constructed to protect me from being overwhelmed. Too much to see. The image in the mirror of the narcissistic wound is such a false self that could not complete her intent of keeping me safe. She was alone in her one-sided fixation and could not access the plurality of Psyche's offering—such a multitude of images, doors, and passages to go through into a new pattern of existence.

Feeling wounded or being a wounder (I am always both) is a clue that this relationship with the wound needs tending, and that the wound needs to find a place to be in my life so that I can take care of it—for my-self and for others' sake. The manner in which I relate to the wound is crucial. This relating is the place and process of soul as crucible, alchemical container of archetypal embodiment. As humans, the wound is the portal to the deepest part of ourselves, connected to Psyche's deeper intent. It is the meeting place of fear/desire, destruction/creation, *Mourning the Dream / Amor Fati*. This is soul work which includes the soul of the world: *anima mundi*.

> The speaking and doing is done.
> Now I turn to this presence that lies within
> And all around in the dreaming bodies that we are

Figure 89. Dreaming Bodies

By recognizing the primacy of interconnectedness, embodied imagination has the ability to re-enchant the world, bringing authentic spirituality back into culture. Like Indra's net—which has a multifaceted jewel at each vertex, each jewel being reflected in all of the other jewels—we are always already embedded in the world; a part of a cosmic process of unfolding. As a form of spiritual phenomenology, this unfolding—the intending and extending—may hold the possibility of deconstructing the modern materialistic mythic narrative that has yet to move from the literal to the symbolic, from myth to mythopoesis. In its deconstruction through the mythopoetic endeavor, this wounded, modern materialistic myth, like our own body and mind, could "unbind . . . and in that un-ravelling, we have a chance to connect with something greater than the small self so identified with our sense of being separate . . . Dying to our story, we pass through loss, and possibly the relief of letting go."[2] As if

2. Halifax, *Being with Dying*, 62.

passing through the eye of a needle, like the Klein bottle in alchemy, the body/psyche is passing through itself into another dimension seamlessly. And so our story can perhaps now loop back through itself, to join with its other end from the "inside." Through the mythopoesis, our myth can pass through itself without a hole. By doing so, it metamorphoses into an alternate alchemical version of itself—with the strength and resilience to contain and create itself. Resilience in grief.

Figure 90. Childhood Enchantment

8

A Mythopoetic Practice

Threading Back, Stitching Forward:
Mythopoetic Inquiry

Field Work: Moving from the Literal to the Symbolic, from the Myth into the Mythopoetic

Fieldwork in a mythopoetic inquiry is about getting into the ima-
ginal world through the apertures of the "flickers," the Morse code
of the ancients, the morphic resonances that live in and amongst
us. Engaging this soul-to-soul language, the texts of body-heart-
mind learning and knowing that are the soul's most intimate
dialogue with its own existence, is the living apprenticeship. This
"living" includes interacting with inner figures and archetypal pat-
terns established by the ancient ones we feel and know but mostly
do not recognize. The field we are "working," which is also work-
ing us, includes the morphic field I am proposing we experience
through those "flickers" described and explored throughout this
book. Becoming attuned to these signals and taking them seri-
ously, we begin inviting them as "guests" of the unconscious, texts
to be studied by learning how they work, live, and play. This form
of fieldwork is a key method for mythopoetic research.

Through mythopoetic research, I come to meet the "guests" as they
come to meet me in the dance of opposites, that space-in-between of the
liminal. By practicing the method developed in the research, I am able to

see how profoundly the ancient ones have been present in my life. I feel how their seemingly invisible and silent presence so affects and directs my way of seeing and, I am proposing, continually influences all inter-connected beings. I have come to see and respond more consciously to these morphic resonances by tracking their flickers in my Klein body and have become intensely curious through their varying multidimensional embodiments in the intersubjective field of *anima mundi*. The new level of awareness this curiosity spawned has literally exploded my previously learned, instinctual methods of perception that were, as I see now, sym-bolically foreshadowed in the bursting of blood vessels in my retinas, resulting in blindness. The writing and imaging that emerged from this mythopoetic "feeling in the dark" experiment for survival formed and molded the body of my field notes as they shaped the directionality of the narrative; the method, the pedagogy, and the practice mythopoetic inquiry generates.

Mythopoeia shapes and is shaped by the autonomy of image and story—the forms created by our myth to speak to us of its need to be lived, listened, and responded to. Re-embodying the laments of the an-cients—the archetypal patterns, archaic remnants rippling through our being—requires listening and heeding the "call" concealed or disguised as "difficulties." Theoretically, as a way of "knowing," the mythopoetic ap-proach is primarily informed by the discourse of Depth Psychology, a psychology of the secret and concealment. A secret creates a container for what will be revealed in its own embodiment in the imaginal—a sym-bolic "truth" resonating in the morphic fields flickering throughout the personal and collective Klein body, and its extensions into symptoms, dreams, art making, performance, dance, poetry, and storytelling—as well as through cultural myths, including the modern materialistic myth of our times. Clues to this shadow truth are tracked in the interconnect-ing mirroring in groups and the individual psyche, each an Indra's web in its own structuring of perception:

> Morphic fields are organizing fields that work by imposing pat-terns on otherwise random or indeterminate patterns of activ-ity. The fields organizing the activity of the nervous system are inherited through morphic resonance, conveying a collective, instinctive memory. Each individual both draws upon and con-tributes to the collective memory of the species. This means that

new patterns of behavior can spread more rapidly than would otherwise be possible.[1]

A living mythopoeia arises and is tracked through these spontaneous phenomena of the unconscious in the midst of the dreamscape of the inter-relational field and its many "guests." In receiving and tracking the secrets and concealments that the "guests" are trying to reveal to consciousness—albeit symbolically, through the performances of animated inner figures—Psyche's deeper intent is offered extension in body-to-body encounters of flesh and paint. In the liminality of the creative process, in the theater of Psyche; the dialogue of the conscious and unconscious and the soul's most intimate conversation with itself, the personifications of these "guests," like actors in a Shakespearean play, animate an alternate plot to one's myth. Through the embodiments of one's wounded story— the myth one is living unconsciously—lost or forgotten loves and betrayals speak their way into our being and find new living stories to be told, danced, and sung, releasing the ancients of their prison of lament upon now hearing the up-to-date version of the mythopoesis.

Mythopoetic inquiry both contains and brings to life unrecognized processes in the morphic field of the group (or the individual) psyche, acting as a mirror that both reflects and is reflected upon by its participants. And so it is ever changing, fluid, continuing in its imaging and storytelling. This love story (*amor fati*) is best described as an image always desiring another image, reclaiming the notion of *amor fati* from its previous life sentence of mourning the personal and collective tragedy of death. However, an amorous relationship with the unconscious requires the ability to see symbolic connections—patterns and metaphors—drawing on history as a means for depth illumination. Through the mythopoetic model, taking on such a responsibility means to understand this relationship with regards to patterns that existed long before our time, archetypal patterns across millennia. Understanding these patterns, which have lived through history and now live through us, is both self affirming and potentially evolutionary. The enormous potency of the symbolic gaze sees into the imaginal, to the liminal space (viewed through the spiral lens), holding a living, moment by moment embodiment of the conscious and unconscious, transcending—as well as descending, into the depths—both beyond and beneath the restrictions that the historical narrative imposes. The mythopoetic apprenticeship is activated once "seeing

1. Sheldrake, *Presence of the Past*, 108.

myself as a way of seeing" becomes the modus operandi. At the same time, this practice is an invitation to a mythopoetic sensibility which has the capacity to lead one beyond the literal and into the symbolic way of perceiving these polarities presented in one's myth diaphorically (di-aphor being that aspect of metaphor which embodies the paradoxical), thereby creating Presence.

The role of the ego, in its transformation as receptor *and* actor, is this willingness to engage the diaphoric imagination fully (that which opens us to a reality of the spiritual through—*dia*—and not just as a comparative relationship to our physical reality), anchoring myself in the metaphor that the mirroring of my experience *is*. As an archetypal activ-ist, this imaginal ego is capable of being subject and object simultane-ously. It surpasses all dualities, particularly that of illness and wholeness (one I would consider to be a core complex of my personal myth). The mercurial nature of the imaginal ego enables it to pass through the mir-ror to the other side of the wounded story, stepping into an archetypal narrative that speaks through Psyche's gestures/movements—the flick-ers that reach as far back as the ancients and ahead, into mythic time. The liminality of the archetypal and reflexive relations of subject and object enables the place of narrative to become a place of humanity. This place, which is the mythopoetic, empowers the imaginal ego to meet the wounded narrative with an equal force of creativity, transforming the very myth it is informed by, as the victim of the original myth becomes a wounded healer. The image of the mirror of my personal experience is being reflected in the cosmic mirror of primordial wisdom.[2]

Field Notes: An Exchange with a Colleague

It seems we are all the hero or anti-hero of our own myth, the family being the original context that then templates the rest of our heroic or non-heroic encounters.

In light of this, how could we not cast ourselves as such, even if the "hero," as you imply, is the anti-hero or victim? Is this not the most powerful of roles? Is the myth then not about power, that is, finding/creating that power within the original context as a sym-bol for engaging our ultimate sense of powerlessness in the face of existence?

2. Trungpa, *Cutting Through Spiritual Materialism*, 24.

I see the mythopoetic as the inquiry that takes us into the
liminal void lying at the core of those unanswerable questions that
catapult us towards no longer asking the impossible, other than
re-framing, "Who am I in the presence of the impossible?"

Who am I in the presence of the impossible? seems to me now to
be an underlying query, an unuttered and unanswered question that the
earlier questions posed in the book—*am I how I see myself?* and *am I*
what I think of myself?—were avoiding. A-voiding. Not facing the void.
The proposed *am I simply a way of seeing?* does not skirt the existential
question of *who am I in the presence of the impossible?* Instead, it acts as a
diaphoric invitation that does not split seeing into the two halves of seer
and seen—knower and known, subject and object, teacher and student.
Seeing myself as simply a way of seeing is the liminal action of the void,
where the imaginal ego takes on the responsibility of being receptor *and*
actor, the reflexive being of the Klein body as it is sitting in the void.

The Klein body as liminal presence *is* and *holds* the tension of the
opposites within its non-dualistic sensibility, freeing practitioners from
an *either/or* perspective into the mythopoetic *both/and*. Mythopoetic
sensibility ushers in an existential shift into a field of awareness that
points to the possibility of both mourning the dream and *amor fati* with
the understanding that these are the same process. Through its practice
and embodiment, a mythopoetic inquiry escorts this possibility into the
symbolic and diaphoric, where the seeds planted by the laments of the
ancients and the unborn can sprout and grow into creative embodiments
of moving the dream forward. Not just through contemplation, but taking seriously Psyche's ulterior motive, her evolutionary intent embedded
deeply in the call between *anima* and *anima mundi*.

Through my threading backwards and stitching forwards in this
mythopoetic inquiry—with my own myth as well as those stories and
images of clients and students—some steps become evident that I would
now like to pass on. Knowing full well that they will change in their continuous re-embodying through others' mythopoetic dance, it is my hope
that they might act as a beginning, an invitation to mythopoetic inquirers, even if they do not—as I did not—initially see themselves as such. I
invite you, reader, to consider the following for your own mythopoetic
endeavor:

The mythopoetic apprenticeship is the container *and* the inquiry.
The writing and image-making becomes the inquiry itself, through
the presence of the archetypal activist who—as visceral Klein bottle,

embodying inside and outside—metamorphosed into the spiral lens. Through the active perception of the spiral lens, the imaginal ego is able to confront the void. The shift from *am I a way of seeing?* to *who am I in the presence of the impossible?* holds the enormity of this inquiry, directly facing the profound void that is life.

The intent of the mythopoetic inquiry is to do heart work upon the images from within Psyche and embody her intent through their expression as the body-in-the-world: those images now found in the dark, things apprehended without "seeing" them—as they move and live within, through, and throughout the mythopoeia. This completes one cycle of the ongoing dialogue of the visible/invisible: stepping into and from the invisible to the visible and stepping into the visible from the invisible (world work). This dance of the visible/invisible lifts the personal and collective myth from the literal to the literary, out of and from the wounded story into a living, mercurial mythopoeia, when the future enters into all of us and a new spiral begins.

To those who might engage the raw material of their own self-story, the apprenticeship offered here is through following Psyche's visible and invisible footprints, re-cognizing the "flickers" as the clues to their own mythopoetic journey. Mythopoetic practice is an embodiment-through-extension into the world of deeper intention and those seeds of the wisdom that Psyche offers through the images that are our direct experience of being in the world *and* the void. This practice, I hope, can act as a guide—it too is an image, both fluid and sound, earnest in its commitment to enter and re-enter the unknown through the symbols of experience, resonating in the Klein body and now re-visioned through the spiral lens. Morphic resonances, seen through the spiral lens, are echoing the experiences of the ancients and unborn, invitations to bring potent personal, cultural, and archetypal symbols—including the lamentations of the ancestors—into consciousness and creative embodiment. That is, an ethical, aesthetic response to the imperative of *Mourning the Dream / Amor Fati*: mourning their dream as it is embodied in us so that we will heed the call, the pull towards *amor fati*.

A mythopoetic response to the stirrings of the collective soul is healing the myth of woundedness, re-membering the narrative of the imagination. It is through the reflexive act, bending back on this myth, that archetypal activists can assist in creating an alternate story to the previously dominant one. Through this kind of response as a practice, the myth changes as we are living it mythopoetically. We are writing the narrative, our history, at the same time as we are "reading" it (to ourselves and to the world), creating a vision while seeing. It is an imaginative vision—about what is and what can be—through stepping into the darkened collective threshold ahead: the twins of the archetype of wounding and wholeness. Such a living inquiry brings seemingly random experiences into a dialogical fold, framing them within the symbolic. Here, images point the way through the mythographic landscape into the mythopoetic.

Embodying presences into Presence.

When one deepens one's perception of one's myth what comes into view is the archetypal.

I would like to leave the reader with a series of questions to be considered sequentially, as clusters of images that together generate a momentum of archetypal dimension.

I leave myself with the following inquiries, to continue . . .

Who do you/I become in the presence of the impossible?

What does the impossible become in your/my presence?

Stop and feel into/out of your Klein body the unspoken response to these questions—your felt-sense.

Figure 91. Mythopoetic Voyage to Underwater Cave Paintings

Mourning the Dream / Amor Fati has offered me the opportunity of seeing through the stories I have been telling myself to get through the day. These stories and images have been important to my survival, much like small boats, sailing crafts that carried me from the shore of each morning to the beaches of each night. Looking through the spiral lens, I was able to see beneath and past those stories of who I thought I was, now knowing that these stories are vehicles, as all images are. Self-images, symbolically pointing to and reflecting something much vaster.

After much wrestling with provisional stories and self-images that were, in fact, cradles holding Presence, *Mourning the Dream / Amor Fati* has brought me to a kind of "faith," as you might call it. I had yet to experience this as an adult. The role of the book now is to invite the reader to consider the same, to become a spiral lens that sees the dimensionality of past-present-future as a synchronistically organized Presence. With this Presence *amor fati* seems natural and inevitable.

Figure 92. I Am a Spiral Lens

What does the impossible become in my presence as simply being a
way of seeing?

The impossible becomes . . .

A place of magic . . .

Figure 93. In Our Presence

Postscript

I am finished with the material in this book for the time being. But I
know the material is not finished with me.

References

Abram, David. *The Spell of the Sensuous: Perception and Language in a More-than-Human World*. New York: Pantheon, 1996.

Abrams, Jeremiah and Connie Zweig. "Noticing, Naming and Embracing the Shadow." http://strategicmodelbuilding.com/uploads/Noticing.pdf.

Albright, Daniel. "Early Cantos I–XLI." In *The Cambridge Companion to Ezra Pound*, edited by Ira Bruce Nadel, 59–92. Cambridge Companions to Literature. Cambridge: Cambridge University Press, 1999.

Alling, Norman, and Newcomb Greenleaf. "Klein Surfaces and Real Algebraic Function Fields." *Bulletin of the American Mathematical Society* 75 (1969) 869–72.

Angelo, Marie "Splendor Solis: Inviting the Image to Teach." *International Journal for Jungian Studies* 11 (2005) 13–25.

Appelbaum, David. *The Stop*. SUNY Series in Western Esoteric Traditions. Albany: SUNY Press, 1995.

Bachelard, Gaston. *The Poetics of Space*. Translated by Maria Jolas. Boston: Beacon, 1958.

Bancroft, Mark. "The History and Psychology of Spirit Possession and Exorcism." http://www.markbancroft.com/info/spirit-possession.

Baynes, Cary F., ed. *The I Ching: Or, Book of Changes*. Translated by Richard Wilhelm. New York: Pantheon, 1950.

Bohm, David. "Meaning and Information." In *The Search for Meaning: The New Spirit in Science and Philosophy*, edited by Paavo Pylkkänen, 43–85. Toronto: HarperCollins Canada, 1989.

Bosnak, Robert. *Embodiment: Creative Imagination in Medicine, Art and Travel*. London: Routledge, 2007.

Bressler, Charles E. *Literary Criticism: An Introduction to Theory and Practice*. 2nd ed. Upper Saddle River, NJ: Prentice-Hall, 1999.

Casey, Edward. *Imagining: A Phenomenological Study*. Markham, ON: Fitzhenry & Whiteside, 1976.

Cimino, Cristiana, and Antonrllo Correaleal. "Projective Identification and Consciousness Alteration: A Bridge between Psychoanalysis and Neuroscience?" *International Journal of Psychoanalysis* 86 (2005) 51–60.

Cleary, Thomas, trans. *The Secret of the Golden Flower: The Classic Chinese Book of Life*. New York: HarperCollins, 1991.

Coppin, Joseph, and Elizabeth Nelson. *The Art of Inquiry*. New York: Springer, 2005.

Corbin, Henri. *Alone with the Alone: Creative Imagination in the Ṣūfism of Ibn ⬚Arabī.* Bollingen Series 91. Princeton: Princeton University Press, 1998.

Cousineau, Phil. *Stoking the Creative Fires: 9 Ways to Rekindle Passion and Imagination.* San Francisco: Conari, 2008.

Csikszentmihalyi, Mihaly. *Flow: The Psychology of Optimal Experience.* New York: Harper & Row, 1990.

Dalai Lama. *Sleeping, Dreaming, and Dying: An Exploration of Consciousness.* Edited by Francisco J. Varela. Somerville, MA: Wisdom, 1997.

"Deep Democracy, Its Impact and Evolution." *Deep Democracy Institute.* http://www.deepdemocracyinstitute.org/deep-democracy-explained.html.

"Depth Psychology." In *New World Encyclopedia.* http://www.newworldencyclopedia.org/p/index.php?title=Depth_psychology&oldid=1007396.

Dirkx, John, et al. "Musings and Reflections on the Meaning, Context, and Process of Transformative Learning: A Dialogue between John M. Dirkx and Jack Mezirow." *Journal of Transformative Education* 4 (2006) 123–39.

Doering, Oscar. *Christliche Symbole.* Freiburg im Breisgau: Herder, 1933.

Doty, William. *Mythography: The Study of Myths and Rituals.* Tuscaloosa: University of Alabama Press, 2000.

Eckhart, Meister. *The Complete Mystical Works of Meister Eckhart.* Translated by Maurice O'Connell Walshe. New York: Crossroad. 2009.

Edinger, Edward F. *The Creation of Consciousness: Jung's Myth for Modern Man.* Studies in Jungian Psychology by Jungian Analysts 14. Toronto: Inner City, 1986.

———. *Ego and Archetype.* Boston: Shambala, 1972.

Faulkner, William. *Requiem for a Nun.* London: Vintage, 1951.

Fels, Lynn. "Complexity, Teacher Education, and the Restless Jury: Pedagogical Moments of Performance." *Complicity: An International Journal of Complexity and Education* 1 (2004) 73–98.

———. "In the Wind: Performative Inquiry." In *Arts-based Research & Praxis in Education.* Vancouver: University of British Columbia Press, 2002.

Frank, Arthur. *The Wounded Storyteller: Body Illness and Ethics.* Chicago: University of Chicago Press, 1995.

Fullagar, Simone. "Narratives of Travel: Desire and the Movement of Feminine Subjectivity." *Leisure Studies* 21 (2010) 57–74.

Gilbert, Sandra, and Susan Gubar, eds. *Shakespeare's Sisters: Feminist Essays on Women Poets.* Bloomington: Indiana University Press, 1979.

Goethe, Johann Wolfgang von. *Scientific Studies.* Edited and translated by Douglas Miller. Collected Works 12. Princeton: Princeton University Press, 1995.

Greene, Maxine. *Releasing the Imagination: Essays on Education, the Arts and Social Change.* Jossey-Bass Education Series. San Francisco, CA: Jossey-Bass, 1995.

Halifax, Joan. *Being with Dying: Cultivating Compassion and Fearlessness in the Presence of Death.* Boston: Shambhala, 2008.

Hillman, James. *Archetypal Psychology: A Brief Account.* Dallas: Spring, 1988.

———. "An Inquiry into Image." *Spring: An Annual of Archetypal Psychology and Jungian Thought* (1977) 62–88.

———. *The Myth of Analysis.* Evanston, IL: Northwestern University Press, 1972.

———. *Re-visioning Psychology.* New York: Harper & Row, 1975.

———. *The Soul's Code: In Search of Character and Calling.* New York: Random House, 1996.

Hillman, James, and Sonu Shamdasani. *Lament of the Dead: Psychology after Jung's Red Book*. New York: Norton, 2013.

Hollis, James. *The Eden Project: In Search of the Magical Other*. Vancouver: Jungian Society, 1999.

———. "Hauntings: Dispelling the Ghosts Who Run Our Lives." https://ashevillejungcenter.org/product/hauntings-dispelling-the-ghosts-who-run-our-lives/.

Holmes, Jeremy. "Defense and Creative Use of Narrative in Psychotherapy: An Attachment Perspective." In *Healing Stories: Narrative in Psychiatry and Psychotherapy*, edited by Glenn Roberts and Jeremy Holmes, 49–66. Oxford: Oxford University Press, 1999.

Irigaray, Luce. *To Speak Is Never Neutral*. Translated by Gail Schwab. London: Continuum, 2002.

Jung, Carl G. *Archetypes and the Collective Unconscious*. Translated by R. F. C. Hull. Collected Works 9. Princeton: Princeton University Press, 1969.

———. *The Basic Writings of C. G. Jung*. Edited by Violet S. De Laszlo. New York: Modern Library, 1959.

———. *The Essential Jung*. Edited by Anthony Storr. Princeton: Princeton University Press, 1983.

———. *Man and His Symbols*. London: Aldus, 1964.

———. *Memories, Dreams, Reflections*. New York: Random House, 1963.

———. *Modern Man in Search of a Soul*. London: Kegan Paul Trench Trubner, Harvest, 1993. (1955 ed.)

———. *Mysterium Coniunctionis*. London: Routledge Kegan Paul, 1963.

———. *Psychology and Religion*. Edited by Sir Herbert Read. Collected Works 11. Princeton: Princeton University Press, 1969.

———. *Psychology of the Unconscious*. New York: Moffat, Yard, 1921.

———. *Red Book=Liber Novus*. Edited by S. Shamdasami. New York: Norton, 2009.

———. *The Structure and Dynamics of the Psyche*. Collected Works 8. Princeton: Princeton University Press, 1960.

———. *Symbols of Transformation*. Edited by Gerhard Adler and R. F. C. Hull. Collected Works 5. Princeton University Press, 1956.

———. *The Transcendent Function*. Collected Works 8. Princeton: Princeton University Press, 1969.

Kalsched, Donald. *The Inner World of Trauma: Archetypal Defenses of the Personal Spirit*. London: Routledge, 1996.

———. *Trauma and the Soul. A Psycho-spiritual Approach to Human Development and Its Interruption*. New York: Routledge, 2013.

Krishnamurti, Jiddu. *Choiceless Awareness*. Chennai: Krishnamurti Foundation India, 2007.

———. *Freedom from the Known*. New York: HarperCollins, 1969.

Kristeva, Julia. *The Black Sun: Depression and Melancholia*. New York: Columbia University Press, 1987.

Lao-tzu. *Tao Te Ching*. Translated by Stephen Mitchell. New York: HarperCollins, 1988.

Lacan, Jacques. "The Mirror Stage as Formative of the Function of the I." In *Écrits: A Selection*, 1–8. Translated by Alan Sheridan. London: Routledge Classics, 2001.

Leclerc, Josee. "The Unconscious as Paradox: Impact on the Epistemological Stance of the Art Psychotherapist." *Art in Psychotherapy* 33 (2006) 130–34.

Leggo, Carl. "Longing for Books: Reasons for Reading Literature." *English in Australia* 46 (2011) 37–45. http://www.aate.org.au/view_journal.php?id=48.

MacKay, Frances. "Mythopoetic Spaces in the (Trans)formation of Counselors and Therapists." In *Pedagogies of the Imagination: Mythopoetic Apprenticeship in Educational Practice*, edited by Timothy Leonard and Peter Willis, 189–202. Chicago: Springer Science, 1990.

Maffei, Giuseppe. "The Experience of Time in Analysis." *International Journal of Jungian Studies* 2 (2010) 102.

May, Rollo. *The Cry for Myth*. New York: Norton, 1991.

Mayes, Clifford. *Inside Education: Depth Psychology in Teaching and Learning*. Madison, WI: Atwood, 2009.

McGaughey, Douglas R. *Strangers and Pilgrims: On the Role of Aporiai in Theology*. Theologische Bibliothek Töpelmann 81. Berlin: de Gruyter, 1997.

McLaren, Peter L. "The Anthropological Roots of Pedagogy: The Teacher as Liminal Servant." *Anthropology and Humanism Quarterly* 12 (1987) 75–85.

McNamara, Jim. "The Evolutionary Challenge in Western Culture: An Archetypal, Existential, Ecological Perspective." *Archetypal Review of Culture* 1 (2010). http://www.archetypalreviewofculture.org/book/export/html/9.

Merleau-Ponty, Maurice. *Phenomenology of Perception*. Translated by Colin Smith. London: Routledge, 1962.

———. *The Primacy of Perception*. Edited by James M. Edie. Translated by William Cobb. Northwestern University Studies in Phenomenology & Existential Philosophy. Evanston, IL: Northwestern University Press, 1964.

———. *The Visible and Invisible*. Edited by Claude Lefort. Translated by Alphonso Lingis. Northwestern University Studies in Phenomenology & Existential Philosophy. Evanston, IL: Northwestern University Press, 1968.

Miller, David, L. *Gods and Games: Toward a Theology of Play*. New York: World, 1970.

———. "Images of a Happy Ending." *Eranos* 44 (1977) 61–90.

Mindell, Arnold. *Dreambody*. Santa Monica, CA: Sigo, 1982.

Needleman, Jacob. *Time and the Soul*. San Francisco: Berrett Koehler, 2003.

Nietzsche, Friedrich. *Basic Writings of Nietzsche*. Translated by Walter Kaufmann. New York: Random House, 2000.

———. *Beyond Good and Evil*. Translated by R. J. Hollingdale. London: Penguin, 2003.

———. *Ecce Homo*. Translated by Walter Kaufmann. New York: Vintage, 1990.

Ozeri, Shahar. "Merleau-Ponty on Seeing." *Perverse Egalitarianism*, 2 June 2009. https://pervegalit.wordpress.com/2009/06/02/merleau-ponty-on-seeing/.

Paris, Ginette. *Wisdom of the Psyche: Depth Psychology after Neuroscience*. New York: Routledge, 2007.

Peat, F. David. "Alchemical Transformation: Consciousness and Matter, Form and Information." *World Future* 48 (1997) 3–22.

Peterson, Jordan. "Why Are We so Complicated?" https://www.youtube.com/watch?v=8suS5Lnf8Io.

"Primordial Word." *Archive for Research in Archetypal Symbolism*. https://aras.org/concordance/content/primordial-word.

Rilke, Rainer Maria. *Ahead of All Parting: The Selected Poetry and Prose of Rainer Maria Rilke*. Edited and translated by Stephen Mitchell. New York: Modern Library, 1995.

———. *Letters on Cézanne*. Translated by Joel Agee. New York: North Point. 2002.

———. *Letters to a Young Poet*. Translated by M. D. Herter Norton. New York: Norton, 1993.

Rinpoche, Sogyal. *The Tibetan Book of Living and Dying*. Edited by Patrick Gaffney and Andrew Harvey. New York: HarperCollins, 2002.

Robbins, Brent Dean. "Maurice Merleau-Ponty." *Mythos and Logos*, 22 July 2008. http://mythosandlogos.com/MerleauPonty.html.

Roberts, Glenn. "Introduction: A Story of Stories." In *Healing Stories: Narrative in Psychiatry and Psychotherapy*, edited by Glenn Roberts and Jeremy Holmes, 3–26. Oxford: Oxford University Press, 1999.

Rosen, Steven. "Quantum Gravity and Taoist Cosmology: Exploring the Ancient Origins of Phenomenological String Theory." *Progress in Biophysics and Molecular Biology* 131 (2017) 34–60.

———. *Topologies of the Flesh: A Multidimensional Exploration of the Lifeworld*. Athens, Ohio: Ohio University Press, 2006.

Rumi, Jalal al-Din. *The Essential Rumi*. Translated by Coleman Barks. New York: Quality Paperback, 1998.

Samuels, Andrew. *A Critical Dictionary of Jungian Analysis*. London: Routledge & Kegan Paul, 1986.

Schutz, Alfred. *The Problem of Social Reality*. Collected Papers 1. Edited by Maurice Natanson. The Hague: Nijhoff, 1967.

Shakespeare, William. *Hamlet*. Penguin Shakespeare. London: Penguin, 2005.

Sheldrake, Rupert. *The Presence of the Past: Morphic Resonance and the Habits of Nature*. London: Icon, 2011.

Smith, David G. "Hermeneutic Inquiry: The Hermeneutic Imagination and the Pedagogic Text." In *Forms of Curriculum Inquiry*, edited by Edmund C. Short. New York: SUNY Press, 1991.

Snowber, Celeste. "Dance as a Way of Knowing." In *Bodies of Knowledge: Embodied Learning in Adult Education in Volume of New Directions for Adult and Continuing Education* 134, edited by Randee L. Lawrence. San Francisco, CA: Jossey Bass, 2012. http://ca.wiley.com/WileyCDA/WileyTitle/productCd-1118358325.html.

———. "What the Body Knows: Dance as Embodied Inquiry." http://abrstudio.wordpress.com/2012/02/14/celeste-snowbers-symposium-presentation.

Stein, Murray. *Carl Jung's Red Book on CD ROM*. Asheville, NC: Asheville Jung Center, 2010.

Trungpa, Chogyam. *Cutting through Spiritual Materialism*. Boston: Shambhala, 1973.

———. *The Sacred Path of the Warrior*. Boston: Shambhala, 1984.

Turner, Victor. *The Ritual Process: Structure and Anti-structure*. New York: Transaction, 1969.

Walhof, Darren. *The Democratic Theory of Hans-Georg Gadamer*. Cham, Switzerland: Springer, 2016.

Ward, Aileen. *John Keats: The Making of a Poet*. New York: Viking, 1963.

Wheelwright, Philip. *Metaphor & Reality*. Bloomington: Indiana University Press, 1962.

Wikipedia. "Persephone." In *Wikipedia*. https://en.wikipedia.org/wiki/Persephone.

Wikipedia. "Theodor Lipps." In *Wikipedia*. https://en.wikipedia.org/wiki/Theodor_Lipps.

Winnicott, David. *Playing and Reality*. London: Routledge, 1971.

Zimmer, Heinrich. *Myths and Symbols in Indian Art and Civilization*. Edited by Joseph Campbell. Princeton: Princeton University Press, 1978.

CPSIA information can be obtained
at www.ICGtesting.com
Printed in the USA
JSHW030944141222
34804JS00006B/78